THE OBJECTS AND TEXTURES OF
EVERYDAY LIFE IN IMPERIAL BRITAIN

The Objects and Textures of Everyday Life in Imperial Britain

Edited by

DEIRDRE H. McMAHON
Drexel University, USA

JANET C. MYERS
Elon University, USA

ASHGATE

Published by
Ashgate Publishing Limited
Wey Court East
Union Road
Farnham
Surrey, GU9 7PT
England

Ashgate Publishing Company
110 Cherry Street
Suite 3-1
Burlington, VT 05401-3818
USA

www.ashgate.com

British Library Cataloguing in Publication Data
A catalogue record for this book is available from the British Library

The Library of Congress has cataloged the printed edition as follows:
Names: McMahon, Deirdre H., editor. | Myers, Janet C., 1969- editor.
Title: The objects and textures of everyday life in imperial Britain / edited
   by Deirdre H. McMahon and Janet C. Myers.
Description: Farnham, Surrey, England : Ashgate, 2016. | Includes
   bibliographical references and index.
Identifiers: LCCN 2015029931 | ISBN 9781409455189 (hardcover)
   | ISBN 9781409455196 (ebook) | ISBN 9781472403582 (ePub)
Subjects: LCSH: Great Britain--Social life and customs--19th century. |
   Material culture--Great Britain--History--19th century. | Home--Great
   Britain--History--19th century. | Personal belongings--Great
   Britain--History--19th century. | House furnishings--Great
   Britain--History--19th century. | Commercial products--Great
   Britain--History--19th century. | Imperialism--Social aspects--Great
   Britain--History--19th century. | National security--Social aspects--Great
   Britain--History--19th century. | Group identity--Great
   Britain--History--19th century.
Classification: LCC DA533 .O25 2016 | DDC 941.081--dc23 LC record available at
http://lccn.loc.gov/2015029931

ISBN 9781409455189 (hbk)
ISBN 9781409455196 (ebk – PDF)
ISBN 9781472403582 (ebk – ePUB)

Printed in the United Kingdom by Henry Ling Limited,
at the Dorset Press, Dorchester, DT1 1HD

Contents

**PART III: IMPERIAL POSSESSIONS, COMMODITY CULTURE,
AND COLONIAL RETURN**

List of Figures

Notes on Contributors

Sumangala Bhattacharya is Associate Professor of English and World Literature at Pitzer College in Claremont, California. She is the author of numerous articles on Victorian literature and culture. Her research and teaching interests center on issues of gender and colonialism, and she has a special interest in the Gothic. She is currently working on a book project on the representations of hunger in the nineteenth century.

Bradley Deane is Professor of English and Morse-Alumni Distinguished Teaching Professor at the University of Minnesota, Morris. He is the author of *The Making of the Victorian Novelist: Anxieties of Authorship in the Mass Market* (Routledge, 2003) and *Masculinity and the New Imperialism: Rewriting Manhood in British Popular Literature, 1870–1914* (Cambridge University Press, 2014).

Clive Edwards is Professor of Design History at Loughborough University. His publications include monographs on aspects of furniture technology, materials and trades, furnishing textiles and the manufacture and retailing of domestic furnishings, as well as contributions to multi-authored works on interiors, architecture and the home. His latest book is *Interior Design: A Critical Introduction* (Berg, 2010). His interest in cross-disciplinary study is evident in his work, which includes research on design, materials and technology, consumption, business and retailing. He has recently published articles on the Victorian furniture makers Collinson and Lock and on the mechanization of nineteenth-century marquetry processes. Edwards is currently Editor-in-Chief of a three-volume reference work on design for Bloomsbury (2015).

Jo Guldi, Assistant Professor of History at Brown University, is a historian of modern Britain. Her first book, *Roads to Power* (Harvard University Press, 2011), tells the story of how Britain built the first nation connected by infrastructure and technology that caused strangers to stop speaking on the public street. She is co-author with David Armitage of *The History Manifesto* (Cambridge University Press, 2014). Most recently, she is writing a history of land use and capitalism.

Kellie Holzer is Assistant Professor of English and faculty affiliate of Women's and Gender Studies at Virginia Wesleyan College. Her research focuses on attitudes toward marriage in Victorian and colonial Indian fiction and periodicals. She has published essays in *South Asian Review, Nineteenth-Century Gender Studies* and *Nineteenth-Century Contexts*.

Victoria Kelley is Reader in the History of Design and Material Culture at the University for the Creative Arts and Senior Lecturer in the School of Fashion and Textiles at Central Saint Martins, University of the Arts London. Her recent publications include *Soap and Water: Cleanliness, Dirt and the Working Classes in Victorian and Edwardian Britain* (I.B. Tauris, 2010). She is the co-editor, with Glenn Adamson, of *Surface Tensions: Surface, Finish and the Meaning of Objects* (Manchester University Press, 2013).

Deirdre H. McMahon is Associate Teaching Professor of English at Drexel University, where she teaches nineteenth- and twentieth-century British literature, postcolonial fiction and theory, and literature for young adults. Her work has appeared in *Studies in the Novel*, *Academe*, *Kronoscope*, and *Other Mothers: Beyond the Maternal Ideal*, edited by Ellen Bayuk Rosenman and Claudia C. Klaver.

Jason Howard Mezey is Associate Professor of English at Saint Joseph's University, where he teaches courses in postcolonial literature and theory as well as South Asian, South African, and contemporary British fiction. His work on Indian fiction, his primary field of research, has been published in *Journal of Commonwealth and Postcolonial Studies*, *Studies in the Novel*, *Interventions: International Journal of Postcolonial Studies*, and *South Asian Review.*

Mary Jeanette Moran is Associate Professor of Children's Literature at Illinois State University. Her interests include fantasy, narrative studies, and feminist ethical theory. In addition to her work on children's and young adult literature, she has also published and presented on eighteenth- and nineteenth-century British literature for adults. She has published articles on the Judy Bolton mystery series, Madeleine L'Engle, and *Anne of Green Gables*, and is currently working on a book project on fantasy and feminist ethics.

Janet C. Myers is Professor of English at Elon University. She is the author of *Antipodal England: Emigration and Portable Domesticity in the Victorian Imagination* (SUNY, 2009), and she has published articles on Victorian emigration and Australian literature in *Victorian Literature and Culture*, *Novel: A Forum on Fiction*, and *Journal of Commonwealth Literature*. Her current work on women and material culture recently appeared in *Nineteenth-Century Gender Studies*.

Acknowledgments

We wish to thank our fellow contributors for sharing their insights and enthusiasm for Victorian material culture with us. We also extend our heartfelt gratitude to Ann Donahue of Ashgate Publishing for her advice and support. We are grateful as well to the anonymous readers whose incisive suggestions improved the collection.

Deirdre McMahon would like to thank Larry Milliken of Drexel University's Hagerty Library and Amey Hutchins and William Keller of the University of Pennsylvania's Rare Book and Manuscript Library for their assistance. My interest in Victorian Studies solidified when studying with Florence Boos, whose scholarship and pedagogy remain models for me today. Many thanks go, too, to the colleagues and friends who have shared their insights and interest as the volume moved forward: Ray Brebach, Tom Brennan, Ted Fristrom, Richard Fusco, Ann Green, Amy Lilly, Mary Moran, John Picker, and Abioseh Michael Porter. Norah, Paul, and Daniel have given me time at the computer and joy away from it, as has Jason, who leaves me speechless.

Janet Myers would like to thank the librarians at Elon University, especially Lynn Melchor, and the University of North Carolina at Chapel Hill, for their assistance in locating source material and in granting access to online resources. Appreciation is also due to Elon University for providing research funding to support this project. Finally, she is grateful to her writing group—Barbara Gordon, Megan Isaac, and Cassie Kircher—for their helpful feedback on this project at various stages.

Introduction: Material Possessions— The Objects and Textures of Everyday Life in Imperial Britain

Deirdre H. McMahon with Janet C. Myers

When leading American art critic Clarence Cook collected his *Scribner's Monthly* columns on décor and household furnishing into his 1878 masterpiece, *The House Beautiful*, he chose English illustrator Walter Crane's "My Lady's Chamber" for the frontispiece, suggesting that the woman pictured and the woman reader could each fashion "a house beautiful" suited to her family's needs. In its depiction of a mythic, idealized domestic realm of order and creature comfort, Crane's illustration captures much of what Victorians and their contemporaries across the Atlantic associated with the upper middle-class "house beautiful" as both a discursive construct and a material site. The image shows a beautifully dressed woman serving tea. Her draped skirt and lace neck and cuffs demonstrate her remove from manual labor, while the laden table associates her with the supposedly feminine acts of nurturing and hospitality. The lady of the house leans toward the center of the frame, but the picture's focal point rests on the teapot, where the heat of the fire merges with the steam of the tea, representing the warmth and intimacy of the household as a whole. In many ways, the beautifully dressed woman becomes another fixture of domestic display in the upper middle-class home, one that effortlessly exerts control over the exquisite surroundings she has designed and that she daily occupies.

Crane's depiction of domesticity in "My Lady's Chamber" is idealized, but its placement in a guide to household furnishing asserts its attainability, specifically through material possessions. This highly stylized design of hearth and home depends on its objects, whose careful assembly and arrangement proclaim the aesthetic as well as financial capital of the bourgeois household. A close look at this moment of stasis in the perfect British interior, however, also suggests how porous the border between home and world may have been in nineteenth-century Britain. The imperial origins of many of the items featured—the blue and white Chinese porcelain plates and ginger jars, Japanese fans, Persian carpet, and the quintessential British drink, tea, available only via colonial import—position the woman as an elegant, tasteful consumer of empire, able to integrate products from around the globe into the private sanctity of the home.

Through the examination of similar common household items, *The Objects and Textures of Everyday Life in Imperial Britain* reveals the plasticity of seemingly distinct senses of domesticity—hearth and home versus the public sphere, and English metropole versus imperial territories. Foundational to the collection is the claim that objects, and particularly objects in use, reveal a great deal about the culture in which they are used, a claim that is especially relevant for discussion of nineteenth-century culture because of the abundance of objects and commodities created by the advent of mass production and the transformation of Britain into both an industrial economy and imperial power. These chapters also advance Victorian material studies by moving beyond the examination of objects in museums, exhibitions, and collections—where prior studies have been ably concentrated—to focus instead on objects in use in everyday contexts. In doing so, *The Objects and Textures of Everyday Life* takes objects out from under the glass of the museum case to interrogate how recursive patterns of daily life led to rituals and practices that gradually came to undergird British self-definition.

By focusing on everyday objects, the chapters gathered here scrutinize domestic spaces similar to that represented in Crane's illustration, but we also seek to complicate the domestic as a category of analysis. For our purposes, "the domestic" connotes both home life and the ideals associated with it as well as the nation as a homeland, distinct from and dependent upon the imperial. Thus the volume adds a materialist bent to the strong critical tradition on the imbrication of the domestic and imperial, including the work of Alison Blunt, Deirdre David, Rosemary Marangoly George, Inderpal Grewal, Susan Meyer, Suvendrini Perera, and Ann Laura Stoler, among others. *The Objects and Textures of Everyday Life* presents a critical reorientation in material studies of nineteenth-century domesticity to examine the functions of "home" as at once both personal (the physical dwelling place and affective ties of family) and national (the geographical boundaries and collective identity of nineteenth-century Britain). Not solely synecdochical or metaphoric, "home" operates as a site and a mechanism for negotiating identity construction in the imperial age. Thus ideas of the domestic helped to order the arrangement of individual households as well as to shape broader understandings of national self-definition and of the public's cognitive map of Great Britain.

By considering the material history of nineteenth-century domesticity, *The Objects and Textures of Everyday Life* seeks to deepen analysis of common practices, which our contributors suggest at times diverged from prevailing discourses and print culture representations of domestic ideology. Our volume thus calls for further investment in materialist as well as textual studies to better understand the contingent and dynamic processes of enacting middle-class Britishness in the period. We are particularly interested in how things—common, everyday items—functioned in the negotiation of domesticity and empire. Building upon Bill Brown's contention that thing theory both enables and requires critical attention to "why and how we use objects to make meaning, to make and re-make ourselves" (4), our approach foregrounds the historicity of *objects in use* as a means to examine the mediation of relationships and social structures, particularly in terms of the range and volatility of gender scripts, class allegiances, and shifting national and imperial subject positions. By analyzing how household artifacts of nineteenth-century Britain and its imperial outposts functioned in their nitty-gritty daily use, *The Objects and Textures of Everyday Life* demonstrates that material possessions served as both a rallying point and flexible register for contouring British self-definition during the period. Moreover, our treatment of the material support of "Imperial Britain" works to illustrate how thoroughly the concepts of household, nation and empire were bound together during the long nineteenth century.

To better address the fluidity and scope of nineteenth-century Britons' use of everyday objects in negotiating identity, our collection builds from the insights of a number of disciplines. In doing so, *The Objects and Textures of Everyday Life in Imperial Britain* demonstrates the utility and value of cross-disciplinary materialist analysis. Informed by and representing diverse fields within historical and literary studies—including history of design, landscape history, childhood studies, and feminist and postcolonial literary criticism—our scholars share a focus on how practices arise out of the customary (and sometimes non-normative) uses to which objects were put. The volume contributes to a materialist understanding of imperial Britain by tracking how preoccupations with common household goods and domestic habits fueled contemporary debates about cultural institutions ranging from personal matters of marriage and family to more overtly political issues of empire building. Such patterns, in turn, created expectations about which things and people mattered, as well as how and why they mattered. As Mary Douglas and Baron Isherwood contend in *The World of Goods*, "[i]nstead of supposing that goods are primarily needed for subsistence or competitive display, let us assume that they are needed for making visible and stable the categories of culture" (38). The stability of such systems of meaning, though, is contingent. Through malfunction, wear, or a change in use, objects may resist or exceed their classification. At different points and from different perspectives, the same objects might be seen as commodities or trash, treasures or junk, evidence of what is valued or what should be discarded. Our volume offers an historically situated examination of how the material traces of nineteenth-century British domesticity demonstrate significant links between homes and museums, between household management and political agency at home and throughout the empire, and between individual acts of conspicuous display and collective pressures toward conformity. The collection's materialist approach thus encourages critical rethinking of Victorian cultural formation through the domestic.

Focusing on common, everyday objects presents readers with the opportunity to view "Imperial Britain" through a double focus, the simultaneous consideration of home and abroad. The result of such scrutiny is, as Homi K. Bhabha and others have argued in different contexts, a collision of familiar and foreign that creates *unheimlich*, the Freudian term for the uncanny that Bhabha identifies as "the unhomely" (141). Discussing Isabel Archer's "suffocating" marriage in Henry James's *The Portrait of a Lady*, Bhabha uses this double lens to debunk related myths of familial sanctity and separate spheres, insisting: "[T]he intimate recesses of the domestic space become sites for history's most intricate invasions. In that displacement, the border between home and world becomes confused; and, uncannily, the private and public become part of each other, forcing upon us a vision that is as divided as it is disorienting" (141). It is exactly such myths of effortless, natural, insulated domestic harmony as those given visual form in "My Lady's Chamber" that prompt uncanny and disorienting shocks when the daily stuff of nineteenth-century life reveals how fully the public and private overlap and become part of one another. This shock finds its most commonly cited form in commodity fetishism, which is a crucial but frequently over-privileged hermeneutical tool specifically for the analysis of things. Building from Marx, scholars of nineteenth-century Britain in a number of excellent critical treatments have examined the ways power and social relations accrue to and are mediated through the alienating effects of the marketplace.[1] As Erin O'Connor explains in *Raw Material*, "capitalism scrambles distinctions between bodies and objects by falsely animating things and fatally mechanizing workers" (16). Products are valued not as things in and of themselves, or for their uses, or for the time, work, and talent necessary to produce them—but for money.

The Objects and Textures of Everyday Life refocuses the study of common objects to situate discussion of their exchange value, consumption and cultural weight within conceptions of domesticity as at once natural and carefully constructed, formative and yet mundane. In this context the exchange of goods as commodities retains limited significance when compared to how domestic objects were utilized. The ubiquity of many everyday items—cups and saucers in the cupboard, a tea kettle on the stove, a book in a child's hands—adds to domesticity's mystique. Recognized as powerful symbols of middle-class identity, and yet often devalued as actual items in terms of market price or association with prevailing gender expectations, such objects and their associated patterns of use were often so commonplace as to be beneath notice. Moreover, our analyses suggest that patterns of use of everyday objects often functioned conservatively, reinforcing divisions within the middle classes even while smoothing over vicissitudes in the cultural formation of Britishness itself.

---

[1]   Earlier studies that inform our volume include, but are not limited to: Raymond Williams, *Culture and Society: 1780–1950*; Terry Eagleton, *Ideology: An Introduction*; Catherine Gallagher, *The Industrial Reformation of English Fiction: Social Discourse and Narrative Form, 1832–1914*; Thomas Richards, *The Commodity Culture of Victorian England: Advertising and Spectacle, 1851–1914* and *The Imperial Archive: Knowledge and the Fantasy of Empire*; Andrew H. Miller, *Novels Behind Glass: Commodity Culture and Victorian Narrative*; Anne McClintock, *Imperial Leather: Race, Gender and Sexuality in the Colonial Contest*; and Catherine Waters, *Commodity Culture in Dickens's* Household Words.

"Foreign countries have come to me":
Object Lessons in Empire and the British Household

If I have not gone to foreign countries, young man, foreign countries have come to me ... Put it that I take an inventory, or make a catalogue ... I see some cups and saucers of Chinese make, equally strangers to me personally: I put my finger on them, then and there, and I say 'Pekin, Nankin, Canton.' It is the same with Japan, with Egypt, and with bamboo and sandal-wood from the East Indies; I put my finger on them all. —Mr Sapsea

(Charles Dickens, *The Mystery of Edwin Drood*, 1870)

Thomas Sapsea in *The Mystery of Edwin Drood* (1870), auctioneer and "the purest jackass in Cloisterham," reminds critics of the powerful draw and concomitant insufficiencies of commodity fetishism as a mode of analysis of material possessions (32). Without his leaving home, "foreign countries have come to" Sapsea in the form of the global goods he auctions; he "puts his finger on" and determines the provenance and initial price of every object he sells, then exhorts the assembled crowd to bid against each other (34). Bypassing the complexities of both imperial trade and the colonial labor that produced these goods, Sapsea emphasizes that until he touches these "cups and saucers" they have no origin or value. As if anticipating the work of J.L. Austin and Judith Butler, Sapsea's pronouncements mark these objects, establishing them as commodities of a particular source and desirability. To a great extent, Sapsea *makes* these objects when he puts his "finger on them all." Ultimately, however, even this labor is denigrated, as Mr Sapsea values items only as far as they sustain his self-styled position as the highest man in Cloisterham. His role as auctioneer gives him such authority that he feels it proper and expedient to conclude sales by "slightly intoning in his pulpit, to make himself more like what he takes to be the genuine ecclesiastical article" (34).

Sapsea, as businessman and then mayor, enables Charles Dickens to hint at how the complicated flow of goods, people, money, and ideas under empire encourages a willful myopia in which imperialism operates without history and capitalism without workers. Somewhere between the auction house where Sapsea takes his pulpit, authenticates his wares, and builds his brand, and the opium den, where the central mystery of the missing Edwin Drood emerges, a narcotic-fumed anxiety coalesces around the uncertain nature of Englishness.[2] Critical attention to Dickens's unfinished final novel has centered most on the act of detection or on the threats posed by imperial trade to the Englishness of individual bodies, the

---

[2] Drood's possible murder by his opium-addicted uncle, John Jasper, casts doubt on the sanctity of familial ties. The novel contrasts Jasper with Neville Landless, an orphan whose obscure Ceylonese background and over-determined name signal Dickens's interrogation of the biological, cultural or moral foundations of English national character. See Perera, *Reaches of Empire: The English Novel from Edgeworth to Dickens.*

family, and the household. To a great extent, though, material goods have fallen out of this analysis.[3] Quietly absorbed into the homes of Cloisterham, the blue and white "cups and saucers of Chinese make" and other imperial goods slip past the critical eye, as their exchange-value and exotic threat are subsumed into the comfort and familiarity of the domestic. Simultaneously foreign and home-like, such objects confound our understanding of normative British identity politics, imperial panic, or the cluttered Victorian interior, thus occluding how these categories may overlap.

Sapsea's fictional auction goods resemble many of the material traces of nineteenth-century British domesticity, which tend to be either overlooked or removed from context. Elaine Freedgood's *The Ideas in Things* argues that readers, including critics, have been trained to skim over materiality, so that we dismiss the "cavalcades" of things that populate Victorian texts "as largely meaningless": "the protocols for reading the realist novel have long focused us on subjects and plots; they have implicitly enjoined us *not* to interpret many or most of its objects" (1). Freedgood's warnings are compounded by Arjun Appadurai, who cautions that when critics do attend to objects, we often interpret them primarily through commodity fetishism, as if capitalism and thus modernity after the onset of empire allow for only one interpretive possibility. *The Objects and Textures of Everyday Life* seeks to extend materialist analyses and theories of commodity fetishism to include additional projections and cultural systems for establishing social value. Our contributors share Appadurai's concern with the intensely political nature of things in everyday use. Appadurai suggests that "relations of privilege and social control" remain embedded in all exchanges of objects, time and money, but "in the mundane, day-to-day, small-scale exchanges of things in ordinary life, this fact is not visible" (57). Our volume turns to everyday life to make visible both the tensions that animate regimes of value and how specific objects may exceed or subvert conventions of exchange. Following Appadurai's dictum that "it is the things-in-motion that illuminate their human and social context" (5), we track the things of this collection to their most common destination, the British home.

Design scholar Tim Putnam calls the home "a prime unexcavated site for an archaeology of sociability" in which material possessions act as "life supports" for a household's organization of space and time as well as for its relational network of familial, gender, generational and class connections (144). Putnam suggests the

---

[3]   The exceptions to this claim include Barry Milligan's work on opium as both commodity and ideological threat in *Pleasures and Pains: Opium and the Orient in Nineteenth-Century British Culture* and, even more fully, Elizabeth Hope Chang's discussion of imperial commodities in *Britain's Chinese Eye: Literature, Empire and Aesthetics in Nineteenth-Century Britain*. Chang's work is especially provocative for our purposes in her argument that "Jasper's dreams give him endless reproductions of the same plot, leaving him forever at the moment of the murder, unable to move forward or in any new direction. As the trappings of English domestic life—bedframes, armchairs, inkbottles—whirl away, 'nothing is left but China'" (133).

normative function of object relations within individual houses: "Changes in the material order of the home—as in the appropriation of domestic space, the choice and arrangement of furnishings and decor, as well as in the domestic routines and provisioning of the household—reflect and indeed define cultural changes" (145). When viewed through such a lens, the materialist analyses of domesticity that comprise *The Objects and Textures of Everyday Life* work together to convey a sense of how the artifacts of daily life in imperial Britain acquired meaning and social function. Charting the contingent and shifting social functions of things in their historical context also provides additional scholarly insight into the processes through which individuals and groups became constituted as gendered, classed, national and imperial subjects. In our focus on patterns of use, our volume underscores that individuals and groups were not just subject to but active subjects in the diverse and elaborate cultural systems, each with its own rituals and internal divisions, that made up imperial Britain.

In examining what Annette B. Weiner has called "the symbolic densities of objects" (394), each chapter in *The Objects and Textures of Everyday Life in Imperial Britain* owes a debt to Judy Attfield's championing of material culture as a compelling site for analyzing the nuanced politics of everyday experience. Despite the growing field of material culture studies of nineteenth-century Britain to which this volume seeks to contribute, the everyday remains under-explored territory, particularly in analyses of the permeable and mutually reinforcing ideological foundations of nineteenth-century Britain: domesticity and imperialism.[4] As Beth Fowkes Tobin argues, "[n]ot only do objects ... participate in the formation of identities and the constitution of embodied subjectivities; subjects can endow objects with subjectivity, and furthermore, objects can act with a kind of agency we tend to think should be reserved for human subjects" (2). This interplay between subject and object is at the heart of the chapters in this collection. Each examines

---

[4]   Our volume represents and participates in what Lyn Pykett calls "The Material Turn in Victorian Studies." Precursors such as Nupur Chaudhuri's "Shawls, Jewelry, Curry, and Rice in Victorian Britain" indicate the durability of this approach, but material analyses of nineteenth-century British culture have gained greater critical momentum in the past decade. In 2007, for example, the North American Victorian Studies Association themed their influential annual convention on "Victorian Materialities." As an outcome of this conference, *Victorian Studies* devoted a special issue on the topic (Winter 2008). *The Journal of British Studies* also devoted a special issue to material culture in April 2009. The ongoing scholarly interest in "the material turn" is reflected in the following, among others: Isobel Armstrong, *Victorian Glassworlds: Glass Culture and the Imagination 1830–1880*; Jennie Batchelor and Cora Kaplan (eds) *Women and Material Culture, 1660–1830*; Goggin and Tobin (eds) *Women and Things, 1750–1950: Gendered Material Strategies*; Daniel Miller, *The Comfort of Things*; John Plotz, *Portable Property: Victorian Culture on the Move*; Leah Price, *How to Do Things with Books in Victorian Britain*; Talia Schaffer, *Novel Craft: Victorian Domestic Handicraft and Nineteenth-Century Fiction*; and John Styles and Amanda Vickery (eds) *Gender, Taste and Material Culture in North America and Britain, 1700–1830*.

the way ordinary household objects generate practices that are so woven into the fabric of everyday life that they exert a seemingly invisible influence over those who use them. Although this volume does not attempt to be comprehensive—one of our arguments is that such an undertaking would be impossible—the range of scholarship represented indicates a cross-disciplinary investment in the everyday as a category of analysis in the study of how things were used to work through the internal contradictions and discomforts associated with British identity construction during the age of empire.

Critical Background: Material Culture Studies of Nineteenth-Century Britain

In its methodology, *The Objects and Textures of Everyday Life in Imperial Britain* builds upon the critical practices of social historian Asa Briggs, who advocated treating Victorian things as "emissaries" of the period's messy, often contradictory political and social thought. Briggs's *Victorian Things* (1988) is a pioneering work within this field, which gathered interest as Marxist, feminist, and postcolonial scholars turned their critical lenses toward the physical traces of nineteenth-century culture. With the rise of industrialism and the advent of mass production, the nineteenth century saw a wider array of consumer goods made available to the burgeoning middle classes. Seismic shifts in consumerism followed and deepened in response, gaining new opportunities via increased imperial exchange. As John Plotz quips at the start of *Portable Property* (2008): "One universally acknowledged truth about the Victorians is that they loved their things" (1). Briggs offers similar observations, tempered by the key contention that "the economic inability of large groups of the population to acquire things was even more significant in Victorian Britain than personal refusal to do so. In 1900/1901 only 17 per cent of the population left enough property for it to be recorded in the probate records" (17). The daily life explored by our volume thus necessarily represents a partial rendering of nineteenth-century Britain. Our analyses remain weighted toward households in the latter half of the century with middle-class or higher resources and status. In addition to greater purchasing power and arrays of material possessions, such households were the subjects of greater record-keeping, which helps to illuminate their relationship with specific objects. The association of new goods and consumption patterns with traditional values encouraged the seeming solidification of the middle classes, but as the chapters collected here demonstrate, internal divisions suggest a broad range of economic realities, allegiances and aspirations within the middle classes.

It becomes evident when surveying materialist studies of nineteenth-century Britain that critical attention has favored static objects rather than objects in use. Considerable materialist scholarship has focused on museums or collections, particularly in analyses of acquisition and display. Perhaps the best-known example of the Victorian fascination with things remains the Great Exhibition of 1851, which gathered 14,000 exhibitors from 77 countries, whose goods represented the best manufactures that the world had to offer. More than 6 million people, the majority British, came to the Crystal Palace in London's Hyde Park to see the massive, spectacular display of objects. Whether the ensuing debate centered on the aesthetic failures of British art and design, the uneasy status afforded to Irish manufacturing, or the Exhibition's representation of a global marketplace, the objects on display were recognized at the time as having multiple and shifting meanings as well as significant cultural import. Described by art historian Francis Klingender as "by far the best documented event in the nineteenth century" (165), the Great Exhibition continues as a primary site for scholarship on midcentury national and imperial imperatives, helping to advance a materialistic approach in nineteenth-century studies.[5]

In large part because of the period's simultaneous professionalization of the museum and the expansion of the middle classes and their ability to afford what Richard Altick called "the shows of London," scholars such as Tony Bennett, Barbara J. Black, and Christopher Whitehead have turned their attention to the cultural reflection and impact of museums' acquisition and exhibition strategies. A crucial strand of criticism on collecting—represented by Annie Coombes, Tim Barringer and Tom Flynn, and Lara Kriegel—has focused specifically on empire in British museology, suggesting that display of imperial artifacts marks and contains not only things, but also colonized geography and peoples, shoring up a complicated British identity in the process. This important critical strand privileges exhibition, however, above the other uses of things; once installed, the objects themselves are valuable in part for their stasis rather than their potential malleability or range of utility.

Despite many fascinating materialist studies of the Great Exhibition and other formal collections, scholars have paid less attention to the household goods, kitchens, roadways, advertisements, routine transactions and daily reckonings of Victorian domestic life. The strong critical engagement with nineteenth-century domestic ideologies—ushered in by literary critics Martha Vicinus, and Sandra M. Gilbert and Susan Gubar, and by historians Leonore Davidoff and Catherine

---

[5] See the following studies, among others: Jeffrey A. Auerbach, *The Great Exhibition of 1851: A Nation on Display*; Jeffrey A. Auerbach and Peter H. Hoffenberg (eds) *Britain, the Empire and the World at the Great Exhibition of 1851* ; Tony Bennett, "The Exhibitionary Complex"; James Buzard, Joseph W. Childers and Eileen Gillooly, *Victorian Prism: Refractions of the Crystal Palace*; Hermione Hobhouse, *The Crystal Palace and the Great Exhibition: Art, Science and Productive Industry: The History of the Royal Commission for the Exhibition of 1851*; Peter H. Hoffenberg, *An Empire on Display: English, Indian, and Australian Exhibitions from the Crystal Palace to the Great War*; Lara Kriegel, *Grand Designs: Labor, Empire and the Museum in Victorian Culture*; Louise Purbrick (ed.) *The Great Exhibition of 1851: New Interdisciplinary Essays*; Thomas Richards, *The Commodity Culture of Victorian England: Advertising and Spectacle, 1851–1914*; Tobin Andrews Sparling, *The Great Exhibition: A Question of Taste*; and Paul Young, *Globalization and the Great Exhibition: The Victorian New World Order*.

Hall—has emphasized gender dynamics and material conditions, but not typically material objects as a primary focus of study.[6] Notable exceptions to this scholarly trend are often either site or craft specific, such as Thad Logan's ground-breaking *The Victorian Parlour* (2001) or Kathryn Ledbetter's *Victorian Needlework* (2012).

Our attention to the materiality of middle-class domesticity—in terms of its construction, aspiration and emulation as well as its inextricability from empire—shares similar impulses with Deborah Cohen's *Household Gods: The British and Their Possessions* (2006) and Suzanne Daly's *The Empire Inside: Indian Commodities in Victorian Domestic Novels* (2011). *The Objects and Textures of Everyday Life in Imperial Britain* complements these studies in important ways. Cohen posits an arc from 1830–1930 in which shifting expectations for interior décor aligned with shifts in popular morality, so that far from ruinous luxuries, domestic comforts came to be seen as evidence of proper investment in the home as a moral compass. Several of our contributors interrogate the gender politics of interior furnishing, as does Cohen, but our emphasis on common objects in use moves away from shops and other sites of acquisition so as to explore the links between domestic maintenance and identity: how keeping a proper home helped to define what it meant to be English and, by extension, to be British. Daly's analysis of the function of specific Indian imports in Victorian domestic novels similarly attends to the definition of Englishness at home in the metropole. In scope and genre, however, Daly's excellent study offers a more narrowly delineated treatment of the cultural work of specifically Indian objects in British domesticity.

Both Cohen and Daly express the need for greater critical analysis of the ideological forces embedded in the familiar artifacts of everyday experience. We attempt to meet this need by stressing the ideological imbrication of domesticity and imperialism, in part because these concepts were foundational to how Britain saw itself during this period but in equally large part because historians have too often polarized national versus imperial history. *The Objects and Textures of Everyday Life* thus directly answers Catherine Hall and Sonya Rose's call that "Historians of Britain need to open up national history and imperial history, challenging that binary and critically scrutinising the ways in which it has functioned as a way of normalising power relations and erasing our dependence on and exploitation of others" (5). The work of Antoinette Burton, Linda Colley, and Philippa Levine has been particularly important in redefining imperial history so that the imperial and domestic are no longer assumed to exist on parallel or oppositional planes. Our study contributes to this effort by demonstrating the complexity and unevenness of empire as experienced by many ordinary Britons, surrounded by and in part negotiating identity through the ordinary objects in their lives.

As the chapters in *The Objects and Textures of Everyday Life in Imperial Britain* indicate, the priorities of ordinary people can be discerned by how they

---

[6]   Instrumental scholars in the study of British domesticity of the period include Nancy Armstrong, Karen Chase and Michael Levenson, Deirdre David, Elizabeth Langland, Mary Poovey, and John Tosh, among others.

used the daily stuff of their lives; at the same time, larger trends in use suggest how individuals negotiated the many and at times contradictory meanings that became attached to things, even as the sociopolitical outlines against which individuals positioned themselves become clear. Furthermore, our study situates Victorian domesticity in a rich cultural and geographical topography that extends beyond the kitchen and parlour, as well as beyond England to diverse locales within the wider empire, including Scotland, India, the tropics and "the Orient."

These material traces of nineteenth-century Britain have significant cultural impact precisely because they are simultaneously ambivalent and yet so often unquestioned. As Rita Felski notes "[t]he distinctiveness of the everyday lies in its lack of distinction and differentiation; it is the air one breathes, the taken-for-granted backdrop, the commonsensical basis for all human activities" (80). The daily practices and rituals engendered by common objects and examined by the authors in this collection accrue weight through repetition. Doing the same thing day after day creates a pattern that is habitual but not predictive in nature. How things are used or understood in one household has limited bearing on how they *might* be used or understood in another. Social forces of conformity, emulation and resistance, however, channel possible and idiosyncratic uses to a smaller and more meaningful array. The routine use of a single object, though seemingly an apolitical matter of habit, may indicate ideological affiliations, evasions and deflections. The chapters that follow move from analyses of specific objects in specific contexts to comment upon what Pierre Bourdieu famously encapsulates in the concept of habitus—the process whereby everyday acts become central to how a group of individuals understand themselves. For nineteenth-century Britons, the daily routines of drinking tea, fixing meals, cleaning the parlour, and rearing children became crucial in constructing a collective social and national identity, one in which domestic and imperial influences continually intertwine. Far from being static, these processes work through—and thus exist uneasily and contingently within—the repetitions and transformations inherent in day-to-day experience. Each chapter in the volume illustrates the self-fashioning made possible through things by examining the recursive cycles of manufacture and consumption in which everyday objects were created, transported, used and repurposed. The practices that emerge from these patterns in turn reveal the dynamics by which individuals and groups formed their identities within the larger and ever-shifting cultural terrain of imperial Britain.

Chapter Overviews

Part I: Mapping Domestic Territories

In its broadest strokes, the collection is organized around three groupings that range chronologically from the early nineteenth century to the *fin de siècle* and thematically from the geographies of domestic space in England, to the intricacies of housekeeping, to the dynamic interchanges between domestic and imperial culture. The chapters that follow thus explore some of the many ways Britons in the nineteenth century negotiated the pressing cognitive and hands-on demands of self-definition in an imperial age. Mindful of Antoinette Burton's critique of postcolonial scholarship that reifies *a priori* an understanding of the nation as cohesive and stable before empire, the chapters in *Part I: Mapping Domestic Territories* focus on the contested edges of the nation as itself under production in the public imagination.[7] Taking seriously Burton's claim that "a nation is never fully realized, but always in-the-making" (148), our first three contributors illustrate how daily acts like consulting road maps, reading children's novels, and furnishing a new home worked to outline the geographical and psychic boundaries of nationhood and to educate middle-class Britons to become both discerning consumers and good citizens.

In the opening chapter of the collection, "The Tangible Shape of the Nation: The State, The Cheap Printed Map, and the Manufacture of British Identity, 1784–1855," Jo Guldi examines the role of the print industry in creating road maps that helped to define the shape of the nation as it was witnessed for the first time by most Britons. She explains how late eighteenth- and early nineteenth-century cartographers began to combine their surveys of distance with topographical and geographical detail, creating the first images that showed roads along with mountains, rivers, and the outlines of coasts. These maps were eagerly adopted by commercial interests and individual travelers. Until the 1850s, however, the accurate representation of the British Isles in map form routinely ended with Edinburgh, leaving the Scottish Highlands to trail into the blank space at the top of the page. Guldi argues that these road maps, designed to instruct travelers and facilitate communication and commercial exchange, constructed a unified image of the nation that was reinforced by subsequent textbooks and historical treatises. As scientifically informed and portable charts of the nation, though, such maps erased Highlanders in the unmapped North, who during the period were being culturally dispossessed and forced off the land. By demonstrating how the geographical representation of Great Britain remained in flux for much of the first half of the century, Guldi asserts that the first modern maps depended upon a fractured and contingent sense of national belonging and of "home."

---

[7]   In "Who Needs the Nation?" Burton identifies a trend in postcolonial scholarship and particularly in British historiography to maintain the centrality of the concept of the nation as if the nation had existed prior to empire. Such assumptions, she argues, limit critical engagement with a fundamental reassessment of how nations and empires come to be. According to Burton, "The extent to which we will succeed in displacing the nation from center stage depends in the end on our willingness to take seriously the ramifications of the claim that a nation is never fully realized, but always in the making—and to interrogate the ways in which our own narrative strategies may help fetishize one of history's most common explanatory frameworks" (148).

In "Establishing Stability: Conforming to Type in British House Furnishings, 1860–1910," Clive Edwards turns from an image of the nation as a whole to consider how expectations about the aesthetics of class allegiance influenced the interior spaces of the Victorian home. Drawing on a range of sources, including books on design, advice columns on household outfitting and maintenance, and magazine articles on "taste," as well as printed estimates from British retail furnishers that meticulously itemized the necessary furnishing and equipment for a range of households, Edwards argues that there were two conflicting generic approaches to house furnishing in the period 1860–1910. One, generally male dominated, followed established parameters of "good taste"; the other, often more female oriented, considered individuality and personality as appropriate bases for furnishings and décor. By looking at these contrasting perspectives, Edwards argues that the practices employed not only re-fashioned interiors but also engendered attitudes toward them, and in doing so established social stability through a degree of conformity in the design and types of furniture supplied for various economic levels.

Mary Jeanette Moran's "The Material Lessons of Children's Literature: Unearthing Class Standards in E. Nesbit's *The Story of the Treasure Seekers*" moves our volume to the engineering of class awareness among late-century children, focusing specifically on scripted uses of things as markers of middle-class conformity. Moran examines the growing market of books for children throughout the second half of the nineteenth century as both objects and narratives. Promoted first as ideal Christmas and birthday gifts, books for children soon became academic and Sunday school prizes, suggesting that parents and educators embraced their didactic potential. At the same time, however, children as a discrete and protected class and childhood as discrete and protected period of development become markers of middle-class identity. Moran analyzes how novels like Edith Nesbit's *The Story of the Treasure Seekers* (1899), which centers upon children rescuing their parents from financial ruin, orient young readers to their own class status. Moran argues that material lessons of children's literature leave young readers in a double bind: to be truly middle-class, they must value ideology—including the innocence and sanctity of childhood—more than things, but fervent allegiance to bourgeois ideals remains insufficient compared to the *deus ex machina* of a wealthy uncle.

Part II: Hearth, Home, and Housekeeping

The second section of the volume shifts discussion from the internal affairs of Great Britain to the internal workings of the middle-class home, paying particular attention to under-recognized trends in daily household objects and management. The opening chapter by Victoria Kelley, "Housekeeping: Shine, Polish and Glaze as Surface Strategies in the Domestic Interior," examines both the processes of degradation to which ordinary domestic objects were subjected as well as the processes of cleaning, polishing and maintaining that were used to stave off decay and to enhance surface integrity. Analyzing household advice in manuals and magazine columns, Kelley identifies what to the present-day reader might seem like a sort of *surface fanaticism*: unrelenting demands for the frequent and regular cleaning, brushing, buffing, polishing, pressing, and ironing of all manner of objects, from stair-rods to bed frames to stoves to larders to shoes to table linen to clothing. By attending to autobiographical accounts of working- and middle-class domestic routines, Kelley demonstrates how the gendered labor implicit in housekeeping standards also encourages an aesthetic of *surface delight*. Her analysis suggests the need for additional critical awareness and scrutiny of the laborious processes of maintenance and wear that shaped everyday objects, connecting nineteenth-century artifacts now often displayed in pristine museum collections to the people who owned, used and cared for them.

Continuing Kelley's emphasis on labor-intensive daily tasks, Sumangala Bhattacharya's "Kitchen Magic: Reforming the Victorian Kitchen with Alexis Soyer" analyzes two types of patent stoves marketed by celebrity chef Alexis Soyer—the "Magic Stove" and the "Kitchen Apparatus"—that promised to simplify the processes of cooking and housekeeping by relying on principles derived from industrial modernity. The Magic Stove, a small, portable appliance that could be used for outdoor cookery and for bachelor jaunts into the near and far east, offered an escape from domesticity, while the Kitchen Apparatus, a bulky multi-purpose gas appliance requiring expensive installation and maintenance, inscribed domesticity within the frameworks of industrial machinery and efficiency. The contrasts between these two appliances and the discourses of cookery that surrounded them thus speak to changing expectations about cooking as feminized domestic labor versus masculine freedom or professional endeavor.

Examining the interdependence of gender and labor politics, "Tea, Gender and Middle–Class Tastes," by co-editor Deirdre McMahon traces the history of the tea trade as a primer of British imperialism. Representations of the trade and consumption of tea in advertising, literature, and product packaging suggest both that the woman of the house would serve tea and that tea helps to make a house a home. In this way, an imperial product becomes an everyday part of the bourgeois household, even as the ritual of drinking tea becomes a code for civilization and for women's conformity to conventional domesticity. By examining first-person accounts by colonial administrators as well as business and legal records, McMahon brings the material conditions of tea production to bear in analyzing how gender dynamics fed the inequitable colonial relations underpinning tea's place in the British psyche. Any violence or coercion inherent in imperial trade is erased, replaced by the image of the smiling English mother offering tea, comfort, and middle-class allegiance in equal measure.

Part III: Imperial Possessions, Commodity Culture, and Colonial Return

The final chapters of the volume move outward to examine the impact of empire on the British domestic interior and vice versa, looking at how imperial commodities circulated throughout the empire, and paying particular attention to the processes of colonial return and appropriation. By discussing the often divergent images and uses of military medals, soap oils, and smoking pastils, these chapters examine how commodity culture functioned in part to mediate the relation between home and the colonies. In their respective contributions, Jason Howard Mezey and Bradley Deane also attend to how objects resist or refuse classification, maintaining their "thing-ness" despite Victorians' or recent critics' attempts at interpretation.

Jason Howard Mezey's "'A cross, a lion and a scroll or two': The Victoria Cross and the Substance of British Imperial Identity" connects the material failures of military command in the Crimea to the institution of the Victoria Cross as a democratizing gesture. Mezey then discusses the largest number of VCs handed out for a single action within a single battle (the Second Relief of Lucknow during Indian Mutiny) to theorize the larger clout of the VC in the imperialist quest for revenge and protection of the women and children associated with British holdings in India. So in many ways, the soldiers represent "every man" in Britain, eager to avenge the actual British casualties of the Mutiny as well as the threats against Britannia. The Victoria Cross itself is rarely awarded, but because the Victoria Cross operates so significantly in public discourses about bravery, masculinity and the British right to rule, it acts as a rhetorical touchstone for a shared vision of empire. This function is in stark contrast to the object itself, which was roundly criticized for its flaws in metal and design. These flaws are instrumental in charting how a thing becomes an object with such mythological grandeur that ironically, its value is now established as a commodity rather than as a relic or award. The ideological value that accrued to the VC is also in stark contrast to the consistent failures of the state to recognize and support the average soldier. To weigh the ideological versus material importance of representations of British valor, Mezey turns to the fate of many soldiers who returned to Great Britain after the war, most of whom faced poverty. The chapter ends with a brief study of Lord Michael Ashcroft, who recently donated the world's largest private collection of Victoria Crosses to be displayed in an eponymous gallery in the Imperial War Museum in London.

Bradley Deane's "Monkeys in the House: Commodities and Competing Fetishisms in Late Victorian Popular Culture" similarly dwells on the complex fantasies Victorians entertained about the objects that circulated throughout their empire. Deane merges analysis of commodity fetishes, specifically those associated with Monkey Brand soap, with discussion of imperial fetishes, such as the one that features prominently in W.W. Jacobs's famous short story, "The Monkey's Paw" (1902). In his analysis of soap advertising and late Victorian popular fiction, Deane theorizes the differences between an economic and anthropological approach to fetishism, showing how these discourses clashed in late Victorian representations of imperial objects entering the Victorian home. He argues that during the romance revival, many stories fantasized about colonial objects with covert magical properties, and by doing so challenged the complacencies of Victorian consumerism. The commodity may be fetishized, but in these stories the fetish refuses to be commodified. By resisting and even reversing the dynamic of commodity fetishism, Deane argues, these colonial objects reveal the dehumanizing and violent conditions of production that commodity fetishism disavows.

The final chapter of the collection, Kellie Holzer's "Lady Montagu's Smokers' Pastils and *The Graphic*: Advertising the Harem in the Home," examines the racial and sexual cross-identifications afforded by a series of advertisements in the first issue of the popular illustrated newspaper. The central advertisement—for Piesse & Lubin's breath mint, or "smoker's pastil"—capitalizes on the mid-nineteenth century British public's fascination with Oriental harems and Indian zenanas by ascribing a laudatory review of the product to Lady Mary Wortley Montagu. Though the review is an anachronistic fiction, as Montagu died a century *before* the firm was founded, the appropriation of Montagu's cultural clout associates the product with the East and with the exotic. In doing so, the advertisement brings the floral-scented lozenge from the harem to England, imparting to a specifically female reader that her breath can be sweetened just like that of the ladies in the harem. Piesse & Lubin link the hookah in the harem with the tobacco-consuming practices of the English drawing room, inviting the female reader to adopt the leisurely behaviors of elite Oriental women and insinuating that an English lady's smoking habit could be glamorous and exotic rather than disreputable and scandalous. Holzer argues that the practices invoked by this and adjacent ads for exotic complexion powders—including women smoking cigarettes, exercising individual purchasing power, recognizing their own sexuality, and identifying with racial and cultural others—were points of power for early feminist thinkers. In the actual advertisements, however, such practices were mediated and to an extent domesticated through a complex scopophilia that exoticizes the home even while fueling and neutralizing imperial commerce. Thus the advertisements come to represent a larger triumph of commodity culture to manipulate conflicting imperial and domestic ideologies, and indeed, to demonstrate that these ideologies work in tandem to reinforce the bottom line of imperial commerce: to buy, buy, buy.

Coda

As a whole, *The Objects and Textures of Everyday Life in Imperial Britain* foregrounds nineteenth-century concerns about the stability and stabilizing structures of life at home, when home itself is increasingly freighted by imperial sojourns, colonial return, class conflict and gender anxieties. Attuned to the tensions that surrounded nineteenth-century ideas of the domestic, our volume suggests that the recursive construction of Britishness itself remained wedded to things. Our volume thus calls for a more concretized criticism of the period, one particularly focused on how contingent and constantly shifting ideas of self, nation and empire were mediated and amplified in part through material possessions. In the mirror that reflects the woman's act of pouring tea, Crane's illustration reminds us that efforts to create and maintain the domestic might be both recursive and frequently overlooked. The chapters that follow seek to attend to the stuff of everyday life, with the recognition that using common objects for social, economic, or political benefit may reveal just how constructed and contested the ordinary might be.

Works Cited

Altick, Richard. *The Shows of London*. Cambridge, MA: Harvard University Press, 1978. Print.

Appadurai, Arjun. *The Social Life of Things: Commodities in Cultural Perspective*. Cambridge: Cambridge University Press, 1986. Print.

Armstrong, Isobel. *Victorian Glassworlds: Glass Culture and the Imagination, 1830–1880*. NY: Oxford University Press, 2008. Print.

Armstrong, Nancy. *Desire and Domestic Fiction: A Political History of the Novel*. NY: Oxford University Press, 1987. Print.

Attfield, Judy. *Wild Things: The Material Culture of Everyday Life*. NY: Berg, 2000. Print.

Auerbach, Jeffrey A. *The Great Exhibition of 1851: A Nation on Display*. New Haven, CT: Yale University Press, 1999. Print.

Auerbach, Jeffrey A., and Peter H. Hoffenberg (eds) *Britain, the Empire, and the World at the Great Exhibition of 1851*. Burlington, VT: Ashgate, 2008. Print.

Austin, J.L. *How to Do Things With Words*. Cambridge, MA: Harvard University Press, 1962. Print.

Barringer, Tim, and Tom Flynn (eds) *Colonialism and the Object: Empire, Material Culture, and the Museum*. NY: Routledge, 1998. Print.

Batchelor, Jennie, and Cora Kaplan (eds) *Women and Material Culture, 1660–1830*. NY: Palgrave Macmillan, 2007. Print.

Bennett, Tony. *The Birth of the Museum: History, Theory, Politics*. NY: Routledge, 1995. Print.

Bhabha, Homi. "The World and the Home." *Social Text* 31/32 (1992): 141–53. Web.

Black, Barbara J. *On Exhibit: The Victorians and Their Museums*. Charlottesville, VA: University of Virginia Press, 2000. Print.

Blunt, Alison. *Domicile and Diaspora: Anglo-Indian Women and the Spatial Politics of Home*. Malden, MA: Blackwell, 2005. Print.

Bourdieu, Pierre. *Distinction: A Social Critique of the Judgment of Taste*. Trans. Richard Nice. Cambridge, MA: Harvard University Press, 1987. Print.

Briggs, Asa. *Victorian Things*. Chicago: University of Chicago Press, 1989. Print.

Brown, Bill. *A Sense of Things: The Object Matter of American Literature*. Chicago: University of Chicago Press, 2003. Print.

Burton, Antoinette. "Who Needs the Nation?" (ed.) Catherine Hall. *Cultures of Empire: Colonizers in Britain and the Empire in the Nineteenth and Twentieth Centuries*. NY: Routledge, 2000. 137–53. Print.

Buzard, James, Joseph W. Childers, and Eileen Gillooly (eds) *Victorian Prism: Refractions of the Crystal Palace*. Charlottesville, VA: University of Virginia Press, 2007. Print.

Chang, Elizabeth Hope. *Britain's Chinese Eye: Literature, Empire and Aesthetics in Nineteenth-Century Britain*. Stanford, CA: Stanford University Press, 2010. Print.

Chase, Karen, and Michael Levenson. *The Spectacle of Intimacy: A Public Life for the Victorian Family*. Princeton, NJ: Princeton University Press, 2000. Print.

Chaudhuri, Nupur. "Shawls, Jewelry, Curry and Rice in Victorian England" (eds) Nupur Chaudhuri and Margaret Strobel. *Western Women and Imperialism: Complicity and Resistance*. Bloomington, IN: Indiana University Press, 1992. 231–46. Print.

Cohen, Deborah. *Household Gods: The British and Their Possessions*. New Haven, CT: Yale University Press, 2009. Print.

Colley, Linda. *Britons: Forging the Nation 1707–1837*. London; Pimlico, 2003. Print.

Cook, Clarence. *The House Beautiful: Essays on Beds and Tables, Stools and Candlesticks*. NY: Scribner, Armstrong and Co., 1878. Print.

Coombes, Annie E. *Reinventing Africa: Museums, Material Culture, and Popular Imagination in Late Victorian and Edwardian England*. New Haven, CT: Yale University Press, 1997. Print.

Daly, Suzanne. *The Empire Inside: Indian Commodities in Victorian Domestic Novels*. Ann Arbor, MI: University of Michigan Press, 2011. Print.

David, Deirdre. *Rule Britannia: Women, Empire and Victorian Writing*. Ithaca, NY: Cornell University Press, 1995. Print.

Davidoff, Leonore, and Catherine Hall. *Family Fortunes: Men and Women of the English Middle Class, 1780–1850*. NY: Routledge, 2003. Print.

Dickens, Charles. *The Mystery of Edwin Drood* (ed.) Margaret Cardwell. Oxford: Oxford University Press, 1999. Print.

Douglas, Mary, and Baron Isherwood. *The World of Goods: Towards an Anthropology of Consumption*. 1979. London: Routledge, 1996. Print.

Eagleton, Terry. *Ideology: An Introduction*. London: Verso, 1991. Print.

Felski, Rita. *Doing Time: Feminist Theory and Postmodern Culture*. NY and London: New York University Press, 2000. Print.

Freedgood, Elaine. *The Ideas in Things: Fugitive Meanings in the Victorian Novel*. Chicago: University of Chicago Press, 2006. Print.

Gallagher, Catherine. *The Industrial Reformation of English Fiction: Social Discourse and Narrative Form, 1832–1914*. Chicago: University of Chicago Press, 1988. Print.

George, Rosemary Marangoly. *The Politics of Home: Postcolonial Relocations and Twentieth-Century Fiction*. Cambridge: Cambridge University Press, 1996. Print.

Gilbert, Sandra M., and Susan Gubar. *The Madwoman in the Attic: The Woman Writer and the Nineteenth-Century Literary Imagination*. New Haven, CT: Yale University Press, 1979. Print.

Goggin, Maureen Daly, and Beth Fowkes Tobin (eds) *Women and Things, 1750–1950: Gendered Material Strategies*. Burlington, VT: Ashgate, 2009. Print.

Grewal, Inderpal. *Home and Harem: Nation, Gender, Empire, and the Cultures of Travel*. Durham and London: Duke University Press, 1996. Print.

Hall, Catherine, and Sonya O. Rose (eds) *At Home With the Empire: Metropolitan Culture and the Imperial World*. NY: Cambridge University Press, 2007. Print.

Hobhouse, Hermione. *Crystal Palace and the Great Exhibition: Art, Science, and Productive Industry: A History of the Royal Commission for the Exhibition of 1851*. London and NY: Continuum, 2004. Print.

Hoffenberg, Peter H. *An Empire on Display: English, Indian, and Australian Exhibitions from the Crystal Palace to the Great War*. Berkeley and Los Angeles: University of California Press, 2001. Print.

Jacobs, W.W. "The Monkey's Paw." *The Lady of the Barge*. 1902. NY: Dodd, Mead and Co., 1911. 27–53. Print.

Klingender, Francis Donald. *Art and the Industrial Revolution*. 1947 (rev. and ed.) Arthur Elton. NY: Schocken, 1970. Print.

Kriegel, Lara. *Grand Design: Labor, Empire and the Museum in Victorian Culture*. Durham: Duke University Press, 2007. Print.

Langland, Elizabeth. *Nobody's Angels: Middle-Class Women and Domestic Ideology in Victorian Culture*. Ithaca, NY: Cornell University Press, 1995. Print.

Ledbetter, Kathryn. *Victorian Needlework*. Santa Barbara, CA: Praeger, 2012. Web.

Levine, Philippa. *Gender and Empire*. NY: Oxford University Press, 2007. Print.

Logan, Thad. *The Victorian Parlour: A Cultural Study*. Cambridge: Cambridge University Press, 2006. Print.

McClintock, Anne. *Imperial Leather: Race, Gender and Sexuality in the Colonial Contest*. NY: Routledge, 1995. Print.

Meyer, Susan. *Imperialism at Home: Race and Victorian Women's Fiction*. Ithaca, NY: Cornell University Press, 1996. Print.

Miller, Andrew H. *Novels Behind Glass: Commodity, Culture and Victorian Narrative*. Cambridge: Cambridge University Press, 1995. Print.

Miller, Daniel. *The Comfort of Things*. Boston: Polity, 2008. Print.

Milligan, Barry. *Pleasures and Pains: Opium and the Orient in 19th-Century British Culture*. Charlottesville, VA: University of Virginia Press, 1995. Print.

Nesbit, E. *The Story of the Treasure Seekers*. 1899. San Francisco: Chronicle Books, 2006. Print.

O'Connor, Erin. *Raw Material: Producing Pathology in Victorian Culture*. Durham, NC: Duke University Press, 2000. Print.

Perera, Suvendrini. *Reaches of Empire: The English Novel From Edgeworth to Dickens*. NY: Columbia University Press, 1991. Print.

Plotz, John. *Portable Property: Victorian Culture on the Move*. Princeton, NJ: Princeton University Press, 2008. Print.

Poovey, Mary. *Uneven Developments: The Ideological Work of Gender in Mid-Victorian England*. Chicago: University of Chicago Press, 1988. Print.

Price, Leah. *How to Do Things With Books in Victorian England*. Princeton, NJ: Princeton University Press, 2012. Print.

Purbrick, Louise (ed.) *The Great Exhibition of 1851: New Interdisciplinary Essays*. NY: Manchester University Press, 2001. Print.

Putnam, Tim. "'Postmodern' Home Life." *At Home: An Anthropology of Domestic Space* (ed.) Irene Cieraad. Syracuse, NY: Syracuse University Press, 1999. 145–54. Print.

Pykett, Lyn. "The Material Turn in Victorian Studies." *Literature Compass* 1.1 (January 2003–December 2004). Web.

Richards, Thomas. *The Commodity Culture of Victorian England: Advertising and Spectacle, 1851–1914*. Stanford, CA: Stanford University Press, 1990. Print.

Richards, Thomas. *The Imperial Archive: Knowledge and the Fantasy of Empire*. London and NY: Verso, 1993. Print.

Schaffer, Talia. *Novel Craft: Victorian Domestic Handicraft and Nineteenth-Century Fiction*. NY: Oxford University Press, 2011. Print.

Sparling, Tobin Andrews. *The Great Exhibition: A Question of Taste*. New Haven, CT: Yale Center for British Art, 1982. Print.

Stoler, Ann Laura. *Carnal Knowledge and Imperial Power: Race and the Intimate in Colonial Rule*. Berkeley and Los Angeles, CA: University of California Press, 2002. Print.

Styles, John, and Amanda Vickery (eds) *Gender, Taste and Material Culture in North America and Britain, 1700–1830*. New Haven, CT: Yale/Paul Mellon Centre, 2007. Print.

Tobin, Beth Fowkes. "Consumption as a Gendered Social Practice." *Material Women, 1750–1950: Consuming Desires and Collecting Practices* (eds) Maureen Daly Goggin and Beth Fowkes Tobin. Burlington, VT: Ashgate, 2009. 1–13. Print.

Tosh, John. *A Man's Place: Masculinity and the Middle-Class Home in Victorian England*. New Haven, CT: Yale, 2007. Print.

Vicinus, Martha. *Suffer and Be Still: Women in the Victorian Age*. Bloomington, IN: Indiana University Press, 1973. Print.

Waters, Catherine. *Commodity Culture in Dickens's* Household Words*: The Social Life of Goods*. Burlington, VT: Ashgate, 2008. Print.

Weiner, Annette B. "Cultural Difference and the Density of Objects." *American Ethnologist* 21.2 (1994): 391–403. Web.

Whitehead, Christopher. *The Public Art Museum in Nineteenth-Century Britain: The Development of the National Gallery*. Burlington, VT: Ashgate, 2005. Print.

Williams, Raymond. *Culture and Society: 1780–1950*. 1958. NY: Columbia University Press, 1983. Print.

Young, Paul. *Globalization and the Great Exhibition: The Victorian New World Order*. NY: Palgrave Macmillan, 2009. Print.

PART I:
Mapping Domestic Territories

Chapter 1

The Tangible Shape of the Nation: The State, the Cheap Printed Map, and the Manufacture of British Identity, 1784–1855

Jo Guldi

In 1775, James Boswell had just heard that parts of the East Indies were better mapped than the Highlands, a fact he found outrageous. As Boswell and Samuel Johnson both knew, no single authority was to blame for the white spaces on available maps of the Highlands, but there were important consequences to follow from those lacunae. The production of maps functioned as a rough gauge of commercial interest, and consequently the hopes for development and enrichment that a region could expect. Johnson only observed coolly, "That a country may be mapped, it must be travelled over" (2: 363). As a native Scot, Boswell resented what he discerned in the tides of history. A lack of travel in Scotland and a lack of maps ordained a continued dearth of interest and investment in the region moving forward. It implied the continuation of poverty by a structured pessimism about Scotland's susceptibility to improvement, and that very attitude, as soon as it became evident in a lack of maps, determined the failure of investment to follow. Wasn't the implication of England's mapping preferences, objected Boswell to Johnson, that Scotland "is not *worth* mapping?" (2: 363). His question belied both puzzlement and resentment. Who had determined that Scotland wasn't worth mapping? Was it the fault of many generations of travelers, or of anonymous investors, or mappers commercial or governmental, or something murkier like cultural opinion, as Johnson seemed to imply? All that Boswell could tell was that the values bound up with that lack of maps would have profound economic consequences for disparities that would impact generations to come.

We tend to think of enlightenment initiatives like surveying, travel, and mapping as coherent and unilateral processes of state control and exploitation, intended by European elites as the predecessor to a program of economic assimilation and inclusion, envisioned from the beginning through desires for control and dominance over other peoples.[1] In histories since Francis Bacon, the technology of mapmaking has played the role of accomplice to enlightenment, and since T.B. Macaulay, British historians have depended upon such a thrust of history to explain how modern Britons came to understand themselves as members of a

---

[1]   See Michael Biggs.

nation united by their experience of modern materiality. More recent historians such as Roy Porter and Matthew Edney have followed Macaulay directly into a privileging of the printing press and paper as tools of assimilative enlightenment.[2] In their histories, material objects like books and maps are represented as the vehicles of power, capable of playing a single role in history, that is, bending the collective psychology of their readership inevitably towards the ideological unity of peoples and nations. In the case of nationalist historians like Linda Colley, the circulation of maps and travelers suggests how objects reproduced enlightenment ideas and helped to create a unified, egalitarian nation with a modern idea of citizenship. In the case of historians of empire like Matthew Edney, the circulation of maps among the elites suggests how European elites reproduced their own hierarchical view of society into the objects they used, which came to embody differentials in power rather than an age of access to all promised by defenders of enlightenment. In both stories, the map as object appears as a mere reflection of elite intent, reproducing and extending the reach of power to assimilate and to exploit.

Yet the maps have a story of their own to tell, one less about reproducing the strategies and ideas of elites than about the efficacy of objects themselves and the law of unintended consequences. Boswell's confusion, as an eighteenth-century map reader wondering at the intentions of map designers, points us to a rift in the life of the object. Was the printed map really the mute vehicle for the transmission of power that recent historians have claimed? Or was it a technology invested with the eerie power to shape mass psychology in directions unanticipated by its designers, a role ascribed to technology by now forgotten theorists like historian of technology, Lewis Mumford?

The distorted borders on Boswell's map were the result of a process of state power as translated through the competing discourses of rival institutions within the state, a process that political historians have conceptualized as "governmentality," after Michel Foucault. Such a process occurs as compounded institutional decisions create unforeseen consequences in the institutionalization of information flow, giving rise to profound after effects in access to power and the market.[3] In Britain, government map making stretched backwards to the nautical maps of the seventeenth century and the military maps of the 1720s before being

---

[2] For the origins of these stories, see Joad Raymond. Also see Roy Porter's *Enlightenment*, which sketches a coffee-house world of pamphlets, books, and public discourse to argue that Britain's early path to modernity produced the political stability that kept it safe during Europe's revolutionary moment of 1848. For comparison with the later, national newspaper press and its role in nationalism, see Bob Harris, Lucy Brown, Joel Howard Wiener, and Simon James Potter. Matthew Edney's *Mapping an Empire* argues that the British used the trigonometric survey of India to establish the subcontinent as a knowable domain ready for exploitation. Like Macaulay and Porter, Edney privileges the politics of an era over a deciphering of material objects and their contested uses.

[3] See Mitchell Dean, Matthew Hannah, Tania Li, and S.A. Marston.

extended to the nationwide collection of data on roads with the launch of the Ordnance Survey. Between 1784 and 1855, as mapmakers directly translated the state's activities for a consuming public, a new industry of stationers and printers benefited from access to the Post and Ordnance Survey data, causing a flourishing tide of maps to be disseminated to commercial travelers and tourists, gradually trickling down into the classroom itself.

In fact, the eighteenth-century map was very much the product of multiple and conflicting intentions, part of a larger chain involving institutional actors such as the military, the state, commercial surveyors and publishers, and readers themselves. In 1784, when government activity with the Post prompted the first modern road maps, government data had become the primary source upon which the printing of maps depended. Commercial cartographers engraved and published maps relying entirely for their data upon government-directed surveys conducted by the military and Post, whose activities were structured according to the hierarchical divisions of the early eighteenth century. The military survey of Scotland conducted between 1747 and 1755 remained the last use of the most advanced surveying methods and technology in Scotland, even while new military surveys were conducted of England and Ireland, creating a far more accurate representation of these territories. By 1800, the original Scottish survey was hopelessly out of date; yet the military's other obligations meant postponing Scottish surveying until the 1860s.

In the transmission of maps down a chain of actors with conflicting aims and readerships, linear intentions were frustrated. Despite complaints from London publishers, initiatives by Edinburgh cartographers, and indeed even the assimilation-bent policies of the government itself after 1790, none of these factors reversed the pattern of exclusion set by eighteenth-century government surveying. As a result, London publishers proved unwilling to incorporate their haphazard knowledge of Scotland in their new, scientific representations of Britain as a whole. Thus the common traveler's map of Britain represented an icon of the nation jarring to modern eyes: through the 1850s, publishers routinely depicted Scotland as a white corner on the map, lopping off everything above Edinburgh with the parchment's edge.

Governmental borders and omissions were converted to general experience through the materiality of the modern road map: the lightweight, folded, mass-produced, bird's-eye view of the roads that appeared only with government subsidies after 1784. Until 1855, when the repeal of the Stamp Acts created a truly national press, the cheap printed map formed the primary point of access by which most Britons grasped how their nation had been connected by the state building of roads and expansion of commerce. This visible shape of the nation, in tangible and portable form, offered Britons a ticket for exploration and a tool for belonging. The new roadmaps immediately began reshaping both the abstract national imaginary of the nation and the daily experience of navigation across territory. Cheap maps, instruments of national imaginary and distortion both, meanwhile spread into every fissure of British life from property speculation and commercial travel to basic education, as children learned to understand the historical necessity of the nation by reading maps. Maps offered one of the primary tools for molding the meaning of British citizenship before 1850.

Contemporaries like Boswell were capable of a critical reading of these objects, wondering how the absence of information would shape decisions down the line. Many eighteenth-century people must have felt similarly frustrated in tracing the ordering of knowledge, power, and investment in the new objects of information acquisition (such as maps) that surrounded them. Their objects were the product of conflicting desires for the nation, a contingent chain of information handing down maps in sometimes arbitrary formats. New actors were playing a role in shaping the flow of investment in ways less rational or consensus-driven than theorists of sentimental economics like Bernard Mandeville and Adam Smith might have predicted.

What they were less able to articulate was how the contingent chain of state and commercial surveyors, as well as the objects that passed between them, structured the flow of events down the line, or how the processes of governmentality continuously thwart the intentions of designers and reformers alike. Just so, the decisions of eighteenth-century investors were being shaped by a new world of information and maps, a world where small choices at the institutional level had potentially disproportionate consequences in the shape of standardized, mass-produced objects of information, like the map and the guidebook, and their potential to influence economic choices.

Yet even though they were the product of contingent and arbitrary inclusions and exclusions of information, maps nevertheless reshaped the way Britons thought about the borders of their world. New maps designed for pedagogy, mineral extraction, and land speculation recopied the fissures in the nation enshrined by the state, enforcing a rule of exclusion and ignorance of the nation's peripheries. Students memorizing the names of every British hamlet and cove so that they could trade there as adults, for example, had no knowledge of the nuances of Scotland or Ireland. As Boswell understood, maps governed imagination, and imagination governed investment. The maps, contingent and arbitrary as they were, nevertheless continued to shape experiences of wealth and poverty for generations to come.

These facts produce a story with subtle but important differences from the established history of how mute objects encouraged the rest of the world to desire both rule by and participation in the European elite. Eighteenth-century maps, the product of mixed intentions and elite confusions, were never intended as the harbingers of English identity inflicted onto Scotland. Rather, the slippages and oversights created by the contradictory impulses of the military, the state, and the investor produced haphazard objects misaligned with their intention, at the very same moment when markets conspired to give these objects a disproportionate power over the imagination of their readers. Far from being the mute vehicle of power, the map was an agent with a mind of its own, capable of diverging from the desires of its designers and reconceptualizing British identity in unintended ways.

The State as Patron of the Public Map

Modern maps were bound up with nation-building and the nation-state. Cheapness and accuracy depended upon the expensive surveys behind the maps having been conducted, for the first time, not by private firms or individual entrepreneurs, but rather by the state itself. Surveys of England, Scotland, and Ireland, initially conducted by the military for reconnaissance purposes, were eventually offered to the public through the instrumentation of the Post Office with its mandate to further national security by another route, the improvement of communications. The coming of the cheap map was thus linked to other means of exploring the nation: military conquest, a national road network, a national coach network, and a national mail, each of them the direct enterprise of the state.

Specifically, the quantitative, standardized practices of eighteenth-century mapmaking and publication were wholly dependent upon the military. Military schools brought England the best of trigonometric research from the continent.[4] Military surveyors themselves became the first serial map publishers. Daniel Paterson, originally surveyor and Assistant Quarter-Master-General of His Majesty's Forces, while on the Board of Ordnance forged the first link between the government and the public road map. During his travels for the Ordnance, Paterson had carefully documented situations when his own estimates of road length differed from the figures in Ogilby's seventeenth-century strip-maps, the contemporary standard for road distances ("Carnan *against* Bowles"). Paterson's *New and Accurate Description of All the Direct and Cross Roads of England* appeared in 1772, offering the first new survey of Britain's roads in a century, its data the direct reflection of individual travels sponsored by the military on the nation's roads.

But it was the Post Office, rather than the military, that was responsible for the graphic layout and physical shape of the single-sheet, folded road map as we know it. The Post Office had been engaged since 1711 in periodically resurveying the distances of England's roads so as to accurately rate postage (Lewins 67). In 1784, that practice received a new stimulus when Britain's Post Office received a mandate to oversee expanding communications in the form of roads and coaches.[5] John Cary, a London printer, had befriended John Palmer, the organizer of the new mail coaches. In 1784, the year when the first mail coaches left the General Post Office in Lombard Street, Palmer commissioned Cary to produce a new kind of map, synthesizing the data that Postal Surveyors had been collecting in the course of appointing new coach routes to carry the mail. Palmer's commission launched two of the most important names in nineteenth-century cartography: both Cary and his surveyor, Aaron Arrowsmith, would set up map shops of their own. Cary's was along the Strand and Arrowsmith's was in Long Acre (Baigent). At Palmer's

---

[4]   I discuss eighteenth-century innovations in trigonometry, surveying, and engineering and their relationship to the military in *Roads to Power*, chapter 1.

[5]   See Frederick Baines, 5–27.

behest, Cary was granted a monopoly on the Post Office survey data and the power to reproduce it.

The maps of both Cary and Arrowsmith were marked by the stamp of the Post. Both depicted the road system that carried the post coaches as their subject. The General Post Office, Lombard Street, served as the center for all distances, being the point from which all mail coaches departed. The Post coach routes meant that the maps' most important feature was a direct relationship to the details of topography and connection that determined whether a coach would be on time. As a result of these official requirements, Cary's maps broke with the seventeenth-century tradition of the strip-map and distance table, oriented to the traveler's plodding course over a single route, by instead supplying a new idiom: the topographically nuanced national road map (Delano-Smith and Kain 168–77).[6] Seventeenth- and early eighteenth-century cartographers of the road network typically offered the road as a horizontal strip—hence the name "strip-map"—to either side of which were houses, towns, bridges, and other landmarks for navigation. A single page icon of the nation, with major corridors, gave the only clue about where highways intersected or how one might choose between alternative routes leading from London to Edinburgh. Users of Emanuel Bowen's *Britannia Depicta* (1764), for instance, would have little sense of how the jags in the road corresponded to nearby property lines or geographical outcroppings. The one source of information for comparing different routes were the numerical "distance tables" that comprised the bulk of most travelers' texts: exhaustive estimates, in miles, of the distance between one town and the next (Figure 1.1). The audience these books catered to was small, well-traveled, and polite. Its travelers needed less topographical information, probably relying on hired guides to help them navigate between towns.

Instead of resorting to limited corridors and numerical abstractions, Cary's maps expanded the bird's-eye overview of the road network from a minimally mapped appendage to the central feature of the text. They borrowed a detailed, topographical, bird's-eye view from military surveys, drawing out the contours of territory for everyday travelers for the first time, and so projecting map users who were visually engaged with the landscape, actively wayfinding their routes through unfamiliar territory.[7]

---

[6]   The first travel-sized road books gave limited information about the roads as a network. Sometimes luxury items painted on expensive vellum sheets, the road books catered to an elite who expected to employ local guides, not maps, to help them through the actual journey. From the 1670s small fold-out maps appeared in the pocket guides carried by travelers. They offered the image of a kingdom joined by a road network. Poorly corresponding to actual topography, they offered little practical help on the road. Early eighteenth-century road books focused on itineraries—the path from one town to the next—rather than on the road network as a whole.

[7]   See John Cary's *A New and Accurate Topographical Survey of the Environs of London, Cary's Actual Survey of the Great Post Roads Between London and Falmouth,*

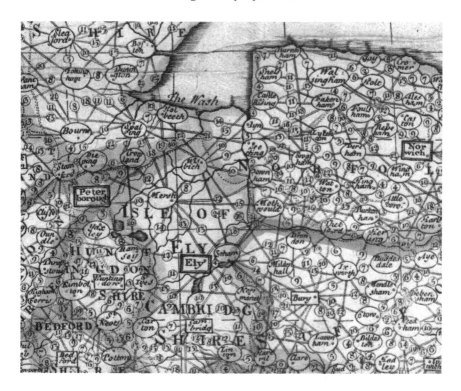

Figure 1.1   Distances reckoned as the crow flies
Source: Detail from John Bowles, *The Travellers Guide through England and Wales.* London: Bowles, 1737.

Cary's were thus the first road maps in the modern sense of the word, combining the visual recognition of landmarks, the comparison of distances, and the plotting of alternative routes into a single, efficient document (Figure 1.2). The format of the topographically nuanced national road map was generalized into accessible travelers' maps by Cary and the London printers who copied him. Beginning in 1824, Cary offered a reduced, six-sheet map, more convenient for travelers.

Cary's maps benefited in accuracy from his monopoly over Ordnance Survey data and notice of distance discrepancies by local postmasters by GPO order (Baines 118). His access to official data was reaffirmed 20 years later when he

---

Cary's New and Accurate Map of the County of Surry [sic], and *Cary's Actual Survey of the Country Ten Miles Round Hampton Court and Richmond.* Also see Yolande Jones.

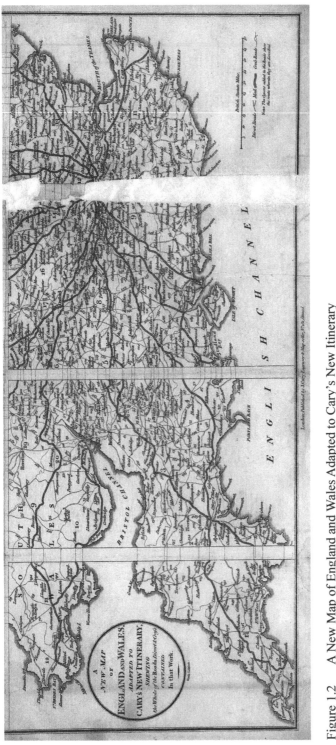

Figure 1.2   A New Map of England and Wales Adapted to Cary's New Itinerary
Source: John Cary. 6th edn London: J. Cary, 1815.

received a commission from the Ordnance Survey to reproduce its maps, again in return for a monopoly over the public reproduction of its data.[8]

The wide adoption and multiple editions of the new maps demonstrate the extent to which consumers also favored the bird's-eye view. By the 1820s, Daniel Paterson, Cary's major competitor, likewise dispatched with the distance tables that had formed his major revenue and began emulating Cary's roadmap. Cary's maps would be published in multiple editions for the next several decades and would form the pattern for widely disseminated maps like those of Crutchley, William and Charles Smith, and Letts and Sons, all of whom depended upon access to government data for their charts.[9] Reduced-sized images of Cary's maps recruited a large audience. From the single-sheet *New Map* to the *New Itinerary* pocket book and its expanded *Travelers Guide* to the larger *English Atlas*—each was released in a new edition every few years. Cary's monopoly on the printed map continued until the 1820s, when new surveys supplied further cheap maps, all of which copied Cary in the format of the topographically nuanced, national system of roads.[10] Even the dominant traveler's manual, *Paterson's Road Book*, became equipped with graphic maps rather than strip-maps and written descriptions in its 1826 edition. With more available data, however, other cheap national maps proliferated. Letts and Sons, for instance, stationers at the Royal Exchange, was one of a dozen firms that trucked in maps printed from the data of the Ordnance Survey. Working from government surveys allowed them, they argued, "to recommend without bias" the form of map most suited to each traveler (*The Annual Commercial Register* 266–9).

The state thus served as the primary patron of public cartography. It was government money that launched an entire industry of map production, located along the Strand, rapidly conveying new images of the nation into the hands of the public. Even into the 1840s, the map-printing firm of Arrowsmith and Basire thrived on the basis of a commission from the Board of Trade to plot the plans for railways that the Board was responsible for overseeing. The publishers then

---

[8] See William Ravenhill, 159–72; Cary v. Faden; Cary v. Longman; George Ticknor Curtis, 175; and Edmund Vale and Thomas Hasker, 2–3.

[9] See George Fordham, "The Work of John Cary and His Successors," and *John Cary, Engraver, Map, Chart and Print-Seller and Globe-Maker, 1754–1835*. Also see maps by John Cary cited in the bibliography.

[10] See George Allen; John Wallis, *Wallis's New Pocket Edition of the English Counties*; Aaron Arrowsmith, *Map of the Hills, Rivers, Canals, and Principal Roads, of England and Wales*; Charles Smith; Lewis Hebert; Edward Mogg, *A New Travelling Map of England, Wales and Scotland* and *Mogg's New Map of England and Wales, with Part of Scotland*; Edward Langley, *Langley's New Map of England & Wales* and *Langley's New Travelling and Commercial Map of England and Wales*; John Bumpus; C. Smith & Son; *Oliver & Boyd's New Travelling Map of England & Wales*; Robert Scott and A. Fullarton & Co.; James Wyld; J. & C. Walker; R. Creighton; John Betts; *Laurie's Travelling Map of England and Scotland*; S. Lewis & Co.; George Kemp; J. Pigot & Co.; J. & C. Walker, *England & Wales, Founded Upon the Grand Trigonometrical Survey*; and *Paterson's Roads*.

"purchased the plates from the Government" and printed a new series of 4' by 6' maps, documenting the categories "in *operation*—in *progress*—*projected*," as well as the railways projected and now defunct ("Railway Map of England and Wales" 176). When the Royal Geographical Society declared in 1841, that the Ordnance Map of England was "insufficient for the present and ever-growing wants of the country," it suggested that the government should commission a "colossal map" of Britain suited "for all imaginable purposes," which would form a "Parent Map" to be consulted by printers working for "all public boards and private individuals: financial maps, municipal maps, military maps, orographic, hydrographic, geological, metallurgic, zoological, botanical, agricultural maps, county maps, parish maps, road maps, historical maps," all of which might "be composed with great facility at very little comparative cost" (Greenough, "Address to the Royal Geographical Society" lxxii).

To contemporaries, the promise of so much data was striking in both its scale and its democratically accessible nature. In 1836, Britain's poet laureate Robert Southey contrasted the general topographical knowledge of his own day with a story of Peter Heylyn, one of England's most famous geographers of the seventeenth century. Walking in the forest with an old family retainer, Heylyn left the path, and became utterly lost. The retainer saw irony in the scholar's confusion: "'That's strange!' said he, 'I have heard my old master, your father, say that you made a book of all the world; and cannot you find our way out of the wood?'" (Southey 1: 167). Southey used the anecdote to suggest how modern printing had revolutionized traveling in his own day. Cheap printed maps represented, Southey implied, something both essentially modern and socially leveling: they encouraged the travel and connectivity that defined modern cosmopolitanism, and they unified the scholar's abstract knowledge with the local's practical skills at wayfinding.[11] Every literate individual in Britain, moreover, could now access the nation's geography with a greater accuracy than earlier generations' most experienced and learned guides for hire. The path out of the woods, an impossibility for even a seventeenth-century geographical genius, was by 1800 the shared inheritance of the British. As a means of putting access over one's wayfinding into the hands of individuals, the map seemed to ratify utopian hopes about how technology would generalize learning, knowledge, and opportunity. Indeed, the printed map represented the marriage of two of the three modern tools that Bacon had identified as the heralds of modernity: the compass and the printing press. The cheap printed map implied the ability to travel throughout the island, a form of intellectual and personal freedom to access the nation at will. That freedom, however, only pertained to individuals who traveled regions documented by the cheap printed map, and the borders of representation were the reflection not of

---

[11]   Catherine Delano-Smith has emphasized the difference between seventeenth-century route-making, writing out in advance the names of places one would pass on an itinerary without knowledge of the road, and wayfinding, which could be done on the road.

consumer demand, but rather of the state's agenda and its sometimes arbitrary role as manager of knowledge.

Commercial Maps as Conduits of Nationalism

As maps became cheaper and more readily available to Britons of all classes, the objects themselves changed, diverging into new families of specialist maps for different expert uses and income levels. These new maps, for all their originality, largely reproduced ideas about the nation as an object of consciousness established by earlier institutions of cartography.

New map objects proliferated to suit the desires of the common commercial traveler. In 1798 wall-size maps of England in these convenient forms were on sale for £3–5 in London. By 1850, the one-inch ordnance map of England and Wales could be purchased for 2s a sheet, or £17 for the whole collection, mounted on cloth for the pocket. Parts of the incomplete, six-inch map of Scotland were also available at 5s a sheet, and a map of Ireland was available at a six-inch scale for 2s 6d a sheet (*The Annual Commercial Register* 266–9). Mapmakers' shop rooms thus boasted, in addition to high-end renditions of the Ordnance Survey, lower-end, reduced-scale versions more affordable to the average Londoner. The *Mechanics' Magazine* encouraged its readers to use a "National Map" published by Tyas and Weale, whose scale at 1/3 inch to a mile (half the scale of the Ordnance), had the advantage of a cheaper distribution. The publishers stipulated that the price of each sheet should "never exceed one shilling, and many are to be charged only sixpence" ("Tyas's National Map" 493). The entire map of 58 sheets would cost no more than 50s. Increasingly priced within reach of the common traveler, the maps were printed and mounted in formats to make them convenient for travel. Maps were especially "divided into sections and pasted on to canvas," so as to form a conveniently folding document that would fit in a pocket, protected "in a neat cover" (*The Annual Commercial Register* 266). New map designs reflected a public invested in information that was accurate, portable, and accessible.

As a point of access, the map shop connected commercial travelers in London's East End to the rest of the nation. Letts and Sons' shop, publishers of a guidebook called *The British Roadster or Stage Coach Companion* boasted about having collected every travelers' map "that has the smallest pretension to accuracy," and encouraged the public "to come and inspect them" whether or not they had an "intention to purchase," in the hopes of the firm benefiting from "the publicity thus afforded" (*The Annual Commercial Register* 270). These smaller traveling maps, also folded in a pocket case, or mounted on rollers and strainers for easy display, ranged from 6d to 53s in price. The firm also eventually boasted guides to watering places, geography, geology, and astronomy, as well as Railway Tables, foreign language dictionaries, and Emigrant's Guides.

These maps made possible a new series of speculative and exploratory practices by travelers who imagined their nation connected into a single, unified system.

Larger, folded maps of the country could represent the road network in enough detail to show simultaneously the roads as a network joining long distances, provide detailed accounts of distances, and allow comparisons between different towns: only this scale of map could serve the needs of carriers, merchants, and travelers, to swiftly compare different possible paths—with relative distance and directness—at a single glance.

Industrial entrepreneurs who used the basic national survey as a matrix upon which to map their own tools of inquiry worked within ideas of the limits of the nation instantiated by the map. On the basis of detailed national maps, the exploding private railways of the 1830s and 40s plotted their routes, using elaborate trigonometric formulas to calculate, based on the towns already surveyed, which directions would be most profitable in terms of potential users. Noting the uses of its data, Parliament commissioned new surveys designed to cater to a novel community of entrepreneurs (Smith and Cary, "A Geological Map").[12] Geological maps could help railways to avoid chalk hills and hidden springs ("Geology" 150). Small users also made use of the surveys to broaden their access to natural resources and the market. Geological maps helped small users find new agricultural returns, as in the case of Dr W. Smith of Scarborough, who opened "a subterranean reservoir on the site of a little spring" and then "regulated the discharge for the benefit of the town" ("Geology" 151). In Ireland, Jonathan Pim dared to hope that the Ordnance Map, once made public, would facilitate the "simplification of the tenure of lands," getting rid of copyhold, fee-farm grants, corporate leases, and the bulk of property types that made transference in land "fluctuate greatly," ranging from "unsaleable" to "too high a value" (Pim 266).

As various channels distributed the cheap printed map for popular use, the outline of Britain's borders became an icon recognizable for the first time, enabling a new identification with the nation as a whole. The shape of the nation became the subject of moral and political education in the classroom. After 1799, William Butler, a schoolteacher who thereafter published his own set of textbooks outfitted with maps, argued that geography had become an essential subject for young persons, both male and female, capable of being mastered at a tender age. Educational theorists like Maria Edgeworth recommended the maps as a tool for teaching children to use hand and eye in conjunction.[13] The first jigsaw puzzles consisted of an ordinary road map, "dissected" into squares, left for the child to recompose on the basis of the whorls, coastlines, and words that fit together. Such tools disappeared among generations who grew up with the shape of the nation familiar as an icon; the cognitive challenge was smaller when the nation's image was more commonplace. Only for children of a generation unfamiliar with the shape of the country, the dissected map was itself a challenge to put back together,

---

[12]   See James Gardner and Peter LeCount.

[13]   See Maria and R.L. Edgeworth, *Essays on Practical Education*, I: 25. See also John Wallis, *Wallis's New Dissected Map of Somerset*; E.R., *Geography and History, Selected by a Lady for the Use of Her Own Children*; and Elder Smith.

the mind struggling to remember the indentures of coasts and the unfamiliar outline of the island viewed from above. The ready access to such maps furthermore encouraged new innovations in the form of reduced maps for children's learning. Tools like Robert Dymond and William Dawson's *Explanatory Key to a Map of England and Wales* (1829) encouraged children to remember the shape of coasts and rivers by providing maps with numbers instead of words to quiz the memory. The exemplary student in Richard Green Parker's *Aids to English Composition* (1851) began his work at essay-writing by describing the landscape visible to him from a nearby windmill mound, using his tutor's spy glass and Cary's country map as aids (Parker 9–10). Such practices implied how deeply contemporaries valued a ready facility with names and geography, hoping perhaps that those children drilled upon maps could, when older, deploy their knowledge with so ready a facility as to easily navigate across every part of the nation.

Such educational map exercises were increasingly informed with a politics that had not held sway in the eighteenth century. A less political use of maps for education was visible in the late eighteenth century, when Samuel Richardson's Pamela aimed, in making herself into an ideal mother, to learn geography so that she could teach basic visual reasoning to her children (563).[14] Yet for the descendants of Richardson's Pamela 50 years later, similar exercises were conceived of less as an exercise of the eye, but rather as a tool for understanding the political nation and geography. The theologian William Paley explained in 1828 the origin of Great Britain's "natural boundaries," arguing that any interior divisions such as once divided the now unified island into kingdoms made the whole vulnerable "against the dangers that surround them" and would result in the conquest of the whole (1: 239). Joseph Priestley argued in his *Lectures on History and General Policy* (1765) that each nation's "natural situation" was of "great consequence either for defending ourselves, or of attacking others" (496). In exercises that patterned Paley's sense of Britain's perfect boundaries, William Butler expected his students to name the southern and northern counties of England and Scotland and their relationship to each of the island's natural boundaries, demonstrating their understanding of the natural relationship between a people and their spaces (Butler 90–93).[15] Hannah More, similarly, had explicitly moral aims in mind when she applauded the turn towards geography in primary education. She exhorted that it would be "proper" always "to read history with a map, in order to keep up in the mind the indissoluble connexion between history and geography; and that

---

[14] Pamela was following Locke's suggestion of learning "the figure of the globe, the situation and boundaries of the four parts of the world, and that of particular kingdoms and countries" (172). In 1780, these geographical facts represented, as they had for Locke, only an "exercise of the eyes and memory" (172).

[15] See also J. Goldsmith, who advised showing the pupil "the place of his residence … and its relation to other places on the map" (2). Originally published in 1804, the book had already gone into 40 editions by 1811, suggesting a rampant and increasing demand for school texts on map-reading.

a glance of the country may recall the exploits of the hero, or the virtues of the patriot who has immortalized it" (More 9). Thus, beyond merely representing the nation's boundaries, the map in practice stood for the geological and heroic origins of the nation, implying a model British subject who could knowledgeably defend the shape of the nation through his grasp of geography and history.

Through these avenues, the image of the nation as described by contemporary cartography was proliferated onto the walls of schoolrooms. Map publishers like The Society for Promoting Christian Knowledge and Crutchley's advertised their wall-sized maps in the back pages of the *Ecclesiastical Gazette*, alongside Latin and Greek grammars, catering to tutors and grammar schools (*Ecclesiastical Gazette* 210, 232). The Statistical Society of London found a typical Westminster school to have a map of the Holy Land and a map of England hanging on its walls, two corollary versions of geographical identity for the Christian Briton (*Journal of the Statistical Society of London* 203). Scotland and Ireland were missing from the catalogues, however, as the maps of the British nation used in schools typically ended with England.

The Invisibility of Scotland

As a tool of citizenship, the artifacts of the maps themselves cut in directions not suggested by the assimilative practices of pedagogy. As English maps of Scotland began to appear after Arrowsmith's map of 1807, Culloden—an insignificant estate and town, but also the battlefield where the last rebellion for Scottish independence had been defeated—was routinely marked by a pair of crossed sabers. It might mean nothing, except that it was the only battlefield marked on any contemporary map of Britain. The difference between England and Scotland, and the mythic opposition of conquest and resistance there implied, was disseminated by the cheap map even as the practices of civic education used maps to indoctrinate a theory of national unity.

While schoolchildren learned to understand the nation as a naturally unified domain through which they could travel with total access, the maps themselves encoded the limits of their knowledge. Schoolchildren taught to recite the boundaries of English rivers and counties had plentiful access to geographical data about England, but their access to information immediately dried up to the north of Edinburgh. The structure of government data, upon which all the cheap printed maps depended, prevented any of these national maps from encompassing Scotland. Frequently, the national map through the 1830s and 40s ended with Carlisle; more often the border extended to Edinburgh or Glasgow, with a few major routes depicted. In almost no case did the regular road maps extend far enough to the north to encompass the Highlands.

Nor was this divided structure of the nation the result, as Johnson had suggested to Boswell, of Englishmen not traveling through Scotland. It was not imperial intention to exclude Scotland from the nation; far from it. Both road-building and tourism took large numbers of English north. In the era between 1790 and 1828, massive parliamentary grants were being directed towards Scottish fisheries and ports, thanks to the readers of Adam Smith who were full of hope that commerce would integrate the border with the economic prosperity that characterized Britain as a whole.[16] Over the first quarter of the nineteenth century, Parliament spent £1,500,000 on the roads of Scotland, constructing 920 miles of roads that by 1828 linked the islands, glens, and furthest abutments into a nationwide network (Dupin 69). The Highlands became in the 1820s and 30s the subject of a blooming tourism that brought bodies north, all of them using guidebooks and reduced maps. But these maps simply bore no resemblance, in sophistication or detail, to the ordinary folded road maps that the British had come to expect.

In contrast to England's carefully documented road network, the Highland's conspicuous lack of specific information reflected the chronology of official surveying. In Britain, surveying practice followed primarily military conquest, secondarily postal communications, and last other scientific interest. In the case of Scotland, the primitive techniques employed in the surveying of military conquest in the 1740s and 50s preceded the advanced, trigonometric methods developed by the time when military surveys of England, Wales, and Ireland were conducted in the course of the Napoleonic Wars. The postal survey of England and Wales similarly did not extend to Scotland. In fact, Scotland's surveying would be neglected longer than that of any other part of the country, put off until it was at last asserted as an urgent matter of national and commercial concern in the 1850s and 60s.

England's first official survey of Scotland was conducted between 1747 and 1755 with the military mapping that followed the defeat at Culloden of Scotland's final rebellion. It took place according to the primitive methods of sighting and sketching that characterized military reconnaissance before the advent of the trigonometric survey. Using a new method that reflected military discipline, teams of surveyors were deployed to different stretches of Scotland for six months at a time, returning long vertical rolls that documented a rough topographical outline of the areas they had covered, which were then synthesized into a single whole by a matter of guesswork and matching the outlines of major landmarks. This map was then archived by the Ordnance in London as a secret instrument held against the possible eruption of new hostilities in Scotland (Skelton 5–16). Military security accordingly forbade the dissemination of information about Scotland's physical territory.

Postal surveying in England did little to supplement this survey. Cary's map was limited in data by that collected by the Post Office of England and Wales, distinct from the Scottish post, which had evolved separately. While Palmer's initiative drove the expansion of mail coaches and the surveying of roads in England after 1784, the mail coaches did not expand in Scotland until after 1810.

---

[16]   The Scots lobby for highway-building is handled in *Roads to Power*, chapter 2. See also Fredrik Albritton Jonsson.

Superficially, both were administered by the same authority, the Superintendent of the Mail Coaches in London, but in fact their operations acted independently, dependent on different roads, appointing postmasters by separate processes, and scheduling their deliveries on different days (Robinson 92, 227–30). As a result, the basic surveying of roads for the post was deferred for Scotland until after 1800, by which time the surveying efforts of the Post Office had been postponed in favor of the Ordnance.

Long after the Ordnance, driven by security concerns in the wars with France, had finished mapping England and Ireland, it began to contemplate the commercial and political advantages of providing a map of Scotland. The Ordnance began mapping the counties of Ayrshire, Wigtownshire and Kirkcudbrightshire between 1819 and 1828, but abandoned the work before any plans were engraved, foreseeing that the English Ordnance was making a transition to a finer scale and that the Scottish survey would have to be redone. Piecemeal work appeared in the 1830s and 40s as the result of commercial lobbying, but the six-inch mapping of Scotland remained incomplete until 1882 (Fleet and Withers).

England continued to rely upon outdated information about Scotland's geography. Because mapmakers such as Cary depended on the sponsorship of the state, cartographers of Scotland as well as the general public had to deal with hopelessly out-of-date information. In 1807 the Military Survey map of Scotland reappeared, when Aaron Arrowsmith, Cary's former surveyor, now an independent publisher of post route maps, followed rumors about the map's existence and wrote letters to the Ordnance that finally produced the 82 rolls of exact north-to-south strip surveys from the King's library, where they had been deposited by the executor of William Roy, the organizer of the eighteenth-century military survey.[17] Arrowsmith confirmed the shape of counties using the surveys being conducted by the Parliamentary Commissioners for Highland Roads and Bridges (Mackenzie 269). As a result of the direct aid of government surveys, then, Arrowsmith's map became the first public map of Scotland to which Englishmen had regular access. It became the basis for the reduced version of Scotland reproduced in gazetteers, and was commonly available for sale in London bookshops ("Modern Geography" 287–93). Another publication, the *Annals of Philosophy*, declared the map "undoubtedly the best that has hitherto been published" (qtd in Mackenzie 269).

Because of the conditions under which Parliament had mapped Scotland, however, the Arrowsmith map was materially lacking. The primary source of geographic information, the Roy data conducted under military mandate, was 60 years out of date, and hardly an accurate or comprehensive survey. Contemporary critics themselves realized the insufficiencies of Arrowsmith's map. Reviewers pointed to inaccurate depictions of the "positions of places" and "courses of rivers" (Mackenzie 269). An Edinburgh learned society complained that "the important Islands of Barra and Rona are misplaced, both in latitude and longitude," and noted "serious errors at the entrance of so important a river as the Clyde" ("Memorial"

---

17   For a detailed account of their reappearance, see D.G. Moir and R.G. Inglis, chapter 10.

503). The *Monthly Review* noted in 1808 that General Roy's survey, as well as being out of date, was also incompetent; the surveyors had "different districts ... allotted to them in each spring," and "when they assembled in Winter to compare their surveys, and could not bring them sometimes to meet by many miles, much altercation often arose, each regarding his own as correct, and that they found it impracticable to form a whole out of them, without a great deal of management and coaxing" ("Modern Geography" 293). Personality and temper determined the making of the Scottish map, which was the product of an era before the institution of triangulation by latitude and longitude.

From a quite early date, attempts to rectify the Scottish map appeared that had no impact whatsoever upon the maps that circulated in England. Scottish cartography began to flourish in Edinburgh, thriving on the tight bonds of intellectuals like Thomas Pennant and George Paton in the 1770s (Walters 121–8). Private cartographic initiatives centered on Edinburgh set out with the explicit intention of correcting the English lack of attention to mapping Scotland. In 1776 the first Scottish strip maps were produced by George Taylor and Andrew Skinner, Aberdeen surveyors who had worked as military surveyors in America.[18] Edinburgh learned societies spurred independent corrections to the haphazard maps available in the South.[19] With John Ainslie's survey of 1789, the first real surveying work to recommence since the 1750s began to appear.[20] In 1791 Thomas Brown's *New and Accurate Travelling Map of Scotland* used such independent surveys to fill in the topography of landscape that lay to both sides of the roads documented in its primitive strip maps. Yet their efforts were modest—mostly restricted to documenting the major highways and their geography. The immediate impact of these independent efforts was limited. Scottish printers provided Scottish traveling maps, printed in Scotland for travelers who made it that far, supplied by the independent initiative of Scottish surveyors.[21] English travelers made do with tools like *Leigh's New Pocket Road-Book*, comprised of written descriptions of crossroads and antiquities. By the 1830s, such private initiatives were still

---

[18] For more on these maps, see R.H. Fairclough and James Holloway, Lindsay Errington and the National Gallery of Scotland.

[19] A circle of improvers centered around Henry Home, Lord Kames, judge and early director of the British Linen Company whose preface to Andrew Wight's *Present State of Husbandry in Scotland* (1776) encouraged the building of roads and turnpikes. Kames had been instrumental in the 1754 founding of the Select Society and its offshoot, the Edinburgh Society for Encouraging Arts, Sciences, Manufactures, and Agriculture in Scotland. These earlier Enlightenment societies were the forerunners of the Society of Antiquaries of Scotland, founded in 1780 in Edinburgh, which played a pivotal role in Scottish geography by inviting cartographers to compete with each other for the Society's prizes.

[20] See Charles W.J. Withers, "How Scotland Came to Know Itself: Geography, National Identity and the Making of a Nation, 1680–1790" and "The Social Nature of Map Making in the Scottish Enlightenment, c. 1682–1832."

[21] Consider the ads for a "Travelling Map of Scotland" in the July 1829 issue of *Edinburgh Literary Journal.*

insufficient to comprise a full survey of the country. Members of the Wernerian Society in Edinburgh petitioned the Treasury to reopen the Trigonometrical Survey of Scotland, referencing how later government-funded surveys of geology had proved useless because they were based on Arrowsmith ("Memorial" 504).[22] The result, from the point of view of the English map reader, was a striking geometry of the shape of Britain as it circulated in practice. The "Map of Britain" typically purchased and shown in Britain until 1840 was a map that ended at Hadrian's Wall, or if it extended, reached only to Edinburgh (Figure 1.3). Though integrated in law, and increasingly interlinked by state-built roads, other state institutions like the Post and the Survey structurally neglected Scotland, thereby excluding this part of the nation from the everyday circulation of ideas and trade.

By the 1850s, as the eruption of guidebooks and railroad travel was greeted as the fulfillment of the seeds of national self-knowledge planted earlier by the roadmap, maps spelled the opportunity for deep access to the nation by the whole of its citizenry. The *Edinburgh Review* enthused, "More, we are convinced, may be learnt of the progress and the changes which have built up this England of ours, and a far deeper insight gained into the real life of the past, by a 'field study' of the country than by the profoundest lectures of the most learned professor" ("Travellers and Handbooks" 506). Yet despite the image of enthusiastic nationalism that sentence conjures, the ones that succeed it break that image, stressing national divisions rather than unity: "English history, although it has a definite unity, has nevertheless been influenced, through much of its course, by the ancient independence of separate provinces, an independence not political only, but of race and of traditions." The editorial continued to delineate the boundaries of Mercia and Wessex—invisible to the political map, yet stamped still by their own "distinct character" ("Travellers and Handbooks" 506). Defying the pedagogy of assimilation and the marginalization of Scotland, the cheap printed map had engraved a sense of difference into understandings of British identity. In the era when maps became tools shaping investment and identity, Scotland was utterly excluded from the kind of map-reading culture visible in England.

*   *   *

It is no secret that the origins of maps have been bound up with agendas of division and exploitation. Readers familiar with the Irish Ordnance, cholera maps, and the survey of India will recognize the whiff of economic exploitation and political control that defined the era of cartographic supremacy.[23] Yet even authors clever

---

[22]   The petition points out a series of errors in surveying and governmental management, including that a Dr MacColluch was paid £7,000 for making a Geological Map "on which unfortunately little reliance can be placed for local details" according to an 1837 volume of *The Edinburgh New Philosophical Journal* (209).

[23]   See E.W. Gilbert, 172–83; C. Close; J.H. Andrews; J.B. Harley; M.H. Edney, "The Patronage of Science and the Creation of Imperial Space: The British Mapping of India,

Figure 1.3   The Post Roads through England and Wales
Source: Thomas Jefferys. London: Jefferys & Faden, 1774.

enough to see state power at work in the map often neglect to recognize how contingent maps were upon the intentions of the creators.

Compiled out of a trail of contingent decisions by eighteenth-century government, surveyors, investors, and schools, nineteenth-century road maps bore

1799–1843" and "British Military Education, Mapmaking, and Military 'Map-Mindedness' in the Later Enlightenment"; J. Black; M.H. Edney, "Mapping an Empire: The Geographical Construction of British India" and "Reconsidering Enlightenment Geography and Map Making: Reconnaissance, Mapping, Archive," J.C. Scott; M.G. Hannah; and P.K. Gilbert.

with them an image of the nation skewed not by intention but rather by accident. Through the lingering importance of government-provided data, the trace of colonial cartographers from the 1740s haunted the work of publishers from the 1770s to the 1830s. Lacunae-ridden maps from the 1740s and triumphalism over Scottish independence lived on even when the state's policy had switched from a military, colonial agenda characterized by its secrecy to a commercial, assimilative agenda characterized by the open sharing of surveying data with former colonies.

As children of divided agendas, cheap printed maps themselves pushed the public in different directions. Maps in schoolrooms spread ideas about the nation's heroic origins to English schoolchildren, but the same children also learned, through the map's omissions, not to travel to or invest in Scotland. Maps overdetermined later English chauvinism and the coherence of late nineteenth-century Irish and Scottish nationalism, bent upon challenging a national imaginary that had structurally excluded them. Cheap printed maps were hardly an assimilative source of national citizenship. Their social effects were as divisive as the grounds of their manufacture: the map's cultural legacy was one of cacophony rather than inclusion.

The map as material artifact was not the reflection of a single, imperial agenda acting with the coherence of a single mind. Rather, the map embodied the mixed conditions of its production across different generations. The map was a palimpsest. From that confused document, schoolchildren learned their identity as citizen-subjects by piecing together the nation, while adult travelers came to understand their places within the national imaginary as they traversed their local landscapes.

Works Cited

Allen, George. *Map of England & Wales*. Stone, Staffordshire: George Allen, 1810. Print.

Andrews, J.H. *A Paper Landscape: The Ordnance Survey in Nineteenth-Century Ireland*. Oxford: Oxford University Press, 1975. Print.

Arrowsmith, Aaron. *Map of the Hills, Rivers, Canals, and Principal Roads, of England and Wales*. London: A. Arrowsmith, 1813. Print.

Baigent, Elizabeth. "Arrowsmith, Aaron, the Elder (1750–1823)." *Oxford Dictionary of National Biography*. (ed.) Lawrence Goldman. Oxford: Oxford University Press, 2004. Web.

Baines, Frederick Ebenezer. *On the Track of the Mail-Coach*. London: Richard Bentley and Son, 1836. Print.

Betts, John. *Betts's New Itinerant and Commercial Map of England & Wales*. London: John Betts, 1839. Print.

Biggs, Michael. "Putting the State on the Map: Cartography, Territory, and European State Formation." *Comparative Studies in Society and History* 41.2 (1999): 374–405. Print.

Black, Jeremy. *Maps and Politics.* Chicago: University of Chicago Press, 1997. Print.

Boswell, James. *The Life of Samuel Johnson.* 4 vols. London: T. Cadell and W. Davies, 1804. Print.

Bowen, Emanuel. *Britannia Depicta.* London: Carington Bowles, 1764. Print.

Bowles, John. *The Travellers Guide Through England and Wales.* London: Bowles, 1737. Web.

Brown, Lucy. *Victorian News and Newspapers.* Oxford: Clarendon Press, 1985. Print.

Brown, Thomas. *New and Accurate Travelling Map of Scotland.* Edinburgh: Thomas Brown, 1791. Print.

Bumpus, John. *New Map of England and Wales.* London: Bumpus, 1820. Print.

Butler, William. *Geographical and Biographical Exercises.* 18th edn, 1799. London: John Harris, 1832. Print.

"Carnan *Against* Bowles." *Reports of Cases Argued and Determined in the High Court of Chancery.* 4 vols. 5th edn, London: Henry Butterworth, 1820. Print.

Cary, John. *A New and Accurate Topographical Survey of the Environs of London.* London: J. Wallis, 1783. Print.

Cary, John. *Cary's Actual Survey of the Great Post Roads Between London and Falmouth.* London: J. Cary, 1784. Print.

Cary, John. *Cary's New and Accurate Map of the County of Surry* [sic]. London: John Cary, 1785. Print.

Cary, John. *Cary's Actual Survey of the Country Ten Miles Round Hampton Court and Richmond.* London: John Cary, 1786. Print.

Cary, John. *Cary's New Map of England and Wales with Part of Scotland.* London: J. Cary, 1794. Print.

Cary, John. *Cary's Reduction of His Large Map of England and Wales, with Part of Scotland.* London: J. Cary, 1796. Print.

Cary, John. *A Map of England & Wales.* London: J. Cary, 1798. Print.

Cary, John. *Cary's New Itinerary.* London: J. Cary, 1798. Print.

Cary, John. *A New Map of the British Isles.* London: J. Cary, 1807. Print.

Cary, John. *A New Map of the British Isles, from the Latest Authorities.* London: J. Cary, 1807. Print.

Cary, John. *A New Map of England from the Latest Authorities.* London: J. Cary, 1807. Print.

Cary, John. *Cary's Traveller's Companion.* London: J. Cary, 1814. Print.

Cary, John. *England and Wales.* London: G. & J. Cary, 1822. Print.

Cary, John. *Cary's Reduction of His Six Sheet Map of the British Isles.* London: J. Cary, 1824. Print.

Cary, John. *Cary's Six Sheet Map of England and Wales, with Part of Scotland.* London: J. Cary, 1826. Print.

Cary, John. *Cary's Six Sheet Map of England and Wales.* London: J. Cary, 1830. Print.

Cary v. Faden. 5 Ves. 24.

Cary v. Longman. 1 East, 358.

Close, Charles. *The Early Years of the Ordnance Survey*. Newton Abbot: David & Charles, 1969. Print.

Colley, Linda. *Britons: Forging the Nation, 1707–1837*. New Haven: Yale University Press, 1992. Print.

Creighton, R. *A Map of England & Wales*. London: S. Lewis, 1838. Print.

Curtis, George Ticknor. *A Treatise on the Copyright in Books*. London: A. Maxwell and Son, 1847. Print.

Dean, Mitchell. *Governmentality: Power and Rule in Modern Society*. London: Sage Publications, 2009. Print.

Delano-Smith, Catherine. "Milieus of Mobility: Itineraries, Route Maps and Road Maps." *Cartographies of Travel and Navigation* (ed.) James R. Ackerman. Chicago: University of Chicago Press, 2006. 16–68. Print.

Delano-Smith, Catherine, and Roger Kain. *English Maps: A History*. London: The British Library, 1999. Print.

Dupin, Charles. *The Commercial Power of Great Britain*. London: C. Knight, 1825. Print.

Dymond, Robert, and William Dawson. *An Explanatory Key to a Map of England and Wales*. London: Longman, 1829. Print.

E.R. *Geography and History, Selected by a Lady for the Use of Her Own Children*. London: Law and Whittaker, 1818. Print.

Ecclesiastical Gazette 5 (1843).

Edgeworth, Maria, and R.L. Edgeworth. *Essays on Practical Education*. 2 vols. London: R. Hunter, 1815. Print.

Edney, Matthew H. "British Military Education, Mapmaking, and Military 'Map-Mindedness' in the later Enlightenment." *The Cartographic Journal* 31 (1994): 14–20. Print.

Edney, Matthew H. *Mapping an Empire: The Geographical Construction of British India, 1765–1843*. Chicago: University of Chicago Press, 1997. Print.

Edney, Matthew H. "The Patronage of Science and the Creation of Imperial Space: The British Mapping of India, 1799–1843." *Cartographica: The International Journal for Geographic Information and Geovisualization* 30.1 (1993): 61–7. Print.

Edney, Matthew H. "Reconsidering Enlightenment Geography and Map Making: Reconnaissance, Mapping, Archive." *Geography and Enlightenment* (eds) David N. Livingstone and Charles W.J. Withers. Chicago: University of Chicago Press, 1999. 165–98. Print.

Fairclough, R.H. "Sketches of the Roads in Scotland, 1785: The Manuscript Roadbook of George Taylor." *Imago Mundi* 27 (1975): 65–72. Print.

Fleet, Christopher, and Charles W.J. Withers. "A Scottish Paper Landscape." Edinburgh: National Library of Scotland. August 2008. Web.

Fordham, Herbert George. *John Cary: Engraver, Map, Chart and Print-Seller, and Globe-Maker, 1754 to 1835*. Folkestone, UK: Dawson, 1976. Print.

Fordham, Herbert George. "The Work of John Cary and His Successors." *The Geographical Journal* 63.5 (1924): 438–40. Print.

Gardner, James. *Geological Map of England and Wales*. London: J. Gardner, 1826. Print.

"Geology." *The Penny Cyclopaedia for the Diffusion of Knowledge*. Vol. 11. London: Charles Knight, 1838. 127–51. Print.

Gilbert, E.W. "Pioneer Maps of Health and Disease in England." *Geographical Journal* 124.2 (1958): 172–83. Print.

Gilbert, Pamela K. *Mapping the Victorian Social Body*. Albany, NY: State University of New York Press, 2004. Print.

Goldsmith, J. *An Easy Grammar of Geography*. London: R. Phillips, 1811. Print.

Greenough, G.B. "Address to the Royal Geographical Society of London." *The Journal of the Royal Geographical Society of London* 11 (1841): lxxii. Print.

Guldi, Jo. *Roads to Power: Britain Invents the Infrastructure State*. Cambridge: Harvard University Press, 2012. Print.

Hannah, Matthew G. *Governmentality and the Mastery of Territory in Nineteenth-Century America*. Cambridge: Cambridge University Press, 2000. Print.

Harley, J.B. "Maps, Knowledge, and Power." *The Iconography of Landscape: Essays on the Symbolic Representation, Design and Use of Past Environments* (eds) Denis Cosgrove and Stephen Daniels. Cambridge: Cambridge University Press, 1988. 277–312. Print.

Harris, Bob. *Politics and the Rise of the Press: Britain and France, 1620–1800*. London: Routledge, 1996. Print.

Hebert, Lewis. *England*. London: Richard Holmes, 1819. Print.

Holloway, James, Lindsay Errington, and the National Gallery of Scotland. *The Discovery of Scotland: The Appreciation of Scottish Scenery Through Two Centuries of Painting*. Edinburgh: National Gallery of Scotland, 1978. Print.

Home, Henry [Lord Kames]. Preface. *Present State of Husbandry in Scotland*. Andrew Wight. Edinburgh: Strahan and T. Cadell, 1778. v–xi. Print.

Jones, Yolande. "Aspects of Relief Portrayal on 19th Century British Military Maps." *The Cartographic Journal* 11.1 (1974): 19–33. Print.

Jonsson, Fredrik Albritton. *The Enlightenment in the Highlands: Natural History and Internal Colonization in the Scottish Enlightenment, 1760–1830*. Diss. University of Chicago, 2005. Print.

Journal of the Statistical Society of London 1 (1839).

Kemp, George. *A New Map of England and Wales with Part of Scotland*. London: Longman, Rees, 1840. Print.

Langley, Edward. *Langley's New Map of England & Wales*. London: J. Phelps, 1820. Print.

Langley, Edward. *Langley's New Travelling and Commercial Map of England and Wales*. London: Langley & Belch, 1817. Print.

Laurie's Travelling Map of England and Scotland. London: Richard Holmes Laurie, 1839. Print.

LeCount, Peter. *A Practical Treatise on Railways*. Edinburgh: Adam & Charles Black, 1839. Print.

Leigh, Samuel. *Leigh's New Pocket Road-Book of England, Wales, and Part of Scotland*. London: Samuel Leigh, 1825.

Lewins, William. *Her Majesty's Mails*. London: Sampson, Low, 1864. Print.

Lewis, S. & Co. *A Map of England & Wales*. London, 1839. Print.

Li, Tania Murray. *The Will to Improve: Governmentality, Development, and the Practice of Politics*. Durham: Duke University Press, 2007. Print.

Locke, John. *The Works of John Locke, in Ten Volumes*. Vol. 9. London: Otridge and Sons, 1812. Print.

Macaulay, Thomas Babington. "Francis Bacon." *Edinburgh Review* lxv (1837): 1–104. Print.

Mackenzie, George. "Extent of the Counties of Scotland." *Annals of Philosophy* (1813): 269. Print.

Marston, S.A. "Space, Culture, State: Uneven Developments in Political Geography." *Political Geography* 23.1 (2004): 1–16. Print.

"Memorial." *Memoirs of the Wernerian Natural History Society*. Vol. 7. Edinburgh: Adam and Charles Black, 1838. 502–4. Print.

"Modern Geography." *The Monthly Review* 55 (1808): 287–93. Print.

Mogg, Edward. *Mogg's New Map of England and Wales, with Part of Scotland*. London: E. Mogg, 1823. Print.

Mogg, Edward. *A New Travelling Map of England, Wales and Scotland*. London: Edward Mogg, 1819. Print.

Moir, D.G., and Harry R.G. Inglis. *The Early Maps of Scotland to 1850*. Edinburgh: Royal Scottish Geographical Society, 1973. Print.

More, Hannah. *The Works of Hannah More*. Vol. 2. NY: Harper & Brother, 1847. Print.

Oliver & Boyd's New Travelling Map of England & Wales. Edinburgh: Oliver & Boyd, 1830. Print.

Paley, William. *The Principles of Moral and Political Philosophy*. 2 vols. Boston: N.H. Whitaker, 1828. Print.

Parker, Richard Green. *Aids to English Composition*. NY: Harper & Brothers, 1845. Print.

Paterson, Daniel. *A New and Accurate Description of all the Direct and Principal Cross Roads in Great Britain*. London: Longman, 1826. Print.

Paterson's Roads. London: Longman, 1826. Print.

Pigot, J. *Pigot & Co.'s New Map of England & Wales*. London: Pigot, 1840. Print.

Pim, Jonathan. *The Condition and Prospects of Ireland*. Dublin: Hodges and Smith, 1848. Print.

Porter, Roy. *The Creation of the Modern World: The Untold Story of the British Enlightenment*. NY: W.W. Norton, 2000. Print.

Potter, Simon James. *Newspapers and Empire in Ireland and Britain: Reporting the British Empire, c. 1857–1921*. Dublin: Four Courts, 2004. Print.

Priestley, Joseph. *Lectures on History and General Policy.* London: Thomas Teggs, 1826. Print.

"Railway Map of England and Wales." *Civil Engineer and Architect's Journal* 9 (1846): 176. Print.

Ravenhill, William. "The Honourable Robert Edward Clifford, 1767–1817, A Cartographer's Response to Napoleon." *Geographical Journal* 160.2 (1994): 159–72. Print.

Raymond, Joad. *News, Newspapers, and Society in Early Modern Britain.* London: Taylor & Francis, 1999. Print.

Richardson, Samuel. *Pamela, or, Virtue Rewarded.* London: T. Kinnersley, 1816. Print.

Robinson, Howard. *The British Post Office: A History.* Princeton, NJ: Princeton University Press, 1948. Print.

Scott, James C. *Seeing Like a State.* New Haven: Yale University Press, 1998. Print.

Scott, Robert, and A. Fullarton & Co., *A Map of England & Wales.* Glasgow: Archibald Fullarton, 1833. Print.

Skelton, R.A. "The Military Survey of Scotland, 1747–1755." *Scottish Geographical Magazine* 83:1 (1967): 5–16. Print.

Smith, C. & Son. *Smith's Map of England & Wales.* London: C. Smith, 1830. Print.

Smith, Charles. *A New Map of England and Wales.* London: C. Smith, 1818. Print.

Smith, Elder. *The Parent's Cabinet of Amusement and Instruction.* London: Smith, Elder, 1835. Print.

Smith, William, and John Cary. *A Delineation of the Strata of England and Wales.* London: J. Cary, 1815. Print.

Smith, William, and John Cary. "A Geological Map." Print.

Southey, Robert. *The Doctor.* 2 vols. NY: Harper's & Brothers. 1872. Print.

The Annual Commercial Register. London: Letts, Son, and Steer. 1850. Print.

The Edinburgh New Philosophical Journal 24 (1837).

"Travellers and Handbooks." *The Edinburgh Review* 138 (1873): 483–506. Print.

"Travelling Map of Scotland." *Edinburgh Literary Journal* (1829): 15. Print.

"Tyas's National Map of England and Wales." *The Mechanics' Magazine* 33 (1840): 493. Print.

Vale, Edmund, and Thomas Hasker. *The Mail-Coach Men of the Late Eighteenth Century.* Newton Abbot: David & Charles, 1967. Print.

Walker, J. & C. *England & Wales.* London: Longman, Rees, Orme, Brown & Co., Paternoster Row, 1837. Print.

Walker, J. & C. *England & Wales, Founded Upon the Grand Trigonometrical Survey.* London: J. & C. Walker, 1840. Print.

Wallis, John. *Wallis's New Dissected Map of Somerset.* London: John Wallis, 1812. Print.

Wallis, John. *Wallis's New Pocket Edition of the English Counties.* London: Davies & Eldridge, Exeter, 1810. Print.

Walters, Gwyn. "Thomas Pennant's Map of Scotland 1777: A Study in Sources, and an Introduction to George Paton's Role in the History of Scottish Cartography." *Imago Mundi* 28 (1976): 121–8. Print.

Wiener, Joel Howard. *Papers for the Millions: The New Journalism in Britain, 1850 to 1914.* NY: Greenwood Press, 1988. Print.

Withers, Charles W.J. "How Scotland Came to Know Itself: Geography, National Identity and the Making of a Nation, 1680–1790." *Journal of Historical Geography* 21.4 (1995): 371–97. Print.

Withers, Charles W.J. "The Social Nature of Map Making in the Scottish Enlightenment, c. 1682–c. 1832." *Imago Mundi* 54.1 (2002): 46–66. Print.

Wyld, James. *A New Map of England & Wales Projected Upon the Trigonometrical Operations Made for the General Survey of the Kingdom.* London: Jas. Wyld, 1836. Print.

Chapter 2

Establishing Stability: Conforming to Type in British House Furnishings, 1860–1910

Clive Edwards

In their 1876 publication, *Suggestions for House Decoration in Painting, Woodwork, and Furniture*, Rhoda and Agnes Garrett urge readers to avoid attempts to inflate their household's economic status via conspicuous consumption, instead promoting simplicity and what they term "good taste" in home decoration. They write:

> Let those who cannot afford the more costly styles of decoration be contented with simple design which they can, if they will, obtain in really good taste at a comparatively small cost. It is the pernicious habit of struggling to imitate costly effects in cheap materials, which has done more than anything else to debase decorative art. (Garrett and Garrett 59)

The authors' advice—presumably targeted to middle-class readers—to spend wisely on "simple design" rather than on cheap copies of more expensive items emphasizes the role of choice in home design; the manual reassures readers that they can, "if they will," maintain respectability and "good taste" while still living within their means. Importantly, while this advice is offered through suggestion rather than coercion, as indicated by the manual's title, the authors also hint at the dire social, economic, and aesthetic consequences that come from inferior imitation of "costly styles." It is worth considering that emulation itself rather than cheap imitation or conspicuous consumption acts as a marker of middle-class conformity. The basis of such emulation, however, may be a desire for aesthetic and consumerist participation—decorating with good taste—rather than envy of surroundings they cannot afford. Garrett and Garrett encourage economic activity, a literal buying in as it were, that maintains finely tuned expectations about "type," in terms of not only the typical furnishings but also the characteristic behaviors and choices at various levels of the middle class. In this way, *Suggestions for Home Decoration* illustrates a tension that is representative of much design advice disseminated through manuals, journal articles, and retail publications between 1860–1910, which provided British readers with prescriptive advice about what and how to consume in order to conform to social position while also celebrating elements of choice and individual taste.

With the rise of the middle classes—for the purposes of this chapter, a diverse and broadly ranging swath of society whose sole distinction was to employ one or more servants—the home functioned as a primary site of negotiation and ultimately stabilization of many of the contradictions inherent in everyday life, including status within and between class divisions, differing gender roles, and the distinctions between labor and leisure, public life and domesticity, and moderation and excess. Given that newlyweds in the latter half of the century often furnished the whole house in one go, the psychological and ideological stakes for setting up house were high. This was particularly so because the vast majority of homes in urban areas were rented, so that home ownership in and of itself was not an assumed marker of class standing. Advisors and critics thus seized the opportunity to counsel the newly married and by extension, middle-class consumers more generally, on the pleasures and pitfalls they might encounter in designing and maintaining the physical spaces of the home.

The Art of Decoration, Mrs Mary [H.R.] Haweis's 1881 guide to household beauty and arrangement, for example, offers a primer of English design history as well as her own theories of "what a room should be" (31). Her guide is illustrative of both the larger cultural anxieties attached to household furnishings and the dizzying array of choices available to consumers outfitting a home. She explains:

> Much remains to be done before England can claim to be an artistic country. Modern teaching has corrected some blots in the intolerable school of design which ushered in the previous century, but it has not yet chased from the domestic field the furniture which makes home hideous, nor taught people to think for themselves … And each of us may aid the nation by self-culture; may make his own house a standing lesson and protest, by merely caring how his walls are covered, and how his goods are placed in juxtaposition. (398–9)

To help readers "think for themselves" while avoiding the "hideous," Haweis provides insight on household matters as large in scale as trees and landscaping and as specific as stove ornaments. Her chapter "On Walls" addresses background color and material applications including tapestry, embroidery, leather, silk, paper, paint, stenciling, and mirroring, among other topics. Equally varied choices were possible for each surface of the home, so that consumers faced a sea of goods, prices, and purveyors.

Customers' decisions were based on cost, convenience, and individual preference, but also were inextricable from domestic display and the representation and construction of household identity in terms of class, gender conventions, religious and political affiliations, etc. The household's taste proved its culture and thus its standing as ideologically as well as materially within the middle classes. Moreover, significant gradations within middle-class respectability could be identified and occupied. Within this highly charged performance of class, choice itself in large part created anxieties as to what the selections said about people and thus how others saw them.

Sociologist Pierre Bourdieu analyzes socially stabilizing structures through the notion of *habitus* whereby various social groupings create particular and for the most part unquestioned patterns and practices for themselves in relation to their distinct economic and cultural capital. *Habitus* in this sense perpetuates itself by shaping new experiences to established ways of seeing and being in the world, so much so that "the practices of the members of the same group, or in a differentiated society, the same class, are always more and better harmonized than the agents know or wish" (59). Bourdieu's description of *habitus* hints at the tensions between homogeneity and the expression of individual identity that were evident in *Suggestions for House Decoration*. While individual agents might "wish" for individuality and uniqueness, the pressures to conform to a group that is differentiated from other groups ironically leads to sameness and imitation.

Linda Young makes the point that middle class status not only revolved around the purchase and consumption of appropriate goods and the subsequent correct usage of them, but these goods themselves influenced behavior and became a tool for reinforcing status. In other words, "[Individuals] shaped their lives to conform to new standards of expectation and reception" (10). This was partly achieved by using "things" to represent taste, which itself was subject to gradations relative to income and position. Contemporary authors recognized this and often referred to the rise and fall from respectability as defined partly by the procurement and subsequent loss of suitable furnishings. Historian Deborah Gorham describes a kind of collective compliance through her description of the "paraphernalia of gentility" as a "generally agreed upon set of possessions ... that form the material base upon which the pattern for a successful middle-class way of life rested" (9). Similarly, Amanda Girling-Budd has persuasively argued that the extensive records of the furnishing firm of Gillow and Co. of Lancaster and London show how "down to the last detail furnishings were both a manifestation of rank and a reinforcement of social hierarchies" (37). Seen from this perspective, trends in home furnishing and furnishing advice imply choice and creativity, but demand conformity.

Part of social stability and personal aspiration came from not only looking the part, but also demonstrating a very particular acumen about which many newly middle-class householders would have felt insecure. Failing to adequately demonstrate aesthetic allegiance to the middle classes (or to a particular middle-class position) by neglecting to follow the dictates of the tastemakers or stepping away from the bounds of what was considered appropriate might constitute a serious social blunder. There would be a break in class allegiance if one's major furnishings fell below or reached above a certain price point, as this would indicate a critical lack of self-awareness or care in the expression of the household's economic status. Deviating too much from the norms could result in being seen as either tasteless or as upstarts, neither of which would be acceptable in polite society.

The burden to already know how to assert one's standing operated unequally along gendered lines, as after midcentury it became increasingly the woman's job to set the aesthetic and economic tone for the household. This does not mean, however, that the gender politics of household furnishing were one-sided or simplistic. The possibility of a harmonized habitus based on both financial and cultural capital allows for and requires participation by both men and women. Indeed, against the long-standing notion of female-centered domestic culture, two decades of feminist and material culture analyses by scholars such as John Tosh and Margot Finn have demolished the related expectations that women's space was the home and that men operated only in public.[1] The economics of home making were generally under the control of the male householder, and the need for men to have some supervision over expenditure was evident. S.P. Walker describes the managerial pressures exerted on the Victorian mistress of the house, particularly in terms of how accounting carried a disciplinary function both for the mistress's control of servants and the husband's control of his wife's spending. Wives were urged to "secure [their] husband's esteem" by scrupulous accounts and regular reports on all aspects of housekeeping, as the man of the house would preside over the familial property (506). Deborah Cohen goes further and reminds us that far from being uninvolved or uninterested in domestic life, in the realm of home decoration, men played a leading role. She writes that the "earliest home decoration manuals were written by married men for married men. Decorators were men; the cause of design reform was led by men; upholsterers were men, as were the clerks on the shop floor" (90). Women, however, suffered the uneasy responsibility of managing and protecting the household's financial integrity while creating a clean, comfortable, and respectable environment that reflected the household's standing and their own aesthetic flair. Thus while men were intimately involved in home decoration and oversight, failures in outfitting or maintaining the middle-class home regularly were attributed to the mistress of the house.

For both men and women the home became a key space in which standards were set and maintained through careful codes of conduct. This meant that the burgeoning middle classes in particular had to develop an understanding of how their homes fit into the hierarchy of society, through, amongst other features, domestic display. As this was a new phenomenon for many, cultural anxieties in matters of both class and identity meant that consumers were constantly looking for advice concerning all facets of choice associated with house furnishing. However, two central ironies marked such mediation in the nineteenth century. Firstly, advice books often preached the importance of individuality in interior design, but then expressed rules, prescriptions and tactics that were seemingly universal. Secondly, the inclusion of commodities that were the products of industrial labor and large-scale production undercut the emphasis placed on creating private, personalized spaces within the home. The result of these contradictions was that an individual's "good taste" was both prescribed and purchased, a process Thad Logan has neatly

---

[1]   See Leonore Davidoff and Catherine Hall, M. Jeanne Peterson, and David Hussey and Margaret Ponsonby. John Tosh has suggested that males indeed had important input into the nineteenth-century home through the enjoyment and maintenance of the household. Additionally, Margot Finn has demonstrated through a selection of men's diaries from the late eighteenth and early nineteenth centuries that men's consumption and enjoyment of things domestic were very apparent.

described as "regulated improvisation" (78). Young has noted that individual expressions of middle-classness should inevitably vary. She explains that "It is therefore astonishing to survey international evidence of the two great mechanisms of gentility, consumerism and etiquette to discover that they are, to all effects and purposes, the same" (37). Young explains how the concept of *habitus* that includes both the attitudes to and the products of a set of choices are related to taste. These choices "remove taste from the common-sense perception of being either a product of personal idiosyncrasy or purely a function of wealth; on the contrary, taste is as systematically defined as any of the conventions of social coherence" (21). In other words, taste is not a function of individual expression of likes and dislikes, but rather, it is an expression of a collective habitus.

When considering the role of advice books, journal articles, and retail publications regarding the systematic fitting out of a home during the second half of the nineteenth century, it seems clear that the advice offered to homemakers frequently followed gendered demarcation lines. For the established rules of good taste, consumers looked to retailers and often male authors for guidance as to how a house might be furnished. For the seemingly more creative and individual approach, customers often relied upon the advice books and particularly the journalism of women writers. The genre of advice mirrors some of the gender dynamics implicit in middle-class expectations of setting up house; in effect, the broad range of advice offered to middle-class consumers worked to reaffirm conformity of both the goods purchased to outfit a home at a particular station and the gender roles of the family who lived there.

Through a comparative analysis of the relationships between retail furnishers' generic estimates and promotional advice for house furnishing requirements, the rest of this chapter considers the tensions—gendered and otherwise—that inform the impulses toward choice and conformity in middle-class decor as well as the contradictions between private and personalized spaces, especially when furnished with the products of mass-produced, rather than handcrafted industry. In many cases, an underlying homogeneity of styles and furnishing types, often arranged within price brackets that related to the property value of houses, was at the core of the advice.[2] Retailers, who supplied estimates of the furnishing requirements of a range of homes, recognized that annual income was an important marker of station. Retailers' estimates were quite prescriptive in managing distinctions within the middle classes; the continuity and authority of their advice suggests an apparently established social agreement as to the most appropriate way of furnishing and decorating a home. Clearly, these visual codes changed over the period in terms of fashionable styles, colors, etc., but there remained a remarkable consistency in the goods associated with or marketed to particular gradations of the middle class.

---

[2] Retail store displays, exhibitions, and advertising sent the same message, but these are beyond the scope of this chapter.

Household Advice and the Emphasis on Conformity

The anthropologist Mary Douglas's comment about goods "making visible and stable the categories of culture" goes a long way to explain the need for conformity to home purchasing and display norms in society (Douglas and Isherwood 62). For Jean Baudrillard, goods have "the sociological function of affiliating [the owner] with the whole class of individuals who possess in the same way" (42). In the nineteenth century, these ideas transferred to particular classes, social groups and lifestyles, as consumers aspired to various tastes and styles that reflected their self-image, class location or ambitions.

Consumers faced uncertainty, however, in how to reflect their self-image, economic status, or class ambition through their home furnishings without exceeding the bounds of conformity foundational to middle-class identity. Consumers found a partial answer in a variety of didactic publications that nonetheless reflect the difficulties inherent in striking this delicate balance. For instance, in 1864 Robert Kerr wrote in *The Gentleman's House* about "an entire class of dwellings, in which it will be found, notwithstanding infinite variety of scale, that the elements of accommodation and arrangements are always the same being based ... [on] the domestic habits of refined persons" (63). Similarly, Haweis's *Art of Decoration* stresses careful, educated choice as central to the proper, appropriate purchasing and display that worked as evidence of one's position. She wrote that "just now every shop bristles with the ready means: books, drawings, and *objets de vertu* from all countries are within everybody's reach, and all that is lacking is the power of choice" (42). The subtext here is that her publication would assist in solving the problem by helping to guide consumers to their best choice of purchases. Like Kerr, Haweis's comment reveals a seemingly impossible balance between the "infinite variety," which implies an element of personal choice, and the necessity of conformity.

The issue of gender further complicated concerns about conformity and advice. Gendered divisions, based on concepts of femininity or masculinity, were usually associated with particular styles, room use, and appropriateness of surroundings. While discussing Robert Kerr's ideal, Karen Chase and Michael Levenson point out how "[t]he gentleman's well-dressed house fuses with his well-adorned wife. They even share a manner" (162). They then quote Kerr directly: "*Elegance*, therefore, unassuming and unelaborated, touching in no way the essentials of home comfort, never suggesting affectation and pride, moderated by unimpassioned refinement, and subdued even to modesty, will invariably be accepted in England" (qtd in Chase and Levenson 162). Kerr's comments might be equally referring to the ideal home or the ideal wife.

Within the confluence of the gender, class and nationalist resonances associated with outfitting a house, women advice writers often asserted theories of home-making that extended beyond decoration. For example, the decorators Rhoda and Agnes Garrett (related to the feminist activists Millicent Garrett Fawcett and Elizabeth Garrett Anderson) used their experience and ability as professional decorators to attempt to subvert what Sylvia Walby has termed the "private patriarchy" of the household (24). They did this through publications aimed directly at women readers and their particular interests. Although not in direct riposte, male authors retaliated. Lewis F. Day described the Garretts' exhibit of a model bedroom in the Paris Exhibition of 1878 as "clumsy and tasteless." He went on to say that the exhibit was proof of "how little is enough to satisfy the ambitions of lady-decorators" (qtd in Adams 151). Clearly, there were contradictory ideas about taste and about the balance between conformity and individuality that existed alongside preoccupations with gender issues, with various social class positions, and with the diverse opportunities for purchase.

Despite these apparent contradictions associated with the tensions between conformity and individuality and complicated by gender, by midcentury, the professionalization of the house furnishing industry ensured that the models of class conformity through household display were recognized. Although individuality could clearly be imported into an interior through choice of color, fabric and decorative bric-a-brac, the social conventions dictating the main items of furniture and fittings considered appropriate for particular rooms existed as "guides," in the same way that behavior was directed by the rules of etiquette. A popular household manual from 1869 highlighted the issue of financial and social appropriateness when outfitting a home, and it emphasized the role of "rules" not only for purchasing but also for displaying and utilizing household artifacts:

The proper furnishing of a house is as much a fine art as painting, and if the rules do not come by an intuitive faculty, they may be acquired. The glaring defects in modern house-furnishing are, first, incongruity of form and size of furniture with the surroundings and means of the possessor, and next, an elaborate decoration of the rooms out of keeping with the position of the owner. And the third is the elaboration of ornament on the furniture, this not being superadded to utility, but subversive of it—ornament being understood to mean a superfluity above utility—permanently fixed or carved upon the article. Decoration means something portable, as vases, glasses, and pictures (*Cassell's Household Guide* 18).

The intention of manuals and advice books such as this one was to be didactic, so that householders would see themselves as possessing both the accoutrements and the sensibility or knowledge necessary to be members of the middle class. In 1881 the architect Robert Edis wrote that "in the houses we live in, it is first of all essential that everything shall be as fitting as possible, and that extravagance of all kinds, or so-called 'high art' shall be subservient to comfort, truth of construction, utility and general convenience" (1–2). Edis's idea of things being "fitting" relates well to the concept of maintaining the appropriateness of one's furnishing to position and status. Because guidebooks presented household decor as a reflection of personal taste, uncertainty as to what would be appropriate opened up professional opportunities; the experts in the field were often men. Deborah Cohen points out that "The best course for most would-be home decorators—or so [the magazine] *The House*'s editors advised—was to turn their interiors over to men who had made the house their profession, in that way many a 'decorative disaster' would be avoided" (32).

The concept of professionalism was important to those who made their living from it, as it not only removed decoration from the realm of the (often female) amateur, but also made links with wider social and political issues such as housing reform. The well-known design reformer Christopher Dresser pointed out that interior decoration was a skilled profession and that decorators should advise their clients on the decoration and furnishing of rooms, much as doctors or solicitors would advise in their own fields. "The decoration of a room," he writes, "is as much bound by laws and by knowledge as the treatment of disease" (39). Indeed, in the later nineteenth century there was a strongly recognized link between home and health, and particularly women's health, with doctors writing what have been called "architectural prescriptions" (Adams 103). These "prescriptions," often written by physicians, reflected the link between home and the body by way of advice on domestic arrangements such as air flow, sanitation and space use as they impacted on female health, especially in childbirth. Cousins Agnes and Rhoda Garrett aligned themselves with these professional attitudes. In their role as interior decorators, they wrote in their book *Suggestions for House Decoration*, "Decorators may be compared to doctors. It is useless to put yourself under their direction unless you mean to carry out their regime" (9–10).

As house furnishing was professionalized, the need for conformity and regulation increased, but even within this new culture, there were occasional detractors. Female commentators, for example, often were positioned to cater for the mass amateur audience. They published practical articles in magazines and journals and answered readers' queries through advice columns. Many of these women writers often appear to be quite harsh in their judgements. Mrs Talbot Coke's response to a correspondent named "Pauline" in *Hearth and Home* in February 1892 is representatively cruel: "As I feared, your furniture etc. is of that hopelessly inartistic green, for which there is no medium between abolition and endurance" (363). In another case, a critic questioned the value of such rulebooks as *Suggestions for House Decoration*. Penelope, whose column appears in *The House* magazine in 1899, levels this charge:

> It is true that there is plenty of idealism and scores of pretty furnishing platitudes to be had for a shilling or two, in various art-at-home manuals, but I doubt whether the economical seeker after tasteful furniture is much informed after perusing scores of dreary sentences as to what constitutes the 'House Beautiful.' ("How to Furnish Tastefully for Five Hundred" 52)

Despite such challenges to professional wisdom, however, the wide range of advice about house furnishing and design ably assisted the network of production, distribution and consumption, as it does today. The advice extended from answers in magazines as to where to buy appropriate materials, to sophisticated feminist evaluations of women and home, such as Frances Power Cobbe's 1881

"Duties of Women as Mistresses of Households." Critics Stephen Cairns and Jane Jacobs's explanation of the "complex and often contradictory relationship between decorative and consumption practices and ideals, orders and grammars that resided both in the site of the home and elsewhere—on design drawing tables, in bureaucracies, in magazines, in commercial premises, in a resident's imaginative and practical world" well reflects the complexity of house furnishing (6). By pointing out the variety of influences on homemakers, Cairns and Jacobs highlight the fact that, despite an emphasis on conformity, the number of agencies, considerations, and potential constraints that influenced their choices in the home were numerous and sometimes contradictory.

Individuality in Home Furnishing and Middle-Class Identity

Although the general guidelines for buying and arranging furniture that were disseminated by household manuals, advice columns, and retail catalogues established some degree of conformity in terms of appropriateness, it was clearly possible to create a more individual interior scheme. Published advice often tried to counter the apparent regulating effects of the retailer's estimates, whilst at the same time maintaining standards (i.e., the conformity or stability) of home furnishings. The trick, according to critic J. Hamlett, was to maintain individual personality, whilst at the same time remaining within the guidelines of orthodoxy and respectability. The lower middle classes who wished for "refinement and cultivation" but who had limited means (Garrett and Garrett 7), for example, were the target market for *Suggestions for House Decoration*—hence their call to buck the trend toward imitation by instead favoring "simple design."

There were some even more stringent detractors against conformity. Haweis, for example, is unstinting in her criticism of aesthetic interiors where "all these fashionable rooms resemble each other ... For the most part these houses reflect no inmate's character, no natural need and requirement—they contain no thought, no sweet little surprise—no touch of genius, nor even of ability" (*The Art of Decoration* 52–3). By contrast, she encouraged homemakers to be slightly more adventurous and individual. This attitude increased the burden on women who had to conform to the established homogeneity of furnishings and arrangement while also demonstrating their superiority in design matters through a studied (but supposedly innate) flair.

Within the rules of interior design, there was thus some scope for self-expression and individuality, as long as one used the "grammar" that sustained the status quo of social hierarchies. In the fitting out of a home, income was often presented as less relevant than education when it came to the distinctions and codes used to identify one's position in society. For Haweis, taste and room arrangement expressed individual personality, which was based on free expression and not on an established orthodoxy of taste; she emphasized originality, not rules. Thus for an accomplished woman homemaking was an opportunity for the display of her aesthetic qualities and abilities. However, a paradox emerges in which women in particular were encouraged to believe that they lived in a world of unfettered personal expression while actually living in a rule-governed society, no less in interiors and homemaking than in any other area. When discussing the role of the professional decorator (tradesman), Haweis suggests that he should "harmonize your individual opinions with the general laws ... of art ... not to make your house a replica of another he has done. A man's house, whilst he is in it, is a part of himself' (*The Art of Decoration* 30). Of course, the retailers' estimates were no doubt valued as useful assistance in planning to a particular budget, ultimately controlled by the husband. She later says in *Beautiful Houses*: "All the houses decorated by Mr William Wallace [a London retailer] have a certain, soft, dainty tone about them, quite individual, and absolutely different from the now-vulgarized 'Empire' frigidities; and (what is very important) Mr Wallace does not deprive the inhabitants of all voice in their own decoration" (106). Women had an opportunity to undertake some of the work of creating a "soft, dainty tone" by producing home-crafted decorative accessories that enabled them to maintain a semblance of financial prudence while also creating a level of individuality.

Nevertheless, the idea of furnishing to a prepared design was important as much to create a "proper scheme" as to avoid going wrong. Haweis explains that

> To make a beautiful and artistic room it is not sufficient to collect a mass of good materials and mix them together. You may spend a fortune at a fashionable decorator's and make your home look like an upholsterer's showroom; or you may fill your house with antiquities of rare merit and calibre, and make it look like an old curiosity shop; but it may be most unpleasing all the same. The furnishing ought to be carried out on some sort of system. (*The Art of Decoration* 201)

Her main point about the interior schemes is clarified in this passage: "It is the delicate, practised perception ... which feels how to craftily mingle richness with paucity of colour, so as not to tire the senses by either—how to avoid both pomposity and barrenness ... This discrimination divides the born decorator from the mere purveyor of reigning fashions, the artist from the upholsterer" (*The Art of Decoration* 369). It is revealing that around this time (1880s onwards) it became possible for women to establish themselves as professional advisors and decorators who appeared to possess "artistic skills," as opposed to the commercial approach of the retailer. These advisors were also expected to consider issues of economy as well as style and aesthetics, and to understand the needs of the household. At the same time, they had to tread a particularly fine path between conformity and individuality.

The problem with trying to avoid conformity (especially without training) was that the display of personality might become overbearing and lack discretion. Many writers of fiction have used the device to poke fun at characters that strive to be above their station. The results of the "problem" of collecting and amassing bric-a-brac without too much thought was described by Henry James in his novel *Spoils of Poynton*: "the abominations ... the little brackets and pink vases, the sweepings of bazaars, the family photographs and illuminated texts," the "household art" which were the mark of a "hideous home" (45). However, these "abominations" were often objects that spoke of the ornamental, the merely pretty (as opposed to beautiful), the domestic, the feminine, and were handcrafted responses to both boredom and the need for decoration. Mrs Haweis tempered her advice about the desirability of the eclectic interior with a sense of taste, to avoid the interior becoming an agglomeration of unrelated objects.

By contrast, Frederick Litchfield commented disdainfully upon the furnishing of homes that were "filled up from the upholsterer's store, the curiosity shop and the auction room," and then added:

> There is of course, in very many cases an individuality to be gained by an 'omnium gatherum' of such as mode of furnishing. The cabinet which reminds its owner of a tour of Italy, the quaint stool from Tangier, and the embroidered piano cover from Spain, are to those who travel, pleasant souvenirs, as are also the presents from friends (when they have taste and judgement) ... The test of the whole question of such arrangement of furniture in our living rooms is the amount of judgement and discretion displayed. (292)

The drive to collect and decorate merges with needlework and other home-making accomplishments, which were characteristic of an educated woman, as a means to achieve the balance of conformity and individualism so often advised. Associated with these practices was the joy of "picking up" or collecting, so encouraged by writers such as Clarence Cook, Edith Wharton, and Elsie De Wolfe.

However, the dangers alluded to by Henry James above were directly noted by other contemporary critics. Hermann Muthesius critiqued the British drawing room. He wrote:

> It suffers in general from having too many odds and ends packed into it and the deliberate informality all too often degenerates into confusion. Actually the province of the lady of the house, it bears the marks of her preferences; lightness, mobility and elegance but usually combined with caprice and that love of frippery and knick-knacks by the thousand that characterises the modern English society woman. (210)

It seems that women were associated with a shallowness of both aesthetic judgment and intellect, for if they are responsible for domestic display, they are also responsible for knowing when and if their domestic interiors speaks for or against a claim to lady-like elegance. The taste for knick-knacks described above reflected in part the dilemma for the Victorian female homemaker who was, on the one hand, encouraged to represent her own and her family's unique qualities and taste, and on the other, to follow formulae for particular rooms as established by the tastemakers. Janna Jones pinpoints the paradoxical nature of this challenge:

> Both popular advertisers and design manual writers laid claim to authority by
> promising women the answer to the dilemma of modern life ... While advertisers
> created desire by helping consumers see their way to a point of purchase amidst
> plentiful product choices, the writers of these design manuals instructed readers
> that what was worth having was nearly impossible to attain. (323)

This paradox suggests the elusiveness of "good taste" and the conflicting
distinctions between the ideal and the real. This situation clearly created significant
insecurities for Victorian homemakers. The phrase "show me your furniture and
I'll tell you what you are" explains it all. The need to strike a balance between
aesthetic good taste and individual expression was clearly a potent cause for
concern for homemakers whether male or female.

Private Spheres and the Public Marketplace

The role of the retailer as a mediator between the manufacturer and the consumer
had developed considerably by the middle of the nineteenth century. The desire for
goods and the creation of self through acquisition meant that the retailer's role was
as important as the literary advisor in assisting consumers in making their homes
in the desired image.

Authors of advice books also often referred to suppliers for particular
sources of goods and whilst not actually advertising their wares, their implied
recommendations were clear. Mrs Talbot Coke's "Home Advice" column in the
magazine *Hearth and Home* is a prime example. Her replies to readers' enquiries
about home decoration and furnishings are scattered with references as to where
one might obtain the recommended goods, and tended to center on well-known
London stores such as Graham and Biddle, Peter Robinson, Hewetson, Wallace's
of Curtain Road and most of all, Shoolbred of Tottenham Court Road. In that
last example, Mrs Coke refers to sales clerks by name who apparently "knew her
taste" (363). The privileged knowledge that Mrs Coke supplied helped individual
readers to confirm their status through the assurance that they were purchasing
the "correct" goods, even while reaffirming Mrs Coke's status as an expert in her
field, whose opinion was well worth the cost of subscription to *Hearth and Home*.

The link between journalists and retailers was made explicit in a series of
articles written by a Lady Sarah M. [pseud.] appearing in *Myra's Journal of Dress
and Fashion* during 1876 and 1877. Each month the "Fashion in Furniture" articles
discussed an aspect of furnishing and went on to extol the virtues of a particular
retailer who would meet the needs described. One example from December 1876
suffices to illustrate the merging of advice column, advertising, and reportage.
The column centers on the business of Goode and Gainsford, London, where "it
would really be possible to go, catalogue in hand, from one department to another
and decide on every article of furniture required in a fourteen-room house, in
the space of about two hours" ("Fashion in Furniture" 258). Knowledge about

which merchants to frequent combined with information about individual pieces of furniture and their pricing fueled both middle-class consumption and the consolidation of middle-class identity during the period. Critic of architectural design Adrian Forty has commented on how the desire of consumers to create an acceptable self-image often meant they had to buy it: "Bereft of other ways of expressing their personalities publicly, people have been driven to catalogues of domestic furnishings to find a persona" (106).

Some firms did not attempt to disguise their selling aims, whilst others wrapped their estimates in a cloak of respectability by employing fashionable decorators to endorse their products, and, in some cases, to design settings and recommend furnishings. Strikingly, the various company estimates (even though they were competitive) illustrate a considerable homogeneity of styles across social hierarchies, financially varying levels, and house sizes that were deemed appropriate for typical lifestyles, thus endorsing the idea of a common understanding of an established taste and reinforcing the ideal of conformity.

The importance of the correct selection of goods became paramount as social commodities increasingly had meanings embedded in them. In the case of the elite and the middle classes, consumers sought the values of gentility, propriety, civility and appropriateness in the goods they purchased. In the case of the aspirational and mass consumers, the values they wanted to emulate were often embodied in less expensive versions of these goods, though they were sometimes simply different. An examination of retailer estimates indicates links between price levels and room types to particular timbers, colors and styles, but such associations do not necessarily represent a filtering down from the expensive to the cheap. It was here that the salesperson's experience and knowledge of customers' desires and aspirations would mix and match to suit the expressed (or hidden) requirements—the individuality—of the customer.

For example, often the advice offered to newlyweds concerned how to make proper choices for the home while avoiding the potential guile of retailers. However, the newlyweds' lack of experience of the furnishing process ensured that retail estimates and ready-made plans were useful and that the process and profitability of guiding and informing newcomers to the business of homemaking remained stable. The advertisement from Smiths Warerooms, Clerkenwell, London, circa 1850s, explains the unwritten hierarchy:

> Those about to marry should obtain the improved book of estimates … where they will find a four-roomed cottage can be completely furnished for 23 guineas; a six-room house completely and neatly for £70; an eight-roomed house with many elegancies and substantialities for £140; and a mansion of fourteen rooms furnished with that style, beauty and durability … for 350 guineas. (Dunbar 40–41)

The four-roomed cottage comprised a hall, drawing room, dining room and one bedroom, whereas the six-room house had a hall, dining room, parlour, two bedrooms and crucially, a servant's bedroom. This arrangement reflects the difference in price as well as the differences in quantity and quality of the furnishings. Although the estimates do not specify colors or patterns, they do recommend appropriate woods, quantities of chairs for example, and the recommended accessories. The pressure placed upon newlyweds to assert their household status through conformity to a particular station within the middle class is evident here.

Although the middle classes were the major target for both estimates and literary advice, many retailers were conscious that the estimates' formulae could work for other social groups as well. Most therefore published other estimates for both higher and lower price ranges. In c. 1910, The Midland Furnishing Company of Southampton Row, Holborn, for example, offered estimates ranging from £27 for a four-roomed house to £655.4s 6d for an eight-roomed house. At the very top of the scale were Hampton and Sons of Pall Mall and Trafalgar Square who in 1892 devised high-end estimates, including one for a 20-room house to be furnished and equipped for £2,000. Even the lower end of the trade used these estimates to sell, although the main selling point there was the credit terms. For example, in the 1890s the Crown Furnishing Company of Seven Sisters Road, London, offered to furnish one room completely for £5: the customer paid a deposit of 10s and 2s a week thereafter.

A brief survey of a range of estimates from eight English retailers over the period 1880–1910, shows evidence of a clear consensus about what constituted appropriate furnishings, and which materials were associated with particular purposes and price points. The most obvious is the use of oak for dining rooms. It was particularly favored for the more expensive estimates, whereas in the lower priced groups some stores offered walnut or mahogany. The drawing room was the most varied, perhaps not surprisingly, with walnut, mahogany and rosewood all featured equally across price ranges and dates. In the bedroom, American walnut was popular in the superior price ranges, whereas ash featured in the middle range, and mahogany or oak in the cheaper end. While the consensus of recommendation reflects the apparent appropriateness of the differing timbers, they also have connotations of their own. Oak reflected the English tradition; mahogany and rosewood suggested luxury; and walnut implied reserve. Looked at another way, oak was perceived as masculine, walnut neutral, and mahogany and rosewood as feminine. Thus, each wood was associated with positive personal characteristics or gender categories that consumers might wish to announce through display.

A slightly different take on the advice system was the use of furnished room settings in retail showrooms. An example from 1906 explains how the model worked:

> Waring's have immensely simplified the task of furnishing for the inexperienced by putting up in their New Galleries five Model Houses completely furnished at a cost ranging from a country cottage at £100, by graduations to £200, £300, £500 and £750. In each of these houses, the prospective furnisher can see the

furniture, carpets and draperies, which he will get for his money, and their effect. ("How to Furnish a Flat" 7)

Wherever the advice came from, the emphasis on conformity to established codes of design and layout was evident in every room.

Within the various rooms of the home, tensions play out in distinctive and important ways between private space and public purchase and display, most particularly in the move from the often symbolic and open "public spaces" to the more private domesticated "personal spaces." The correlation between social status and the range of separate spaces is clear from the estimates relating to income and house size that reflect a clear hierarchy.

The entrance set the social tone of a home. Whether passage or hall-room, it was the location for a number of activities, including entry and exit, the reception of guests, and the all-important first impressions of the household's standing in the community. These activities were transient in themselves, but essential in establishing and maintaining the domestic order. In addition, the hall and its furnishing supported elements of conformity to ritual and etiquette, such as the use of calling cards that were crucial to the maintenance of Victorian society.

Robert Edis noted that there was not much room for furniture in the hall except for a chair and a "small stand for wet umbrellas; this latter need not be one of the usual cast-iron abominations" (156). Charles Eastlake concurs with this judgement against fashion: "The hall table is generally made of oak, in a plain and substantial manner, flanked by chairs of the same material" (69). The retail estimates also confirm this. Most of my examples suggest oak stands in the less expensive estimates, but the addition of chairs, or more substantial hallstands in the more expensive estimates, was evident. Yet despite solid-seated oak chairs being *de rigueur*, there is room for some personal touches in the hall. Rhoda and Agnes Garrett, for instance, suggested a Windsor armchair with a brightly colored cushion which "looks severe enough to discourage unbecoming lounging, and yet sufficiently comfortable to secure a degree of rest for the weary" (41). The front hall thus functioned as a social line of defense, at once the most public area of the home and the literal zone of demarcation between those belonging to and welcomed within the household, and those left cooling their heels.

The dining room and drawing room introduce the concept of gendered space inasmuch as they demonstrate the distinction between the masculine and feminine domains.[3] Kerr suggests that the dining room's appearance "ought to be that of masculine importance" (94), whilst the drawing room should be "entirely ladylike" (107). As Juliet Kinchin has shown, Robert Edis invoked a gendered vocabulary of design when he referred to dining chairs as "broad seated and strong, compared to their light-waisted curvaceous counterparts in the drawing room" (qtd in Kinchin 15). On the other hand, the Garretts wrote that the gloomy London dining rooms "remind one of the British boast that every Englishman's house is his castle, and

---

[3]   See for example, recent work such as Hamlett.

that he wishes neither to observe or be observed when he retires into the dignified seclusion of this, the especially masculine department of the household" (28).

Of course, the gendering of household spaces was far from straightforward or static, but such distinctions were in clear circulation and would have been known to both suppliers and homemakers. The dining room is a useful focus for understanding some of the changes in the nineteenth-century home as it encapsulates the way that middle-class society operated and adapted to change. Rachel Rich's analysis of dining rooms uses three considerations: the architectural, the decorative and the organizational (50). The architectural aim refers to the separation and isolation of the dining room, the decorative for personal pleasure and the impressing of visitors, and the organizational as a partial feminization of the room through table settings and layouts. However, as the most public of spaces, after the hall, much furnishing advice seems to reinforce the idea that the dining room was a male space. The dining room represented the success of the middle-class family that was dependent on the man of the house. In addition, the convention of a dining room with only a single purpose reflected the standing of a household and would attest to a particular socioeconomic status.

The iconography of sideboards and pictures used in dining rooms that often showed scenes of hunting, and the results thereof, follow this trend. These surely represent the primeval male activities of hunting for food for the family. However, Kenneth Ames notes that the iconography changes in the latter part of the century, reflecting the trend towards making a home more of a place of retreat and seclusion from the outside world (44). By implication, imagery applied to sideboards or painted on canvas depicting acts of violence between man and nature appeared disruptive to the comforting process that home and food represented. Although critics such as Harriet Spofford and the Garretts decried such celebrations of the violence of food production, the sellers were aware of the desires of their customers. In scale, material, and decoration, these pieces reinforced the masculinity and formality of the dining space.

However, adaptability was required on occasion. For example, changes in dining room use occurred over the period, which the retailer was quick to spot. The catalogue of Holland and Sons, a London furniture business, noted a significant change in use from simply a place for dining to one that could function as a second sitting room:

> This room is so arranged as to be suitable as dining or sitting room, and can be furnished completely for £100.00. The articles included are enumerated below: A sideboard bookcase, a dining table, 6 dining chairs, a writing table, 2 easy chairs, a corner cabinet, a pair of tapestry curtains, a Brussels carpet. (Symonds and Whineray 104)

The listing demonstrates the increasing range of activities undertaken in a dining room by this time, with reference to writing, reading, and an emphasis on comfort. This was in line with other advice, which recognized that not all people could maintain a dining room for a single purpose. Mrs Loftie wrote, "It thus arises that the eating room, perhaps the best in the house, must in large families often serve as parlour, study, or schoolroom." Nevertheless, she still warned, "This entails a considerable amount of inconvenience, to be avoided if possible" (3). The inconvenience might refer to the children who put away their study materials when a dinner was scheduled, or it might be more subtle in that allowing children to use the dining room for activities could undermine the cultural power it might otherwise have had.

Even if the furnishings on offer changed to suit new ideas about the decoration and furnishings of rooms, other influences far beyond the control of the retailer and tastemaker occurred in room use. These influences included the personal taste or circumstances of individuals and the messages they read into the furnishings. Nowhere were these more obvious than in the parlour.

The drawing room or parlour was originally a smaller room set apart from the medieval great hall, designated as a space for private conversation and display of property. Its particular reinvention for most levels of society in the nineteenth century was crucial to the cult and culture of domesticity. The main characteristic of a refined house was a parlour that represented the front space of the occupiers' lives. This room functioned as a public space for reception and entertainment, in which the right furniture, suitably arranged, was part of the stage management. The parlour was furnished and decorated in a manner that appeared to deny the world of business or production, in favor of some domestic ideal. Yet, the way to achieve this state of affairs was to spend large sums of money with shopkeepers and artisans who provided manufactured products to make this room into a ritual space. Ironically, the very mechanization of many industrial processes, but especially textiles, enabled the manufacture of goods for the parlour and other spaces within the home at a price that was affordable to the growing market.

Richard Bushman perceptively discusses the contradictions in the nineteenth-century home in which there is a clear disjuncture between the economically useless, decorative parlour which itself is a product of much activity in the market and the factory that produced it. He recognizes that the basis for this disjuncture was that aristocratic culture became the conceptual basis for parlours: they were not natural developments growing from everyday experience (262–5). Therefore, other spaces in the home offered the real comfort, away from the applied decorum of the parlour.

Indeed, Allen Clarke in *The Effects of the Factory System* (1899) wrote about the symbolic function of the British parlour: "It is shut up for six days of the week, and is only kept for brag: ostentatious superfluity in the idea of the artisan's wife is, as with those in higher grades of society, a sign of superiority" (qtd in Barrett and Phillips 58). This comment demonstrates how the function of the parlour was often for display rather than use; it allowed Britons to conform to but not enjoy the material goods associated with middle-class domesticity.

One of the main ways of simply achieving these effects was to purchase a parlour "suite." The connotations of the courtly style established in the eighteenth century transferred themselves to the idea of the suite of matching furniture. The image of cohesion afforded by the suite gave the impression not only of the ability to make a single purchase of matching goods but also of social standing through the preference for supposedly more elite furniture aesthetics. Retailers played upon such snobbery. Oetzmann and Co. reminded readers of their 1871 catalogue that "a room furnished out of a saleroom has a saleroom look which will cling to it so long as the articles hang together" (295). The inference was that while "a saleroom look" conveyed stylishness and polish, mismatched furniture would reflect badly on the occupants.

In homes that were either too small or where families were not able to afford the furnishings of a parlour, the ideal of appropriateness was attempted through paraphrase, in the use of multi-purpose convertible furniture and other simulations of gentility. Louise Boland More's influential year-long study of New York's Lower West Side provides an example of a typical, respectable working-class home in 1907 that illustrates both the attempt at parlour-making and the necessity of convertible furniture:

> The 'parlor' is usually gaudy with plush furniture (sometimes covered with washable covers), carpet on the floor, cheap lace-curtains at the windows, crayon portraits of the family on the walls ... sometimes a couch, and the ubiquitous folding bed [which usually hid its true use in a case of some description]. (qtd in Grier 85)

The widespread purchase and use of objects such as these, which were increasingly available through mail order, especially in the United States, demonstrate how the conjunction of improved technologies and distribution systems helped to meet the aspirations of a burgeoning working class, albeit in often cramped spaces.

In contrast to the parlour, the bedroom was one of the more recessed, private spaces of the home, which offered wider scope for expressions of individuality and self-expression. These spaces, often seen as functional places, had prescribed locations for particular objects, clearly related to sensible practices. For example, beds ought to have their sides to the window; writing tables were placed near the fire; the washstand placed in the light, a pier glass located with its back to the light and a wardrobe should face the light in a central position. By the mid-nineteenth century, the bedroom had a much more rounded use. The 1880s catalogue of the furnishing company Oetzmann of London included an anonymous article written by the home decorator employed by *The Lady* magazine. She describes how "many girls like to turn their sleeping apartment into cosy rooms wherein they can study, read, write or do a little amateur dressmaking now and then during the day" (Oetzmann 106). To achieve this arrangement they simply purchased the adaptable items and drapery shown in the catalogue. Oetzmann's catalogue also had an example of "safe" furnishing where economy and appropriateness combined: "for the spare bedroom we found we really could not do better than again avail ourselves of the 'furnished room' system by having the 8½ guineas 'bedroom furnished complete'" (94).

As the bedroom was in the private zone of the house commentators regulated it less, but this did not stop them from establishing rules. Charles Eastlake was harsh in his prescriptions: "As a lady's taste is generally allowed to reign supreme in regards to the furniture of bedrooms, I must protest humbly but emphatically against the practice which exists of encircling toilet tables with a sort of muslin petticoat ... They just represent a milliner's notion of the 'pretty' and nothing more" (212). A little later, Robert Edis, though more conciliatory, still laid down rules:

> [A] bedroom should be essentially clear of everything that can collect or hold dust in any form: should be bright and cheerful, pleasantly furnished ... in which everything shall be carefully arranged and studied for use, not show. The good taste of the lady inhabitants of the house will soon add to the general home feeling of rest and comfort, by innumerable knick-knacks. (219–20)

As the bedroom was essentially a private space, it was the individuality of these "knick-knacks" and other personal possessions that allowed conformity to be disturbed, without destabilizing the Victorian home.

Conclusion

In the contradictory world of the long nineteenth century, the benefits of conformity and the framework of rules for home decoration and furnishings, amongst others, ensured a degree of security that was clearly welcome. Advice guide authors and retailers alike understood the potential anxieties, the issues of respectability and conformity to roles, and they were adept at fomenting and then meeting these demands. The advice in the books and journals of the time reinforced the need for conformity to appropriate taste, whilst often at the same time offering an outlet for the expression of individuality and personality. The retailers were able to meet the varying demands and encouraged them all. However, for the consumer this mix of "regulated taste" and individuality appeared to have created as many difficulties and contradictions as it offered to help. Conforming to gender and class expectations through a shared *habitus* that emphasized choice as voluntary and individualistic, yet at the same time directed, became part of a claim to middle-class identity. It was the family's role to try to make themselves and their homes at once as representative of the household's social position, unremarkable in terms of errors of vulgarity or over-reaching, yet unique in displays of individual "good taste."

Works Cited

Adams, Annmarie. *Architecture in the Family Way: Doctors, Houses and Women, 1870–1900*. Montreal: McGill-Queen's Press, 2001. Print.

Ames, Kenneth. *Death in the Dining Room and Other Tales of Victorian Culture*. Philadelphia: Temple University Press, 1992. Print.

Barrett, Helena, and John Phillips. *Suburban Style: The British Home, 1840–1960*. London: Macdonald, 1987. Print.

Baudrillard, Jean. *For a Critique of the Political Economy of the Sign*. St. Louis: Telos, 1981. Print.

Bourdieu, Pierre. *The Logic of Practice*. Stanford: Stanford University Press, 1990. Print.

Bushman, Richard L. *The Refinement of America: Persons, Houses, Cities*. NY: Alfred Knopf, 1992. Print.

Cairns, Stephen, and Jane M. Jacobs. "The Modern Touch: Interior Design and Modernisation in Post-Independence Singapore." *Institute of Geography Online Paper Series*. School of Geosciences, University of Edinburgh, 2006. Web.

Cassell's Household Guide. 4 vols. London: Cassell, 1869. Print.

Chase, Karen, and Michael Levenson. *The Spectacle of Intimacy: A Public Life for the Victorian Family*. Princeton: Princeton University Press, 2000. Print.

Cobbe, Frances Power. "Duties of Women as Mistresses of Households." *The Duties of Women: A Course of Lectures*. London: Williams & Norgate, 1881. Web.

Cohen, Deborah. *Household Gods: The British and Their Possessions*. New Haven, CT: Yale University Press, 2007. Print.

Coke [Mrs Talbot]. "Home Advice." *Hearth and Home*, 4 February, 1892: 363. Print.

Davidoff, Leonore, and Catherine Hall. *Family Fortunes, Men and Women of the English Middle Class, 1780–1850*. Chicago: University of Chicago Press, 1987. Print.

Douglas, Mary, and Baron Isherwood. *The World of Goods*. NY: Basic Books, 1979. Print.

Dresser, Christopher. *Studies in Design*. 1879. London: Studio Editions, 1988. Print.

Dunbar, Janet. *The Early Victorian Woman*. London: Harrap, 1953. Print.

Eastlake, Charles L. *Hints on Household Taste*. 1868. NY: Dover, 1969. Print.

Edis, Robert William. *Decoration and Furniture of Town Houses*. London: Kegan Paul, 1881. Print.

"Fashion in Furniture." *Myra's Journal of Dress and Fashion*, 1 December, 1876: 258. Web.

Finn, Margot. "Men's Things: Masculine Possession in the Consumer Revolution." *Social History* 25.2 (2000): 133–55. Web.

Forty, Adrian. *Objects of Desire*. London: Thames and Hudson, 1986. Print.

Garrett, Rhoda, and Agnes Garrett. *Suggestions for House Decoration in Painting, Woodwork, and Furniture*. London: Macmillan, 1876. Print.

Girling-Budd, Amanda. "Comfort and Gentility: Furnishings by Gillows, Lancaster 1840–55." *Interior Design and Identity* (eds) S. McKellar and P. Sparke. Manchester: Manchester University Press, 2004. Print.

Gorham, Deborah. *The Victorian Girl and the Feminine Ideal*. Bloomington, IN: Indiana University Press, 1982. Print.

Grier, Katherine C. *Culture & Comfort: People, Parlors, and Upholstery, 1850–1930*. Rochester, NY: Strong Museum, 1988. Print.

Hamlett, J. "'The Dining Room Should Be the Man's Paradise, as the Drawing Room is the Woman's': Gender and Middle-Class Domestic Space in England, 1850–1910." *Gender & History* 21.3 (2009): 576–91. Print.

Haweis, Mary Eliza. *The Art of Decoration*. London: Chatto and Windus, 1881. Web.

Haweis, Mary Eliza. *Beautiful Houses; Being a Description of Certain Well-Known Artistic Houses*. 2nd edn, London: Sampson Low, 1882. Web.

"How to Furnish Tastefully for Five Hundred." *The House* 6 (1899): 52–5. Print.

"How to Furnish a Flat." Unsigned Appendix. *Flats, Urban Houses and Cottage Homes* (ed.) Walter Shaw Sparrow. London: Hodder and Stoughton, 1906. 1–8. Print.

Hussey, David, and Margaret Ponsonby. *Buying for the Home: Shopping for the Domestic from the Seventeenth Century to the Present*. Aldershot: Ashgate, 2008. Print.

James, Henry. *The Spoils of Poynton*. London: Heinemann, 1897. Print.

Jones, Janna. "The Distance from Home: The Domestication of Desire in Interior Design Manuals." *Journal of Social History* 31.2 (1997): 307–26. Web.

Kerr, Robert. *The Gentleman's House*. London: John Murray, 1865. Web.

Kinchin, Juliet. "Interiors: Nineteenth-Century Essays on the 'Masculine' and the 'Feminine' Room." *The Gendered Object* (ed.) Pat Kirkham. Manchester: Manchester University Press, 1996. 12–29. Print.

Litchfield, Frederick. *History of Furniture*. London: Truslove and Shirley, 1892. Web.

Loftie [Martha Jane]. *The Dining Room*. London: Macmillan, 1878. Web.

Logan, Thad. *The Victorian Parlour*. Cambridge: Cambridge University Press, 2001. Print.

Muthesius, Hermann. *The English House*. 1904. Oxford: Blackwell, 1987. Print.

Oetzmann and Co. *Guide to House Furnishings* (including *Hints on House Furnishing and Decoration*). London: Oetzmann, 1871. Print.

Peterson, M. Jeanne. *Family, Love and Work in the Lives of Victorian Gentlewomen*. Bloomington, IN: Indiana University Press, 1989. Print.

Rich, Rachel. "Advice on Dining and Décor in London and Paris 1860–1914." *Journal of Design History* 16.1 (2003): 49–61. Web.

Symonds, Robert, and Bruce Whineray. *Victorian Furniture*. London: Country Life, 1962. Print.

Tosh, John. *A Man's Place: Masculinity and the Middle-Class Home in Victorian England*. New Haven, CT: Yale University Press, 1999. Print.

Walby, Sylvia. *Theorizing Patriarchy*. Oxford: Blackwell, 1990. Print.

Walker, S.P. "How to Secure Your Husband's Esteem. Accounting and Private Patriarchy in the British Middle Class Household during the Nineteenth Century." *Accounting, Organizations and Society* 23.5 (1998): 485–514. Web.

Young, Linda. *Middle-Class Culture in the Nineteenth Century: America, Australia and Britain*. London: Palgrave Macmillan, 2003. Print.

Chapter 3

The Material Lessons of Children's Literature: Unearthing Class Standards in E. Nesbit's *The Story of the Treasure Seekers*

Mary Jeanette Moran

The nineteenth century witnessed intense debate over the nature of childhood and the place of children in modern society. At stake were questions about how much work, loyalty, and obedience children owed their families and nations, and how much protection, care, and autonomy these communities owed their youngest members. The pendulum swung toward more protection, for example, as British Factory Acts in 1833, 1844, and 1867 gradually limited the hours and conditions in which children could work and helped to redefine the proper place of children, including those of the lower classes, as home and school instead of the workplace. Literature for adults explored this changing relationship between children and the market; portraits of children in peril from early responsibilities, workload, or the actions of adults who exploit rather than nurture them—such as Dickens's Artful Dodger, Jenny Wren, or Little Nell—sold well, in large part because of escalating public concern with the proper distinction between child and adult as well as continuing debates about appropriate educational and vocational training across classes. Meanwhile, the burgeoning children's literature market categorized children as consumers, not producers, of material goods. As the century progressed and children became increasingly associated with the domestic realm rather than the working world, the Romantic image of the innocent, pre-cultural naïf battled with ideas of the prematurely knowing and desperate child. In Hans Christian Andersen's "The Little Match-Girl," popularized in England by Charles Beckwith's 1847 translation, such a child froze to death on city streets because she dared not return home to the father who would beat her for failing to sell her quota of matches; in William Booth's *In Darkest England and The Way Out* (1890) the pretty orphan girl described in the opening pages must choose between starvation and prostitution, knowing that once she sells herself she will be "treated as a slave and outcast by the very men who have ruined her" (13). What unites these two images of childhood, innocent and victimized, is the child's need for protection, particularly from the dangers of the public sphere.

The rhetoric redefining children as a protected group produced a number of cultural expectations about children's behavior that reality—and literature—did not always reflect. If children of any class evinced an understanding of the workings of the marketplace akin to that of Booth's orphan girl, they risked undermining the developing separation between children and adults that allowed for limitations on young people's labor. Furthermore, given that lower-class children needed to be rescued from various kinds of work by reform-minded adults, by definition middle-class youngsters could not participate in the world of producing and selling lest they endanger their class status. According to this paradigm, the only appropriate role in the economy for middle-class young people was as consumers, particularly when their consumption habits, such as a desire for books, could help to reinforce their families' bourgeois positions by demonstrating the ability both to indulge in leisure activities and to spend money on decorative objects. Whether the children *read* the books was to a certain extent unimportant, for the mere presence of these material possessions in the home signaled the family's desire to invest in class-specific notions of literacy, education, and an image of childhood as a unique and impressionable stage of life. Given that children did not need to buy or even read the books designed for them, the burgeoning genre of children's literature, while it encouraged youthful autonomy in many ways, did not necessarily construct children as economic agents.

Yet despite these cultural expectations, it is clear that children *did* participate in the Victorian marketplace in many ways—as consumers, as sellers, and as products—thus requiring literary texts to mediate and maintain the uneasy popular myths associating children at once with innocence and delinquency as well as with bourgeois creature comforts and particular, dire economic vulnerabilities. Edith Nesbit's *The Story of the Treasure Seekers*, for example, shows how texts helped train children to position themselves as both innocent of economic strategizing and deeply savvy about potential agency through consumption. Nesbit's Bastable siblings entertain themselves with their imaginations during an absence from school necessitated by their father's failing business; in the process, they demonstrate how anxieties about financial status and class position affect even those children located squarely within the domestic realm. Ultimately, while *The Story of the Treasure Seekers* validates a certain level of autonomy for children, it does so by teaching them to value as treasure not material goods themselves, but culturally approved ways of producing, consuming, and disseminating those enticing objects.

Materiality and Children's Literature

At first glance, children's imaginative play of any period might seem to be free from the pressures of materiality, for in the world of make-believe, children need only creativity, not financial wherewithal, to produce any object they might desire. On the contrary, Gillian Brown argues that materiality is *inherent* to the genre of children's literature, given the influence of John Locke's theories of knowledge development during the eighteenth-century rise of children's book publishing in England. Locke proposed that every new idea results from a sensory experience that connects the new idea with an established one. In turn, Brown contends, "The materiality of children's books—their status as attractive objects and their close relation to other objects—recapitulates Locke's sense of reading as an associative activity" (352). As the children's literature market developed, books for young people retained an emphasis on their material nature not just because it was educationally effective, but because it was attractive to buyers; Brown points out that although "movables"—precursors to modern pop-up books—had been popular with both adults and children in the eighteenth century, "[t]he fact that movables become almost exclusively children's books by the nineteenth century underscores how Locke's recognition of the importance of materiality in reading and education developed through children's book publishing into a prevailing identification of children with materiality" (359). As Peter Hunt reminds us, children's publishers have encouraged this identification by using toys to sell books since at least 1744, when John Newbery[1] marketed his *A Little Pretty Pocket-Book* along with "a Ball and Pincushion, the use of which will infallibly make Tommy a good boy and Polly a good girl" (qtd in Hunt 43).[2] In addition to publishers who created the delightful prospect of receiving a plaything along with a book, some authors promised, if not toys, then more significant material rewards to readers of their texts, such as the eighteenth-century children's books that Gillian Avery summarizes thusly: "Be punctual and diligent, obedient and dutiful, do not lie or thieve or blow up your sister, beware of mad dogs and gaming, and you will live to be a successful sugar planter and to give your rivals a handsome funeral" (24). Comic though they may appear to modern readers, the threats and rewards in these didactic texts imply that children cannot escape their connection with the material world. From the earliest appearance of English-language children's books, then, educational philosophy has linked hands with marketing ploys to produce enduring connections among children's literature, materiality, and early training in ways to establish a middle-class identity.

As with adults, children's ability to make physical contact with particular kinds of books both highlights class divisions and provides opportunities to surmount those boundaries. While reading material was cheap enough to be accessible to poor children through the mid-eighteenth-century, by the 1840s the rise of children's book publishing created a prestige market aimed at the growing middle class and a "cottage literature" for the less privileged, so that different classes of children did not even see the same texts (Avery 16–18, 71). With basic literacy a significant class marker, the Sunday schools that began in the eighteenth century had to struggle against the disapproval of those who believed that encouraging

---

[1]   Further enshrining the materialist history of children's books, Newbery is now the namesake of the most well-known award for excellence in children's literature.

[2]   Lissa Paul describes a similar "holy trinity of children's book advertising: instruction, delight, and toys" that has existed since Newbery's day (137). Hunt also remarks on how, "[a]lmost from the beginning," material rewards for reading are "suitably sexually stereotyped" (43).

working-class children to read was tantamount to inciting revolution.[3] On the contrary, prizes given for academic performance and good behavior motivated students to internalize their evangelical lessons and identify with the ideologies of the current hierarchy. The first Sunday-school awards took the form of basic necessities like clothing that the laboring children lacked; however, throughout the nineteenth century books became more and more popular as prizes, driving a significant increase in the market for children's literature (Avery 68, 74–5). But as book prizes grew more appealing to students and families, in many ways narrative itself grew subordinate to the book as a tangible object. By the latter part of the nineteenth century, the appearance of a book determined its attractiveness as a reward, and publishers tended to advertise their wares by appearance and price rather than content; as Avery points out, "There were shilling books and two shilling books and very handsome ones for three shillings and sixpence for the top scholars or the school with a really munificent benefactor" (76). The presence of any kind of children's books in a house indicated a desire for upward mobility, if not middle-class status itself, signifying that rather than relying on the physical labor of its youngest members, the family could afford to provide them with enough leisure for pleasure reading or at least with the skills necessary to rise above the working classes. The interest in the outward attractiveness of the book transforms its value from potential (future opportunities or experiences its content could offer readers) to immediate (a visible sign of the family's current achievements); however, in both cases the child also becomes a kind of material possession, since the book signifies or enhances the family's class status only through its connection with the child.

This material history of children's books demonstrates that by the end of the nineteenth century the image of the child had acquired a new set of associations that could evoke a great deal of adult anxiety. Children had been marked out as a separate group and given special accommodations, even a distinct literature, but in the process they acquired a symbolic meaning that adults needed to control. In her much-cited study of the complex reception history of *Peter Pan*, Jacqueline Rose illuminates some of the ways in which turn-of-the-century adults continued to project their preoccupations about class distinctions onto the identity of the child. She theorizes that at the time *Peter Pan* appeared (the first performance of the play was in 1904), "the market [for children's books] was divided between the child *recipient* of the Christmas gift and the child *reader*, the former the object of a new and increasing commercial attention (aesthetic luxury and value), the latter the displaced focus of anxieties about the commercial and literary effects on the book trade of the changing educational policy of the state (overproduction, devaluation)" (108).[4]

---

[3] For more details on opposition to Sunday schools on religious and class-based terms, see Thomas Laqueur. See also Roy Porter and Neil J. Smelser.

[4] According to Mavis Reimer, Rose and other children's literature critics such as James Kincaid and Perry Nodelman suggest that adults "reproduce children as commodities" when they author texts for young people (51).

While both conceptions of young book consumers reflect Rose's larger argument that children's literature embodies "what the adult desires—desires in the very act of construing the child as the object of its speech" (2), the difference between the passive "recipient" and the potentially active "reader" also suggests that the latter category could be more threatening than the former, especially if it aligned with class anxieties. As Rose puts it, "The distinction between the two different types of child reader was, therefore, a distinction between a classic children's literary culture still largely dominated by the adult market (literary tradition) and the emergence of an autonomous children's literature which was being negatively identified with aspects of working-class culture" (Rose 108). These conflicting models of children's interactions with books—the passive recipient of classic texts and the active reader of autonomous literature—closely parallel the persistent opposition between the Romantic vision of the innocent child, which would serve to encourage adults' perceptions of themselves and their class identity, and that of the knowing child, who would threaten the division between child and adult and thus endanger his or her own protected status. In other words, at the end of the nineteenth century children's relationships to books signaled their identity as either defined by adults and therefore protected by them, or as containing a certain level of anxiety-producing agency.

"For of Course We Knew": The Child's Point of View

The protagonists in *The Story of the Treasure Seekers*, the Bastable siblings, have a very active relationship with the books they read. Rather than passively digesting texts given to them by adults, they use the stories to stimulate their creativity. In fact, they model all of their imaginative games on their reading, which comprises everything from penny dreadfuls to Sherlock Holmes to Kipling to adult newspapers. This approach to reading appears to grant the siblings a great deal of agency; however, when we consider the complex ways the children must position themselves with regard to a variety of material possessions and to the conflicting images of childhood as innocent and knowing, it becomes clear that their agency remains contingent on conformity to middle-class values. The Bastables (and, by extension, their young readers) must learn that while acquiring money might seem to offer a secure class position, it can actually undermine their status if the methods of obtaining cash associate them with images of degraded or manipulative children. By contrast, when the siblings fully accept the role of a particular kind of consumer, one who desires material objects not out of acquisitiveness but for the experiences and interpersonal connections those objects enable, they manage to reverse their family's financial downfall. Moreover, if the children function as a product themselves—as a physical representation of the kind of childhood made possible by financial security and social standing—then by "marketing" this product to those in power, they can doubly reinforce their middle-class identity.

Nesbit's first book for children and the first of three novels focusing on the Bastable family, *The Story of the Treasure Seekers* marks a significant moment not only in her career but also in the history of children's literature. Oswald, the oldest boy of the six Bastable siblings, narrates his family's adventures while offering ongoing commentary on how to craft such a story for a child audience. Many critics have commented on the significance of this narratorial voice to Nesbit's writing for young people and to children's literature as a whole; Anita Moss, for example, argues that "Nesbit's self-conscious use of metafiction ... produced ... a work which was to usher in modern children's literature" ("Varieties" 91). According to Moss, the novel breaks new ground by positively depicting children's imaginative play rather than seeking to inculcate adult standards of behavior, as well as by including a sympathetic and realistically childlike narrator, who fails to understand the adult world completely but tries to behave well toward both adults and children.[5] Among the ideas not fully understood by the Bastable children is their family's precarious financial position following the disappearance of their father's business partner (presumably along with a large amount of money). Despite their incomplete comprehension of the monetary challenges facing their family, an air of class anxiety permeates all of the siblings' adventures, so that the imaginative, age-appropriate play celebrated by critics contains threads of very mature economic concerns. Consequently, this watershed text in children's literature, which narratively distinguishes a child's perspective from that of an adult, ironically also blurs the boundaries between juvenile and supposedly adult worries.

These anxieties do more than complicate the division between adult responsibilities and childhood freedom; they also depict middle-class existence as both respectable and desirable. While the children aim to "restore the fallen fortunes of the House of Bastable," they do not aspire to the upper-class identity connoted by the idea of an established line of inheritance. Instead, their efforts at finding treasure tend to validate middle-class values of entrepreneurship, creativity, and compassion. The Bastables' treasure-seeking endeavors also underline the importance of material goods to the establishment and maintenance of a middle-class identity. The family's current lack of material luxuries signals their tenuous class status, and the children count themselves successful each time they acquire enough money to purchase items that formerly would have entered their home without effort or remark—scissors, pencil and paper, and apples, for example. Moreover, consumer products seem to offer the children a variety of avenues through which they can secure financial stability for their family, although not all of these avenues prove to be consistent with the respectable status they seek; the products must be the right kind, acquired the right way, through partnerships with the right kinds of people.

---

[5]   Many scholars agree with Moss; Erika Rothwell summarizes the prevailing critical perspective on Nesbit by stating that she "is typically defined as a juvenile author who writes for children as equals and as an uncompromising advocate of the child's viewpoint, rights, and freedoms" (61). However, Rothwell goes on to argue that, as a whole, Nesbit's writing still presents the child as inferior to adults.

The novel opens with the six children (Dora, Oswald, twins Alice and Noël, Dicky, and Horace Octavius, known as H.O.) sharing their individual plans for obtaining enough money to re-establish the most important elements of their former lifestyle—returning to their schools and having something for dinner other than mutton, for example.[6] Mr Bastable wishes to preserve his children's innocence about economic realities, conforming to what Moss calls a "Romantic vision ... of childhood as a time of special, Pan-like vitality and pleasure" ("E. Nesbit" 226). When their father attempts to hide from his children the true reason they can no longer attend school, he tells them "a holiday would do us all good," but although the children are certainly willing to give themselves up to pleasure, their vitality does not preclude an awareness of their father's financial difficulties; instead, they "wished he had told us he couldn't afford it. For of course we knew" (3). The siblings' reaction to their financial situation stresses how thoroughly economic exchange and material culture structure their experiences. As Oswald comments, "Father does not like you to ask for new things. That was one way we had of knowing that the fortunes of the ancient House of Bastable were really fallen. Another way was that there was no more pocket money" (2). In other words, the children notice their descent in class status because they are attuned to the presence of material goods in their lives, and they feel this descent more sharply when their purchasing power decreases. Although the children cannot always discern the precise chain of events that their father hides from them, they do see through to the underlying reality; for example, while they accept Mr Bastable's explanation that he has sent the good silver away to be cleaned, they notice that it has been replaced by "yellowy-white [flatware that was] not so heavy as the old ones, and [that] never shone after the first day or two" and surmise that their father cannot afford to pay for the cleaning (3). Although he has difficulty maintaining the patriarchal role of provider, Mr Bastable does his best to perpetuate, for both his children and himself, an image of childhood as a time free of adult worries and devoted to imaginative exploration. His children prove to be markedly creative, but they express their inventiveness in ways that demonstrate how enmeshed they are in material culture and its attendant pressures, and thus how remote they are from the kind of childhood their father envisions. While their recognition of the family's economic realities gives the Bastable siblings a greater sense of agency, it also makes them more vulnerable to what their father thinks of as adult worries about the precariousness of their position in society.

---

[6]   Julia Briggs observes that the children "cannot attend the free Board Schools because that would have involved an open acknowledgment that they had lost their middle-class status" (81–2).

The Bastables as Agents and Objects

In each chapter, the Bastable children try out another plan for generating income, and although they enjoy the ensuing adventures, their continuing efforts to acquire money emphasize the economic anxiety lying just underneath their suburban, seemingly middle-class life. These anxieties surface most obviously when the Bastables attempt direct entry into commerce through a variety of schemes, such as selling port wine on commission, concocting a patent medicine, and peddling Noël's poetry to newspapers. While their efforts often earn the sympathy of adults—and perhaps a little pocket money as well—they also reveal how easily their family could slip even further down in the social hierarchy, should they associate themselves with the wrong products or types of exchange. The port-selling escapade, for example, begins when the children answer an advertisement claiming that "ladies and gentlemen can easily earn two pounds a week in their spare time, and to send two shillings for sample and instructions, carefully packed free from observation" (7). The ad contradictorily suggests that selling port to one's friends and relatives is an activity perfectly suited to "ladies and gentlemen," but that these genteel people will not want their neighbors to realize that they are engaged in trade. Dora, the eldest sibling, discerns what the ad attempts to occlude, voicing the worry that "I don't think it's quite nice to sell wine ... and besides, it's not easy to suddenly begin to sell things when you're not used to it" (102). When the children entice casual callers inside in order to give their sales pitch, they elicit sympathy from the adults—the butcher who comes to see their father about an unpaid bill, for example, gives them a shilling and goes away—but they also open themselves up to the observation and judgment of their community, as we can see when the prospective port buyers notice the holes in the carpet and the peeling wallpaper. More importantly, their innocent choice of product (predictably, the advertisement describes only the potential profits, not the item to be sold) reveals the inappropriateness of their foray into the market. Associating themselves with alcohol could only reflect negatively on the Bastables, given the iconic images of tots swilling gin because their parents were too poor (or too neglectful) to purchase any other nourishment.[7] When the siblings make a sales pitch to a clergyman who has called to invite them to his Sunday school, their marketing spiel—"[A]n exceptional opportunity. Full bodied and nutty ... of a quality never before offered at the price"—fails to evoke the intended sense of luxury consumerism.[8] Instead, the minister sees them as promoting a morally reprehensible form of consumption, one which warrants a temperance lecture:

---

[7]   In her book *Artful Dodgers*, Marah Gubar comments, for example, that "poor children in [John] Leech's [*Punch*] cartoons exhibit prematurely developed street smarts, class consciousness, and a propensity to drown their troubles in drink" (17).

[8]   Attendance at Sunday school carried different meanings depending on the era; while eighteenth-century reformers collected poor and unwashed children to teach them to read as they saved their souls, by the mid-nineteenth century attending Sunday school "was

"it is the drinking of *wine* and *spirits*—yes, and *beer*, which makes half the homes in England full of *wretched* little children, and *degraded, miserable* parents" (110–11). Reduced by the lecture from miniature businesspeople to "nasty, sordid little things," the children retire in defeat and tears (111). By associating themselves with this disreputable form of commerce, the Bastables unwittingly emphasize their tenuous hold on middle-class respectability, providing an indication of how children's games exist within and even influence the economic realities that surround them.[9] Moreover, in attempting to take control of their financial situation, the siblings evoke the unchildlike child—the one with adult knowledge of spirits and the market—thereby endangering rather than re-establishing their middle-class status.

If the "Castilian Amoroso" incident appears to warn the children away from peddling certain material goods, however, the following chapter complicates this message; "The Nobleness of Oswald" suggests that while products such as alcohol may be irredeemably inappropriate for middle-class children to promote or consume, trade itself does not necessarily lower one's class status, provided that the merchant's behavior promotes middle-class standards such as a lack of greed and the protection of women. The primary focus of this chapter concerns the siblings' attempts to invent a patent medicine. The effort fails nearly as soundly as did their previous plan, although since they never advance past the product development stage, they avoid the individual and familial humiliation caused by the Castilian Amoroso. Neither wine nor medicine is appropriate for the Bastables to sell, for both products evoke patterns of exploitative consumerism and destructive consumption. In this case, it is Noël who suffers, falling seriously ill after the children try to give him a cold so they can test their medicines. Since their father is away, a worried Alice uses their "bad sixpence" (which they have always kept in their money box "for luck") in order to afford a telegram asking for advice from a neighbor, who carries Noël off to the seaside to recuperate (4: 124). Taking up the male role of provider that Mr Bastable seems ill equipped to handle, Oswald assumes the responsibility for Alice's debt. When no other opportunity presents itself, he earns the money by selling bunches of flowers at the train station. Though aware of the lower-class implications of such an act, he undergoes a personal shame in order to preserve the honor of his sister, and thus his family. As the chapter heading suggests, Oswald narrates the incident with his habitual pretended modesty and actual pride, so this might seem to be one of the cases that Rothwell describes where "the joke is ... between the adult reader and

---

the respectable thing to do" (Avery 54). Therefore, the clergyman could be leveraging the expectations of religion, class status, or both.

[9]   Gubar makes a similar but more broad-ranging point as part of her argument that Nesbit and her contemporaries encourage children to become more informed and critical readers: "Golden Age children's authors ... generally conceive of child characters and adult readers as socially saturated beings, profoundly shaped by the culture, manners, and morals of their time, precisely in order to explore the vexed issue of the child's agency" (4).

the author at Oswald's expense" (62). However, Oswald's self-satisfaction does not negate the fact that his actions uphold middle-class values of chivalry and family honor without tarnishing the myth of childhood innocence, as the siblings do by either consuming or peddling alcohol and snake oil; moreover, his behavior in this case demonstrates a version of the personal agency that is the children's goal throughout the novel. Although Oswald cannot resist revealing his actions to the reader, he practices discretion with adults within the text, even sympathetic ones, like his father, the fun-loving neighbor, and Nesbit's double Mrs Leslie, who provide advice or rewards during most of the other adventures. Oswald alone reassures Alice when she lies awake worrying about being damned as a thief; he then finds a way to satisfy her conscience and her debt without any explicit advice or help from an adult.[10] Because Oswald enters into trade out of a gendered sense of honor, neither the product nor the method of selling matters—he can even "put on his oldest clothes" and masquerade as a lower-class child without damaging his class status (126). In other words, the children's actions during these two chapters show how the relationship between middle-class identity and the cultural weight of material goods is mutually constitutive; only when the children respond correctly to these interlocking codes by treating their ultimate goal—reestablishment of their class status—as the real treasure, remaining constantly aware of how their interactions with consumer products reflect on their identity, do they increase their sense of control over their financial situation and social position.

In order to perpetuate an image of childhood that bolsters middle-class ideals, the Bastables must defend those ideals against incursions by the upper classes as staunchly as they learn to resist those from below. Whereas associations with deceptive and debased products and selling practices threaten the middle-class idea of innocence that grants a level of protection to children, the siblings can also maintain their protected status by converting the upper classes—or those with high-class pretensions—to a middle-class lifestyle. For example, when the Bastables cannot afford to travel to the seashore during the hot summer months, they decide to become detectives patterned on their readings of Sherlock Holmes and penny dreadfuls. Much to their delight, they think they have found a mystery close to home when they see lights in the house next door, supposedly vacant while the occupants are on holiday. When Oswald and Dicky peer through the windows, though, they discover not counterfeiters or robbers, as they had hoped, but the daughters of the house, comparing bargains on tinned salmon and produce since, "We must save as much as ever we can on our housekeeping money if we want to go away decent next year" (24). This family clearly wishes to present itself as socially superior; as Noël says, their neighbors "are very grand. They won't know us—and they go out in a real private carriage sometimes. And they have an 'At Home' day, and people come in cabs" (19). Instead of uncovering criminal activity, the Bastables' detecting reveals the superficiality and performativity of class markers.

---

[10]   Mrs Leslie does give Oswald the flowers as a gift, but she never learns what use he made of them.

But even as the novel deflates the imaginary grandeur of the neighbors, it replaces those pretensions with a different kind of pride, which Oswald demonstrates when he apologizes to the young ladies for startling them, admitting that "it is very dishonourable to pry into other people's secrets, especially ladies'" (25–6). His gendered, middle-class sense of chivalric honor influences the neighbors to follow his example, as the youngest of the ladies thanks him for his "nice, manly little speech" and tells him "*You've* nothing to be ashamed of, at any rate ... I'm going to—I'm going to pull up the blinds and open the shutters, and I want to do it at *once*, before it gets dark, so that everyone can see we're at home, and not at Scarborough" (26). Although the Bastables do not encounter any real criminals in this adventure, their talk of counterfeiters and burglars equates the class pride of the neighbors with antisocial behavior. These children might not possess the skill or resources to earn money as detectives, but they can still defend their middle-class honor against the neighbors' snobbery and convert adults from the emptiness of upper-class pretense to an honest acceptance of financial realities.

Similarly, when the Bastables encounter a young princess who proves unimaginative and trapped by her role, not only do they convince her to prefer their way of life, but their interactions also suggest to readers that upper-class sensibilities sap the strength and imagination of their proponents. Reversing standard gender expectations in which women marry for material and social advancement, Noël has been planning since the beginning to marry a princess who, presumably, would have enough money to support his family.[11] Consequently, nothing seems more natural than that the little girl the Bastables meet in the park would introduce herself as a princess. The children assume that the girl is only playing at a royal identity, as they are, but the text emphasizes her high breeding by marking her as both immobile and fragile; Oswald comments, "She was like a china doll—the sixpenny kind; her forehead was very big and lumpy, and her cheeks came high up, like little shelves under her eyes ... She had on a funny black frock with curly braid on it, and button boots that went almost up to her knees. Her legs were very thin" (48). Although, as I have argued, the Bastables function as the material embodiment of the middle-class identity to which their family desperately clings, their interest in experiential knowledge has saved them from transforming into the almost completely inanimate artifact that the princess seems to be. Princess Pauline serves as a warning that children who signify their class status run the risk of becoming objectified, important only for what they represent instead of what they can do or imagine. The siblings misread Pauline as a kindred spirit, thinking that she enters into imaginative play as wholeheartedly as they do, since she so confidently states "I am a princess," without the need to specify that her role is a fantasy (48). As they soon discover, though, what they interpret as imagination is actually a mental rigidity that matches Pauline's china-doll looks.

---

[11] Oswald's narration often aligns 10-year-old Noël with the girls and criticizes his lack of conformity to gender norms, as when he tells him to "be a man and not a sniveling pig" (6).

At first, she accepts as truth everything that her new playmates say, believing that she has come upon a whole clutch of royal children and admonishing Noël that he is "old enough to know [his] own name" (51) when he stumbles on the long and elaborate list of monikers he has just concocted for himself. Eventually, though, the automaton-like girl unbends enough to play tag, at which point "she really [begins] to laugh at last and not to look so much like a doll" (53). But Pauline cannot evade her restrictive upper-class identity, which degrades the Bastables simply by association; her governess soon sweeps in and carries her away from the "common children" (53). Aware of the insult to their class, the elder siblings reject the designation of commonness; Dora "[turns] very red and [begins] to speak" as if to defend her family (53), while Oswald carefully draws a distinction between his behavior and what a "common boy" would have done (54). Although they fear a further reduction in their class status, the Bastables have already convinced Pauline of the superiority of their way of life; she cries defiantly to her caretakers, "When I am grown up, I'll always play with common children!" (53). Of course, by the time Pauline has the power to determine her own companions, her childhood will be long gone. Far from being the solution to the Bastables' financial troubles, as the children expect, the stultifying nature of Princess Pauline's wealth and position implicitly threatens all children's physical vigor and intellectual flexibility. Once again, the Bastables reinforce their middle-class status by unintentionally advertising—to readers as well as to other characters—a model of childhood that is simultaneously innocent of economic manipulation and quietly aware of the pressures of the class system.

The novel further reinforces the power of this image of childhood when it becomes an actual object of exchange—when the children receive monetary compensation in return for the idea of childhood they embody. In one instance, the children visit a moneylender, whom they nickname the "Generous Benefactor—like in Miss Edgeworth" and further familiarize as the "G.B." (80, 81). While the Bastables hope to regain their ability to acquire possessions in order to reassert their middle-class status, or in other words, to purchase elements of domestic display that serve as a means to an end, the moneylender—who of course is Jewish—represents an inappropriate attachment to objects. Oswald comments that Mr Rosenbaum's room "had velvet curtains and a soft, soft carpet, and it was full of the most splendid things. Black and gold cabinets, and china, and statues, and pictures ... [T]here were clocks and candlesticks and vases, and gilt looking glasses, and boxes of cigars and scent and things littered all over the chairs and tables" (83). The excessive display of things not only diminishes their individual value, thus turning them into litter, but also implies a fetishization of material objects that Rosenbaum's attitude towards money further emphasizes; before giving the children a coin (at 60 percent interest!) he sits "stroking the sovereign and looking at it as if he thought it very beautiful" (86). Because the moneylender fetishizes material goods, this scene suggests, possessions reinforce his outsider status rather than allowing him access to middle-class respectability. By contrast, the children seem to have traded their youthful charm not only for a small amount of money, like that they have received from other adults, but also for something of significant value, for after their visit their father receives a letter that he confesses "took a weight off my mind" (87). Given that the children have seen Mr Rosenbaum's name "on a circular in father's study" (80) and that Father mentions that the two "have done some business together" (87), we can only assume that the moneylender has decided to extend the term of Mr Bastable's loan. While the children remain innocent of the corruption caused by too great a dependence on possessions, their actions do have a discernible and significant effect on their family's fortunes by encouraging the man they imagine as a "generous benefactor" to behave more like one in reality. At the same time, this episode illustrates the world outside middle-class respectability in the person of Mr Rosenbaum and, by revealing Mr Bastable's interactions with the moneylender, clarifies how narrowly the family remains within those bounds of respectability.

While the adventure of the Generous Benefactor illustrates the potential power of imaginative play in the marketplace by depicting the children's charm as a commodity that can be used in service of an enhanced class status, the final escapade in the novel suggests that the Bastables' amusements have enough commercial power to redeem their middle-class identity entirely. Their father invites his deceased wife's uncle to dinner, referring to him as the "Indian Uncle" because he has earned his fortune in the colonies, and Mr Bastable hopes to convince him to invest in his business. Misunderstanding the term "Indian" to mean Native American (their only point of reference being the stanza of Pope's *Essay on Man* that begins "Lo, the poor Indian" [Pope 1.99]), the children think that he must be hungry—especially after the dinner with their father, about which Oswald comments, "Something got burned, I'm sure—for we smelled it. It was an extra smell, besides the mutton. I know *that* got burned" (155). Unfortunately, it seems that the uncle's initial impression of Mr Bastable is no more favorable than his response to what he mutters has been a "shocking bad dinner," since the children overhear him saying "he was afraid that what some businesses wanted was not capital, but management" (157). Filled with pity for this apparently impoverished and starving Indian, the children invite him to a dinner they have bought with the spoils of their treasure-hunting—rabbit, almonds, raisins, figs, and coconut, along with a currant pudding. It is this act of compassion that brings him into contact with the children's imaginative play, since each course of the dinner provides fodder for another make-believe scenario: the rabbit becomes a deer "slain in the green forest with ... trusty yew bows" and roasted in the fireplace, the almonds and raisins must be "[plucked] from the boughs of the great trees" (the top of the bureau), and the pudding transforms into "a wild boar at bay, and very hard indeed to kill, even with forks" (163).[12] Throughout the course of the evening,

---

[12]   Reimer points out that the play dinner "reproduces three roles in the colonial project—that of the trophy hunter, that of the European traveler/adventurer, and that of the consumer back home," in the process romanticizing and softening their uncle's role in imperial conquest.

the uncle comes to understand the precariousness of the family's class status from the children's point of view, as he learns everything that they know about their financial woes: no school, no pocket money, and the family silver spirited away. Contrary to the image of childhood as completely free from economic concerns, the Bastables' comprehension of their family's situation helps the uncle see what his refusal to invest must have meant to their father. These revelations make it all the more poignant when the children insist that their uncle take the remainder of the money they have collected on their escapades. Unlike Mr Bastable's business pitch (which is no more successful than the Castilian Amoroso spiel), this "play dinner" and example of generosity locate the uncle firmly within the family setting, where he realizes that Dora is "the image of poor Janey" (169). The loan to Mr Bastable becomes possible within this context, refigured as an expression of family responsibility rather than a demonstration of business acumen. But just as the siblings are not unaware of financial realities, neither does this family setting exist apart from the marketplace. This time, however, the children have found an appropriate product to sell: their own imaginative youthfulness, which arises in large part from their reading habits and engenders both playful fantasies and the ability to empathize with others. The uncle makes clear that he values these qualities by conflating them and the children with material possessions; he tells them that the threepenny piece they donated to the "poor Indian" is "a present ... I value more than anything else I own," and implies that the children themselves are his reward when he opines, "I don't think I've done so badly either, if it comes to that, though I was never a regular professional treasure seeker, eh, what?" (177). The Bastables also find the treasure they seek, not simply in the person of a generous benefactor but in an identity that *in and of itself* validates the very middle-class existence that they desire. As children who combine the leisure and the safety to indulge in fantasy with an awareness of how economics affects people's lives, they *are* middle-class, and thus the uncle's intervention is not a *deus ex machina* but a natural result of their interaction with him.

Continuing the message that middle-class youngsters cannot demonstrate too great a familiarity with economic processes, the novel masks the importance of children (and their reading) to middle-class identity by emphasizing the uncle's role in the Bastables' return to societal grace. His enthusiastic adoption of the whole family, particularly his choice of gifts, reminds us that although middle-class identity gives children a certain level of privilege and protection, it also defines them as necessarily subservient to adults. Having been won over by the children, the uncle returns to the house as a seemingly magical granter of wishes—Oswald identifies his carriage as "the coach of the Fairy Godmother" even before he realizes to whom the carriage belongs or how he intends to help the Bastable family (168). The uncle has decided that he will support Mr Bastable's business, and he marks his new relationship with the family by giving them a dizzying array of gifts, particularly artifacts of his colonial enterprise. I quote the section at length to give a sense of how this parade of treasures signifies the Bastables' return from the exile of financial insecurity:

> There were toys ... and model engines ... and a lot of books, and Japanese
> china tea sets for the girls ... There were sweets by the pound and by the box,
> and long yards and yards of soft silk from India ... and a real Indian sword for
> Oswald and a book of Japanese pictures for Noël and some ivory chessmen for
> Dicky: the castles of the chessmen were elephant-and-castles. [Even beyond
> these entertaining gifts are] the Indian things: carved fans and silver bangles and
> strings of amber beads, and necklaces of uncut gems—turquoises and garnets ...
> and shawls and scarves of silk, and cabinets of brown and gold, and ivory boxes
> and silver trays, and brass things. (170, 171)

Presumably the uncle's experience abroad garnered him not only this load of
booty, but also the wealth and connections that allow him to save Mr Bastable's
business. Signifiers of the leisure enjoyed by the middle class as well as of
the colonial engagements on which the wealth of Britain rests, these treasures
reward the children for their adherence to middle-class ideals of honor, energy,
and creativity, much as the eighteenth-century chapbooks described by Gillian
Avery promised a successful sugar-planter's life to obedient boys. However, while
some of the gifts could provide material for further imaginative play—the book,
the toys, and the chess set, for example—items such as the ivory boxes, silver
trays, and vaguely defined brass "things" seem destined merely for an ornamental
function, a display of imperial power subsumed into a display of domestic wealth
that would reinforce the Bastables' reacquired position. Indeed, by the end of the
list, the gifts' value as signifiers of colonial wealth overtakes their overt purpose as
presents for the children. Surely children (especially such imaginative ones) could
have done without the cabinets, boxes, and trays, and certainly the "necklaces of
uncut gems—turquoises and garnets" seem a bit excessive. But these gifts cement
the uncle's status as "fairy godfather" by evoking a moment earlier in the book
when Noël expresses a wish that "a fairy would come down the chimney and drop
a jewel on the table—a jewel worth just a hundred pounds" (79). At the time, the
rest of the children defuse this romantic desire by suggesting that the fairy "might
just as well give you the hundred pounds while she was about it"—or, better yet, a
regular weekly allowance (79). This practical approach to good fortune dominates
the uncle's intervention as well; though marked as the fairy godfather, he does not
elevate the family to a magical life of leisure. Instead, with his help, the Bastable
family regains the ability to do the kind of intellectual labor that leads to middle-
class success: Father can now engage in profitable work, the boys will go to Rugby
"and perhaps to Balliol afterward," and Dicky already plans to join his father's
business (176). The siblings' quest to regain the good life—including material
possessions valued not for themselves but for what they represent, like educated
minds and palates—thus culminates in an excessive display of things that matches
the clutter of Mr Rosenbaum's room and that ironically limits the children's
freedom in a number of ways. Going back to school means less time for play,
and the children align with traditional gender roles much as their gifts do. Their
uncle assigns a sword and chessmen to the boys, tea sets and dresses to the girls,

and while the boys quickly take up their places in the patriarchal power structure, Oswald's triumphant summing-up of future plans includes no mention of Dora, or even Alice, who had often played boys' roles during the hunt for treasure.

The return to middle-class privilege comes with a price in other ways as well. The children's capacity for creative play and imaginative identification with others serves as a kind of coin with their uncle just as it had with the moneylender. However, whereas Mr Rosenbaum's status as ethnic other suggests that he can only postpone the Bastables' descent into a lower class, the "Indian Uncle," who has made his fortune through colonial enterprise and, quite likely, the exploitation of ethnic others, can rescue the children and their father permanently from that change in status. Just as the means of the family's rescue both originate from and reinforce a notion of middle-class British identity bound by family ties and racial homogeneity, the Bastables' return to middle-class standing similarly defines that happy position through the explicit exclusion of others—in this case, those marked as not English or as associated with unsavory occupations. At the Christmas party that closes the novel and celebrates the Bastable family's move into their uncle's house, the children are delighted to see some of the people who have helped them in their treasure-hunting. However, when they ask about the tabloid newspaper editor who gave them money for Noël's poetry, the kind butcher who forgave their father's bill, and Mr Rosenbaum, the adults laugh and put them off, saying that "you could not ask all your business friends to a private dinner" (175). The children are taught through adult condescension not to ask after or invite "business friends" into their home, as if this celebratory moment were only a family affair, and as if the family, Indian Uncle included, came together without any intervention from the marketplace or the children's more materialistic "treasure seeking."

With domesticity reconstituted in their uncle's well-appointed "jolly, big … house with a lot of windows," the children can once again be children without any connection to commerce, their father is rescued financially without loss of status, and the Indian Uncle learns that his far-flung adventures and accumulated wealth pale in value to the family he had left behind (172). Marah Gubar argues that the apparent altruism of the uncle reveals a seamy underside once we compare the two characters who lend Mr Bastable money; she says that Rosenbaum's "slimy turnaround after being 'touched' by the children encourages readers to question the motives, merits, and dependability of the Indian Uncle, another 'kind gentleman who has a lot of money' and who seems to desire, out of the goodness of his heart, to give it to the poor" (146). If this is the case, then the novel also encourages readers to notice how the forces of middle-class "respectability"—not to mention the cultural significance of material possessions—work to exclude one and lionize the other of these gentlemen who behave in similar fashion. However, such potential critiques of the Indian Uncle or of the system of "respectability" fade away with the close of the novel, in which Noël concludes that "the best treasure of all is the Uncle good and kind" (176). Thus *The Story of the Treasure Seekers* concludes with the family reunited, restored in fortune and affection so that the children are the true treasures of the household and any efforts at "professional" upward mobility—by the children, their father or their "Indian Uncle"—have been erased.

Although direct participation in commerce cannot provide the Bastable children with enough money to restore their family's fortunes, when they learn to "market" successfully the model of creative, energetic, and compassionate childhood brought to life by their imaginative play, they reinforce their middle-class status both symbolically (as they learn to appreciate material objects not for their monetary value but for the experiences they provide and represent) and actually (when they remind their uncle that imperialist financial successes do not absolve him of his responsibility to uphold the British family unit). Because the children's desired goal of middle-class identity depends so heavily on traditional gender roles, it even influences the tenor of the narrative voice. At the beginning of the novel, the narrator introduces the six children and then confides, "It is one of us that tells this story—but I shall not tell you which" (2). It soon becomes clear, however, that Oswald is the narrator, due to his tendency to fall into the first person when talking about himself. I would argue that Oswald cannot help revealing his identity because of the gender role he believes he must fill in order to meet the expectations of his desired class. As the oldest son, he feels responsible for his younger siblings and tries to maintain the family's respectability through gentlemanly conduct. This masculine, middle-class ethos arises from Oswald's actions as both narrator and character. As the narrator, Oswald's efforts to uphold a gentlemanly code of moral behavior can be quite humorous, for he tends to congratulate himself for adhering to this code and to reprove his siblings for any infractions; in his own words, he "is too much of a man to quarrel about a little thing" (16), "hates injustice of every kind" (27), "is always willing to give other people's ideas a fair trial" (31), "always remembers what he is told" (35), and much more. Despite their self-congratulatory tone, though, these asides to the reader demonstrate that Oswald has internalized the gender- and class-based rules for polite behavior that he has learned from reading Kipling and rags-to-riches stories. We can see that this is not mere rhetoric, for Oswald *acts* on these rules when he rescues Alice from her debt by selling the flowers (123–6) and when he comforts Dora, who fears she has failed to live up to the legacy of their mother (112). Through his self-aware narration and observations on his role as a character in the story he is telling, Oswald unites the person who can comment on these cultural mores with the person who embodies them—the person who is, moreover, the son and heir to the Bastable name—thereby doubly reinforcing his gentlemanly ethos. The class aspirations of the Bastable family thus necessitate Oswald's apparently unwitting betrayal of himself as narrator.

The Story of the Treasure Seekers intervenes in the continuing debates over the nature of childhood by depicting young protagonists who counteract the model of the naïve, prattling youngster. The Bastables demonstrate an awareness of their family's financial woes, but they find that if they try to address those problems directly, they appear preternaturally knowing, threaten the self-image of adults, and undermine rather than reinforce their middle-class status. If, instead, they can position themselves as savvy consumers who value material goods not for their monetary worth but for their ability to provide experiences and interpersonal connections, they become avatars of the class status they seek, and, in the process, enable the reclamation of that status for their family. Despite the societal pressure on the children to appreciate the conceptual worth of material objects, the presence of the objects themselves still remains central to their family's class standing. But within the context of the material history of children's literature, books remain the most important possessions not only for the Bastables, who have constructed an appropriately middle-class model of childhood from their reading, but for the child reader holding a copy of *The Story of the Treasure Seekers* and learning to fulfill that role as well.

Works Cited

Andersen, Hans Christian. "The Little Match Girl." Trans. Charles Beckwith. *Bentley's Miscellany* 21 (1847): 105–6. Web.

Avery, Gillian. *Childhood's Pattern: A Study of the Heroes and Heroines of Children's Fiction 1770–1950.* London: Hodder and Stoughton, 1975. Print.

Booth, William. *In Darkest England and the Way Out.* London: Salvation Army, n.d. [1890]. Web.

Briggs, Julia. "E. Nesbit, the Bastables, and *The Red House*: A Response." *Children's Literature* 25 (1997): 71–85. Web.

Brown, Gillian. "The Metamorphic Book: Children's Print Culture in the Eighteenth Century." *Eighteenth-Century Studies* 39.3 (2006): 351–62. Web.

Gubar, Marah. *Artful Dodgers: Reconceiving the Golden Age of Children's Literature.* Oxford: Oxford University Press, 2009. Print.

Hade, Daniel, John Mason, and Lissa Paul. "Are Children's Book Publishers Changing the Way Children Read? A Panel Discussion." *Children's Literature Association Quarterly* 28.3 (2003): 137–43. Web.

Hunt, Peter. *An Introduction to Children's Literature.* Oxford: Oxford University Press, 1994. Print.

Laqueur, Thomas. *Religion and Respectability: Sunday Schools and Working-Class Structure, 1750–1850.* New Haven, CT: Yale University Press, 1976. Print.

Moss, Anita. "E. Nesbit's Romantic Child in Modern Dress." *Romanticism and Children's Literature in Nineteenth-Century England.* (ed.) James Holt McGavran, Jr. Athens: University of Georgia Press, 1991. 225–47. Print.

Moss, Anita. "Varieties of Children's Metafiction." *Studies in the Literary Imagination* 18.2 (1985): 75–92. Web.

Nesbit, E. *The Story of the Treasure Seekers: Being the Adventures of the Bastable Children in Search of a Fortune.* 1899. San Francisco: Chronicle Books, 2006. Print.

Pope, Alexander. "An Essay on Man." *Norton Anthology of English Literature: Volume 1*. 5th edn (ed.) M.H. Abrams. NY: Norton, 1986. 2264–71. Print.

Porter, Roy. "Education: A Panacea?" *The Creation of the Modern World: The Untold Story of the British Enlightenment*. NY: W.W. Norton, 2000. 339–63. Print.

Reimer, Mavis. "Treasure Seekers and Invaders: E. Nesbit's Cross-Writing of the Bastables." *Children's Literature* 25 (1997): 50–59. Web.

Rose, Jacqueline. *The Case of Peter Pan or: The Impossibility of Children's Fiction*. London: Macmillan, 1984. Print.

Rothwell, Erika. "'You Catch It If You Try to Do Otherwise': The Limitations of E. Nesbit's Cross-Written Vision of the Child." *Children's Literature* 25 (1997): 60–70. Web.

Smelser, Neil J. *Social Paralysis and Social Change: British Working-Class Education in the Nineteenth Century*. Berkeley, CA: University of California Press, 1991. Print.

PART II:
Hearth, Home, and Housekeeping

Chapter 4

Housekeeping: Shine, Polish, Gloss and Glaze as Surface Strategies in the Domestic Interior

Victoria Kelley

Introduction: Glass-Case Objects

In our great museums of decorative arts, the things that represent the domesticity of the Victorian and Edwardian period—whether clothes, furniture, furnishings, ceramics, silver or other household objects—give the impression, on the whole, of being pristine. They may carry subtle signs of age, but they have certainly not had a hard life. And even if the marks of bodies, the imprints of use, ingrained dirt and stains *are* detectable, the isolation of the glass case encourages us not to notice them; strategies of display conceal process in favor of discrete and frozen objects, objects that Constance Classen, in her analysis of touch in museums, describes as "timeless" and "eternal" (282). This is not perhaps surprising: the connoisseurs who first assembled the collections that many of our museums are based upon often sought the "best" examples of every category of art and design, in terms of state of preservation, as well as of original conception, materials or execution (Pearce 387–9). In recent years, museums have begun to acknowledge that their pristine objects were once part of life outside the glass case: captions and labels now often reference the *relationships* between objects and owners, referring perhaps to the preferences and purchasing decisions of a real or hypothetical consumer. An example is the Victoria and Albert Museum in London, where, in the British Galleries, elite consumption is demonstrated through objects that belonged to the eighteenth-century actor David Garrick (V&A Room 118a). Yet we are not encouraged to think about the *ongoing, physical* interactions between museum objects and the people who once owned and used them, or to consider processes, the fact that things became dirtied, broken and worn, and that their owners washed and cleaned and polished them. This reflects the assumption that objects that are battered, tattered or dirty are somehow spoiled, a notion that is long-standing, widespread, and in many respects perfectly reasonable, in museum-keeping as in house-keeping. But however reasonable the notion, it has kept hidden both the effects of wear and tear, and, perhaps more importantly, the complicated efforts that people (housekeepers of the nineteenth century, museum conservators of the twenty-first) put into forestalling such processes, or attempting to wind back their effects.

Yet despite the lack of acknowledged attention paid by museums to the processes of dirtying and cleansing, of wear and tear and maintenance, it is almost a truism to declare that Victorian and Edwardian society attached great importance to keeping things clean, maintained and in good order, and particularly in the domestic sphere. Beneath Victorian practices of maintenance lie many contested ideologies and practices, which this chapter will attempt to trace. In all of this, *surface qualities* are paramount: both wear and tear and maintenance are played out across the surfaces of objects. Surface is a comparatively neglected issue in the history of design and material culture. It could be argued that the surface qualities of objects have been played down in a rhetoric of design that has valued form over surface, applied decoration or finish, prioritizing "depth" over the "superficiality" of applied techniques in an ontological opposition of surface and depth, with greater value accorded to the latter (Miller 71–96). If the starting point for this analysis is to consider surface in relation to wear and tear and maintenance, this suggests that it is also necessary to look at the surface qualities of newly-made goods, the original effects before processes of maintenance have commenced. I will argue that the two issues—new surfaces and surface maintenance—interact with each other in systems of aesthetic preference that in turn relate to class, gender, and even modernity.

Evidence: Object and Process

The primary sources that tell us about late nineteenth and early twentieth-century domestic interiors are varied: diverse visual representations; factual written accounts in the form of diaries and autobiographies; fictional descriptions; the abundant genre of advice literature; inventories that document the contents of rooms and homes; and a huge range of commercial sources listing, describing, representing and promoting the goods available to consumers.[1] The secondary literature on the subject uses all these sources, and constitutes a rich and developed field of historical inquiry into the material embodiment of complicated value systems, in which ideas about morality, religion, political economy, gender, social status, taste and comfort were all played out. The writings of Thad Logan on the Victorian parlour, of Deborah Cohen on nineteenth-century material possessions more generally, and of Margaret Ponsonby on the early nineteenth-century home, are all recent examples of scholarship that proposes sensitive strategies for understanding the material culture of domesticity. All acknowledge or even

---

[1]   A good introduction to such sources can be gained from reading articles, reviews and particularly editorials in the *Journal of Design History* (see for instance Grace Lees-Maffei, "Studying Advice"; Lees-Maffei, "Introduction"; Jeremy Aynsley and Francesca Berry).

emphasize the relationships between people and their domestic things. What requires further exploration is the fact that these interactions occur most obviously on the surfaces of objects, as wear and tear and dirt degrade them, and techniques of maintenance and housekeeping repudiate that process of degradation. In the initial exercise of taste in consuming decisions, qualities such as style, form, balance, proportion, material and color are important, alongside surface effects of finish or polish. Yet in the day-to-day relationship of a person and an object, surface is the physical quality that registers the greatest interaction, as it is the only attribute that can be changed with relative ease. And not only *can* it be changed, but it may well change, regardless of its owner's intent: many surfaces are mutable, fragile and demanding of attention.[2]

Which of the sources on the domestic interior can best allow an understanding of surface, both in its original condition and as the site of ongoing processes of interaction between people and things? When it comes to process, advice literature is by far the richest source. By their very nature, books that advise tend to advise *action*: things to do, routines to establish, processes to follow. A cluster of didactic books on interior decoration published in the 1870s and 1880s aligned themselves with attempts, dating back to midcentury, to reform design and taste in response to the perceived inadequacies of Victorian industrial manufactures. Examples include Charles Locke Eastlake's very influential *Hints on Household Taste* (1868), Rhoda and Agnes Garrett's *Suggestions for House Decoration* (1876), Mrs (Lucy) Orrinsmith's *The Drawing Room* (1878) and Robert Edis's *Decoration and Furniture of Town Houses* (1881). All of these books demonstrate an interest in the aesthetics of surface effects, and in wear and tear and maintenance in furniture and furnishings. An example is Edis's consideration of floor coverings for a hallway:

> Oilcloth and linoleum are generally unsatisfactory; the painted pattern of the one soon becomes unsightly, while the general tone of the latter used in plain colours is unpleasant, the pattern work being liable to wear out in a few years, and, as in oilcloth, to present an untidy and unsatisfactory appearance. (*Decoration and Furniture* 41–2)

"How to do" advice on housekeeping focuses less on the decoration of the home than on the physical and moral repercussions of its upkeep. Published both as household advice manuals and as numerous magazine advice columns, this genre shows an interest in wear and tear and maintenance, alongside the pressing and closely related issue of domestic cleanliness. Phillis Browne, for instance, in a chapter on "House-cleaning" in an 1883 book entitled *Our Homes and How to Make Them Healthy*, prescribes in minute detail all the many tasks that must be

---

[2]   This chapter deals with domestic interiors and objects: for a related analysis of textile surfaces (clothing and portable household textiles) see Victoria Kelley, "The Interpretation of Surface." For a collection of essays that deals with surfaces in design and material culture more generally, see Glenn Adamson and Kelley.

carried out to keep a home clean and tidy (869–94). The emphasis is on cleanliness, methods to remove dirt and dust of every description from every crevice and cranny of the home, from basement kitchen to bedroom fireplace, from front step to back door. The advice given is characterized by its exactitude and temporal prescriptiveness: the frequency with which tasks must be repeated is strictly set. The reader is left with no doubt, from the opening rhetoric—"where dirt reigns, disease, misery, and crime stand erect around his throne" to the closing rallying cry (869), "when we have once realized the fact that dirt is the parent of disease ... we shall not hesitate to take trouble to lay down plans and adopt methods for its removal" (894)—that the dominant message is one of morally-inflected soap-and-water cleanliness in the pursuit of health. Not surprisingly, many of the techniques described concern surfaces; yet alongside the emphasis on cleanliness, there is also a consideration of the sorts of surface that will be damaged or compromised by water, soap and scrubbing. Thus Browne acknowledges Florence Nightingale's well-known condemnation of dry dusting, with its tendency to stir up, rather than to remove, dust particles, yet she admits that the damp cloth recommended by Nightingale cannot be used on polished furniture without damaging that polish (875). She also notes that "all brass and steel work in a kitchen should be kept bright and shining. The general aspect of the place depends greatly upon this being done" (886). These and other examples suggest that Browne's concerns extend beyond cleanliness as hygiene, pure and simple, and take us into the realm of the symbolic and aesthetic properties of, in particular, shiny, polished and highly finished surfaces. Textile examples from the period reinforce this point. Linen, whether used for garments or for household textiles such as tablecloths, was often given a smooth "glossed" finish, laboriously achieved both in original manufacture and in domestic maintenance by the application of heat and pressure via a glass or metal calendar or metal iron. Such finish had no practical purpose or hygienic function, but was nevertheless strongly advocated in advice literature, including that by Browne (*Common-sense Housekeeping* 191–3).

Browne's prescriptions read like surface *fanaticism*. I suggest that this emanated from a central concern with cleanliness and dirt, wear and tear and maintenance, but that it circled widely to capture a number of other related issues to do with the quality and nature of manufactured surface effects, and the relationship of the home to a dynamic and often chaotic urban environment. It has been rightly argued that written advice does not always translate directly into actual practice (Lees-Maffei, "Studying Advice" 3–5): it is often more about ideals than realities. Yet in a subject as symbolically rich as this one, ideals can be just as interesting as realities. As Alison Clarke has noted, discussing the domestic interiors of more recent times, what people *aspire to* may be just as important to them as what they actually achieve (23–45). Advice literature can indeed be extreme, mirroring in over-exaggerated and dogmatic ways ideas that may be much more muted and nuanced in practice. For this reason, I do not propose Mrs Browne's surface fanaticism as a condition of most Victorian householders and housekeepers; rather I suggest that writings such as hers shaped and reflected a condition of *surface anxiety*, a nagging unease that characterized many of the relationships between people and objects. And I also suggest that alongside this was an opposite tendency to *surface delight*—the other point of the triangle, where material surface qualities became both aesthetically pleasing and expressive of positive social values. Other sources reinforce this point, and provide a useful counterbalance to advice literature: autobiographies are often descriptive of the minutiae of domestic life and its repetitive processes, and in them we find much stronger evidence of the potential for delight, as well as a record of the anxiety that a concern with surface could bring. The descriptions of late nineteenth-century social investigators, who often described the material culture of their subjects in great detail, are also useful. Both these latter sets of sources take us into working-class life: one of the aims of this chapter is to extend the consideration of the domestic interior from the middle-class parlour into other, more humble homes, and to begin to consider how class and economic difference were reflected in taste.

Surface Anxiety

Slick New Surfaces

By the mid-nineteenth century the significant growth of the urban middle classes fuelled an ever-growing demand for new houses, furniture and furnishings. This demand was met in part with increasingly industrial rather than craft-based production, or at least production that employed industrial or semi-industrial techniques, such as batch-production and the use of machinery in some processes (Edwards 24–32). One of the results was a crisis of confidence, not only in the design of consumer goods, but also in their perceived quality (Garrett and Garrett 13–14; Edwards 31). Robert Edis, writing in 1881, noted the "wretched, scamping" nature of houses constructed by speculative builders: "the miserable deal joiners' work is glossed over with imitation graining of other woods, the still worse plaster work is made to look fair and pleasant to the eye by a coat or two of distemper" (*Decoration and Furniture* 91–2). His emphasis is on the poor quality of workmanship, poor quality that cannot be hidden by attempts at surface disguise.

Part of Edis's argument concerns decoration, reflecting a fierce debate over the correct approach to surface pattern that had raged since midcentury or before.[3] The issue of decorative pattern is beyond the scope of this chapter, which concentrates on other sorts of surface qualities to do with polish, varnish, wear and tear, but these two classes of surface effects are clearly linked in the notion of *honesty*, or its opposite. Many reformers detested the sort of illusionistic representational patterns that were often applied to wallpapers and household textiles. Their rhetoric was

---

[3]   Jules Lubbock's *The Tyranny of Taste* gives a detailed and lively, if perhaps over-polemical, account of mid-nineteenth-century design reform.

satirized by Charles Dickens in *Hard Times* when he had the unfortunate schoolgirl Sissy Jupe reprimanded for her fondness for wallpaper decorated with pictures of horses: "you never meet with quadrupeds going up and down walls; you must not have quadrupeds represented upon walls" (52). There was also disapproval of the sort of surface techniques that attempted to make one material look like another (Lubbock 243, 256). Writing in the 1880s, Edis is emphatic upon this point, on the grounds of quality, but also on the grounds of truth:

> To carry into our houses the shadow of unreality, by graining or marbling in imitation of the real materials, by giving to cast iron the semblance of wrought, by putting up papers painted to represent various woods, tiles, or marble, is simply teaching a lie, and asserting in the worst possible taste the semblance of a truth which does not exist; and when the best graining or marbling in the world is done, it is but a miserable satire on the real material. All striving after imitation and unreality is utterly at variance with good taste in decoration, as in life. (*Decoration and Furniture* 21–2)

Edis's outcry would seem to offer evidence both of the commonplace use of imitative surface techniques and of one influential commentator's distrust of them. Yet techniques such as graining, marbling and veneering had not always been so criticized. In skilled hands they could produce refined effects. Historians Clive Edwards and Margaret Ponsonby both note the change in status of wood veneering, which had been a staple of furniture making and interior decoration since the late seventeenth century (Edwards 32–4; Ponsonby 96). Ponsonby describes how it declined from "highly skilled work" associated with "expensive and smart goods" in the eighteenth century to become in the nineteenth "an inexpensive way of making cheap furniture look more expensive" and a sign of "superficiality and sham" (96).

Robert Edis's dislike of the imitative surface is echoed by his contemporaries. Both Mrs Orrinsmith and Agnes and Rhoda Garrett critique dominant taste, their comments focused on surface effects and the lack of quality they are seen to express. Mrs Orrinsmith notes that the typical "ordinary lower middle-class drawing room" is a room of "showy discomfort," characterized by "brand-new gloss," "the pursuit of brightness," and "tawdry garishness" (2). Agnes and Rhoda Garrett condemn "cheap and showy" furniture marred by unwanted "brilliance" (16) and goods in which "faulty construction" (29) is concealed by "a mass of senseless ornament and a misleading shimmer of French polish" (34). Margaret Ponsonby invokes Charles Dickens's Veneering family from *Our Mutual Friend*, whose "bran-new" house is the very embodiment of *nouveau riche* pretension, and whose name itself is taken from that degraded process of dressing up cheap furniture to showy effect. Ponsonby also cites John Ruskin's letter to the editor *of The Times* analyzing William Holman Hunt's painting *The Awakening Conscience*, in which a kept mistress entertains her lover in a room furnished with objects of "fatal newness" that signal her moral degradation (96–7).[4] Ponsonby's argument is that both of these examples evidence the extent to which new things in too great a profusion betrayed the recent origins of a family's money: if no inherited goods were available, the remedy was to buy a sprinkling of second-hand furniture: "it is possible that good-quality, if slightly old goods were seen as desirable since they carried status with their patina" (97).[5] Certainly in the case of the Veneerings, the newness and shininess of their furniture seems intended by Dickens to symbolize the newness and superficiality of their social relationships, which he satirizes fiercely. Ruskin's letter speaks of "terrible lustre" as well as "fatal newness" (334), and Dickens claimed of both the Veneerings themselves and their "bran-new" possessions that "the surface smelt a little too much of the workshop, and was a trifle stickey" (17). The surfaces described by Ruskin and Dickens, by Edis, Orrinsmith, and the Garretts, are heavily decorated, shiny and glossy, tacky with barely-dried varnish and slick with excessive polish: as such, they appear to have provoked anxiety in many contemporary commentators.

Anthropologist Daniel Miller suggests that anxiety over surface effects seen to be "excessive" is not accidental, but rather the result of "the pervasive ideology of what may be called 'depth ontology' whereby we tend to assume that everything that is important for our sense of being lies in some deep interior and must be long-lasting and solid, as against the dangers of things we regard as ephemeral, shallow or lacking in content" (71). Miller's remarks come in the context of an ethnographic analysis of fashion in Trinidad. The conspicuous consumption he documents (based on fieldwork of the late 1980s) functions as part of a social and aesthetic system that prioritizes the "superficial" in both objects and interpersonal relations, but which is misunderstood and condemned on that account by its many critics. Yet Miller finds a rationale for the behavior he describes, in both black diasporic experience and in his subjects' responses to modernity. This example functions as a gentle reminder to consider the values and the meanings of aesthetic effects to the people who create and consume them, as well as to those who criticize them. Another reminder comes from historian Peter Thornton, in his description of decorative "density," or the Victorian "cluttered look" (320), a feature of some nineteenth-century domestic interiors condemned by reformist critics in its own time and derided even more fiercely through satire by a generation of "post-Victorians" in the early decades of the twentieth century (Woolf 163). The cluttered look might stand as a parallel case to the too-glossy surface. It is a domestic design strategy characterized by its extreme nature that is today aesthetically indigestible, though it may be socially intelligible. Thornton urges his readers, simply and generously, to "remember that most Victorians liked it: it did not seem cluttered to them" (320). And indeed much of the recent historiography of the Victorian domestic interior is generous to the cluttered look, analyzing it on its own terms and finding ways to explore its meanings to the people who created it and lived

---

[4]   See also Edwards 33, 76.
[5]   For more on patina, see McCracken 37–43.

with it. I make a plea for as generous and complex an understanding of the material surfaces of objects, of all types and qualities, and in use and wear.

Dirt, Germs and Urban Chaos

Certain surfaces provoked anxiety because of their association with poor quality goods of high aspiration but low actual status; a further source of surface anxiety arose from a concern with hygiene and dirt's perceived relationship to disease. This is where new surface effects come together with wear and tear and maintenance.

Shirley Forster Murphy's *Our Homes and How to Make Them Healthy* (the volume which contains Phillis Browne's advice on house-cleaning, cited earlier) opens with a chapter by Benjamin Ward Richardson, which sets out the basic principles of "Health in the Home." After describing all the diseases that may arise from unhealthy homes (a very long list, starting with typhus), Richardson articulates the "seven principles" of a "healthy home." The first is: "it must present no facilities for holding dusts or the poisonous particles of disease; if it retain one it is likely to retain the other" (31–2).

Our Homes also contains a section on "Internal Decoration" written by Robert Edis. As might be expected, Edis reiterates much of the advice given in his *Decoration and Furniture of Town Houses*, but with the addition of a detailed consideration of hygiene and its relationship to decorative taste. He starts with lengthy quotations from a recent letter to *The Times* by a "well-known surgeon" describing his experience in moving into a London house. The correspondent dwells in detail upon the dangers of dust:

> There were wardrobes and other pieces of furniture, which had their apparent height increased by cornices, within which were hollow spaces, seemingly made on purpose to form harbours for dirt. There were ponderous bookshelves, containing a formidable amount of printed lumber, and a still more formidable amount of dust. The walls were old with uneven surfaces, and to these uneven surfaces dirt clung with an almost touching tenacity. There were all sorts of fluffy things about, which were supposed to be ornamental, fancy mats and the like, and which blackened the fingers of any one bold enough to touch them ... Upon all these things the dirt of a London street poured in without intermission. In dry weather the dust found its way through every chink; in wet weather the feet of visitors brought in mud, which dried into dust speedily. ("Internal Decoration" 325–6)

The 1870s and 1880s saw the development of germ theory and the beginnings of scientific understanding of the spread of disease. In the 1880s echoes of germ theory found their way into the popular press and advice literature, and from there into the public consciousness. Gwen Raverat, born in Cambridge in the 1880s, recalls an incident from her early childhood: "a mischief-making doctor promulgated the revolting theory that all milk must be BOILED! Because of

Germs; of which we now heard for the first time, and in which we vehemently declined to believe" (55). One result of germ theory was that dust (in which germs were found under microscopic investigation) was feared as a potent carrier of disease. A later domestic advice writer emphasized how germs were both *invisible* and *ever-present*:

> Disease, in the majority of cases, comes from microbes, or as they are often called, *germs*. These are actually *disease seeds*. They are seeds so small that they cannot be seen by the naked eye. They gain entrance to the body through the air breathed, or in liquid drunk, or in some other way. No matter how careful we are none of us can be sure of keeping out of their way. (Stacpoole 8)

Edis's advice in *Our Homes* includes detailed recommendations for dust-free floor coverings, furniture and wallpapers (326–32, 338). This sort of advice is a feature of the writings of Agnes and Rhoda Garrett and Mrs Orrinsmith too, with a particular emphasis on the evils of the fitted carpet, seen as an enormous and uncleanable dust-trap: "the thicker, the woollier, the richer [a carpet], the greater its capacity for the reception and retention of dust" (Orrinsmith 53). Edis, the Garretts, Orrinsmith, and Browne all recommend hard surfaces for floors, such as parquet blocks or floorboards that have been stained and varnished or painted. Mrs Orrinsmith recommends staining and polishing with "ancient and wholesome beeswax and turpentine … If the polishing is effectually done in the first instance, it requires but a slight amount of daily brushing to preserve brightness" (54). On top could be laid rugs small enough to be regularly taken outside and beaten clean (Garrett and Garrett 69; Orrinsmith 50–55; Browne, "House-cleaning" 881).

Thus fear of dust lay behind many of the edicts of domestic advice literature, and had a particularly strong relationship to the polished surface and its maintenance. If the excessive polish of newly-made and pretentiously ostentatious furniture could show up social insecurities, then the smooth, impermeable surfaces of polished objects more generally were also perfectly suited to showing up dust, rendering it visible, in contrast to the textured or permeable surfaces of items such as carpets or flocked wallpapers. As applied to parquet blocks or varnished floorboards, polish (preferably the right sort of not too excessive polish) could be indicative of cleanliness because it kept dust and dirt on the surface, where it could be both seen and easily removed. This returns us to surface ontology: what is of the surface is unimportant, trivial—and trivial dirt is easily dealt with. Yet the constant reappearance of dust on polished surfaces meant that however easily removed, it could also never be forgotten. Those responsible for its removal could never rest. As Browne noted, with an air of almost sadistic melancholy, "the moment which finds a room perfectly clean is the moment in which it begins to get dirty again" ("House-cleaning" 869).

The anxiety associated with surfaces and dirt was strongly affected by the relationship of the home to the world around it, particularly in urban areas. The nineteenth-century industrial city was sufficiently filthy that numerous commentators decried the smoky, sooty atmosphere that insinuated grime into every crevice, inside and out. Robert Edis raged against coal, questioning how long society would be "content to pollute the common air with smoke ... to sow broadcast the evils which work the destruction of everything within our homes, and cover the delicate leaves of the trees in our squares, and the flowers of the earth, with black, filthy corruption?" ("Internal Decoration" 169). He also denounced the "marvellous impurity" of gas lighting, the uncertain quality of water supplies, and the constant chaos caused by excavations to lay or repair gas and water mains, to repave streets and to construct new urban projects ("Internal Decoration" 169–70). We have already seen, in the letter that Edis cites, how external chaos was felt to impinge upon the home; "the dirt of a London street poured in without intermission. In dry weather the dust found its way through every chink; in wet weather the feet of visitors brought in mud, which dried into dust speedily" ("Internal Decoration" 325–6). Historian Lynda Nead, in *Victorian Babylon*, shows a photograph of the construction of London's Underground system in its early phases in the 1860s (44), which depicts both domesticity and the encroaching chaos caused by development in shocking proximity: a group of women and children pose in conventional family portrait style on the terrace of their house, but "nothing stands between this house and the immense excavation works next door. The terrace wall literally marks the limit of demolition" (40).

Rapid urban growth and development meant that the nineteenth-century city was in a state of constant flux, as modernity was constructed in a piecemeal frenzy upon foundations of varying age and decrepitude. In this context, the clean and polished surfaces of the domestic interior were vulnerable and hard of maintenance, but they were also perhaps an important psychological bulwark against external chaos. The preservation of order, on a small scale and in a strictly defined and bounded locality (the home) constituted an important symbol of domesticity, particularly for the women who were chiefly responsible for the battle against the dirt and disorder that both originated in and represented the external environment.

Women's Work and Surface Maintenance

Despite the many modifications and caveats to the idea of the nineteenth-century "separate spheres,"[6] it is undoubtedly true that the domestic work of cleanliness and maintenance was largely the responsibility of women, whose social identity was bound up with the home to a far greater extent than was most men's. Browne, in her detailed advice, describes a normative middle-class household in which a mistress directs work, and female servants carry it out ("House-cleaning" 869–94). The work required to keep a large household clean and orderly was considerable, its difficulties compounded by the additional requirement that processes of cleaning and maintaining be *kept invisible* to those who were not responsible

---

[6]   For more on challenges to the Victorian notion of "separate spheres," see Amanda Vickery.

for them (Browne, "Common-sense Housekeeping" 41–2). Mark Girouard has described how in the English country house of the nineteenth century servants and their work were physically segregated. Kitchens, sculleries and laundry rooms were located in service wings and basements, linked to other parts of the house by networks of back stairs and service corridors (285). Less grand urban homes were organized around a vertical separation, with service rooms in the basement and servants' bedrooms in the attic.[7] Segregation was also achieved temporally, with servants carrying out processes of maintenance in the main rooms of the home at periods when they were not inhabited. Thus in tracing out the anxieties associated with the wear and tear and maintenance of domestic objects and their surfaces, it is necessary to consider the unacknowledged character of much domestic labor. Servants were often overloaded with work, but were nevertheless condemned to be discrete, even furtive, in its completion. Except in the grandest houses, where managerial duties were delegated to senior servants, mistresses suffered from the anxiety of the middle-manager who has to direct the labor of often poorly skilled or unreliable staff, but in a way that did not disturb the notion of home as a site of leisure, and not of labor. In lower middle-class households with few or perhaps just one servant, mistresses also had to contribute physically to a great deal of the labor of maintenance, although again in an unobtrusive manner.

The analysis above is based on upper and middle-class experience. Much of the literature on the nineteenth-century interior, which has burgeoned in recent years, is predominantly focused on upper- and middle-class homes. This stems, perhaps, from an assumption that the working classes were too poor to make interesting choices in their domestic furnishings. I would like to bring in a brief consideration of working-class experience. It seems short-sighted not to extend the issue of surface to the working-class context, especially as there is evidence to support such an analysis, which promises distinctive insights.

Working-class wives and mothers, like their middle-class counterparts, faced pressure to keep the domestic labors of cleanliness and maintenance invisible: there is evidence from autobiographical sources and the accounts of social investigators that husbands and fathers expected domestic work to conform to a timetable that would not disturb their mealtimes or leisure.[8] Women of the working classes often lived extremely restricted lives, bounded by the home and its immediate environment, and with little scope for leisure or individualistic self-expression. Yet domestic tasks of cleanliness and maintenance, while an instrument of that restriction, also provided an opportunity for the material demonstration of values such as respectability and pride. Eileen Baillie, a clergyman's daughter who grew up in a poor community in the East End of London, described the home of a railway worker's family that she visited regularly:

---

[7] For more on these urban arrangements, see Hermann Muthesius's *The English House* and Stefan Muthesius's *The English Terraced House.*

[8] See for instance Maud Pember Reeves 88; M.E. Loane 42.

> It was the most ordinary house in an ordinary side-street … but you could tell at
> once what sort of people lived there, for the front door was neatly painted and
> the doorstep well scrubbed and 'stoned.' Once inside you were conscious of
> spotless cleanliness, despite the smallness of the rooms and the worn condition
> of much of the furniture. Nanny used to say that we could eat our dinners off the
> floor … (138–9).

Here, despite the absence of new and status laden objects, despite the "worn"
furniture, there is nevertheless a suggestion of almost ostentatious display in the
extreme cleanliness and the attention to polish (the doorstep was not just scrubbed
but also "stoned," i.e., coated with whitening). Social pressure to achieve such
display was no doubt onerous, but there are instances of working-class women
who record some satisfaction gained through the achievement of carefully or even
enthusiastically scrubbed or polished surfaces, as will be discussed later.

Surface Delight

Antiques

Earlier we considered the anxiety that new and poor quality furniture and
furnishings provoked in design reformers, anxiety that was particularly focused on
surface qualities—the excessive polish of slick and sticky varnish, the supposed
tastelessness and dishonesty of cheap veneers and imitative surface effects. The
adjectives used in these critiques were expressive; however we might oppose
to them another set of descriptive terms, from the same writers, but describing
the surface qualities of a very different class of objects. Mrs Orrinsmith, for
instance, who despised the "tawdry garishness" of conventional taste (2), gives the
following description of the sort of fireplace she recommends for a comfortable
and tasteful room: "by the side of the brazen fender stands an elderly coal-scuttle
of gleaming copper, whose rich red glow loses nothing by its juxtaposition to the
golden brass of the fender" (38). Again the adjectives stress surface qualities, but
here the objects described are antiques, and the surfaces are depicted as richly
patinated rather than vulgarly glossy. The vogue for furnishing with antiques was
new in the 1870s, and, as Margaret Ponsonby notes, it was partly a strategy to
counter the effects of too much newness amongst the possessions of the recently
wealthy. In the literature produced by Edis, Orrinsmith and the Garretts, which
was influenced by design reform, the appreciation of antiques appears to have
been a direct response to the perceived inadequacies of contemporary furniture
and furnishings, and particularly their lack of surface integrity. Edis contrasts past
styles to the sham of modern, imitative products:

> If we examine any of the best work of past ages, either in textile fabrics, furniture,
> or decoration, we shall see that truth and fitness in design and construction, and

harmony in colour and arrangement, are carefully carried out; that there is no sham or imitation, but, so far as practicable, the work is essentially real and true. (*Decoration and Furniture* 21–2)

Peter Thornton documents the rise of the fashion for antiques that went with the Queen Anne style of the 1870s, with its "stress on informality, its love of irregularity and asymmetrical arrangements" (311–12). This was in contrast to the emphasis on new and glossy surfaces that had symbolized status in previous decades: "in a modern house everything had to look smart, un-worn and un-faded. Tattered covers, signs of repair and patina were not at all desirable in such surroundings" (311–12). But antiques expressed an altogether different aesthetic that was less to do with newness and the brash demonstration of purchasing power, and more to do with a nostalgic indulgence in the comfortable properties of old things, a strategy that has recurred in many periods since. If antique furniture was desirable for the way in which its surfaces had aged, then new goods could also be judged on the way they might age in the future. Mrs Orrinsmith praised the dignified acquisition of patina as a desirable quality in new furnishings: "oak only requires age and polish to acquire golden-brown colour" (54), a surface effect that was, presumably, considered to be consistent with hygiene.

Edis, Orrinsmith and the Garretts' condemnation of imitative surface effects and excessive gloss and polish suggests anxiety: their praise of antiques and new furnishings with the capacity to acquire a pleasing patina suggests the delights of surface, the positive enjoyment that the deployment of attractive surface finishes could bring. Similarly, the process of maintaining such surfaces, while an anxious one because it demanded constant work and unrelenting routine, and brought with it the frustration of a task that could never be done once and for all, also offered the possibility of delight. Here again we can turn to evidence of working-class experience. The memoir of Elizabeth Bryson, who grew up in Scotland in the late nineteenth century, records the satisfaction she derived from cleaning the stone stair up to the door of her tenement home: "the real fun in washing a stair is doing it better than anyone has ever done it before—doing it so well that you have to stop to admire the cleanness of each step as you do it" (32).

And even working-class women who worked as servants in other people's homes sometimes recorded the pleasure they could take in surface maintenance (though they record many frustrations, injustices and tyrannies too). This is Jean Rennie, maid in a large Scottish house, and responsible for polishing the gun-room floor every day: "it was always very muddy and the floor had to be polished every morning. I didn't mind that, because I could see results, and I used to polish until the wood felt shiny and soft to my cloth. And it looked so good and smelled so rich after it was done" (qtd in Burnett 244). What follows will discuss surface delight in more detail, with particular reference to the shiny, polished object: in doing so it will examine further the varying approaches taken by people of different social class to surface and its maintenance.

Shine, Polish, Class, Taste

As has been noted, the working-class home has received relatively little attention from historians of material culture. Yet social investigator Maud Pember Reeves, writing in 1913, described the home of a working-class woman in London who decorated her front windowsill with "a row of red and yellow cocoa tins to make a bright effect" (6), and it does not seem immediately obvious why the cocoa tins should not be just as interesting as any of the many objects used to decorate the drawing rooms of the comfortable middle classes. Within the academic field of aesthetics, Thomas Leddy has analyzed the appeal of what he calls "everyday surface qualities" and the attractions of "sparkle and shine," surface effects that may be valued in certain contexts, yet condemned as "glitzy" or "gaudy" in others ("Everyday Surface Aesthetic Qualities 259–68; "Sparkle and Shine" 259–73). He cites the contemporary Mexican and Chicano *rasquache* style, which makes use of found objects and materials to produce decorative surface effects characterized by sparkle and shine: "in the realm of taste, to be *rasquache* is to be unfettered and unrestrained, to favor the elaborate over the simple, the flamboyant over the severe. Bright colors (*chillantes*) are preferred to somber, high intensity to low, the shimmering and sparkling over the muted and subdued" ("Sparkle and Shine" 260). Is it too much of a leap to identify the red and yellow cocoa tins described by Maud Pember Reeves as a small-scale flowering of something akin to *rasquachismo* in early twentieth-century London? I would argue that there is evidence, in both autobiographical accounts and in the descriptions of social investigators and observers such as Reeves, of a distinct working-class aesthetic that had an interesting and particular relationship to surface qualities. We have seen already how the shine and polish of maintenance were valued within some sections of the working-class community, allowing the material demonstration of social values by people who could not often purchase new things, and who therefore had to make the best display they could through the conspicuous upkeep of the things they had. This was not a universal trait, and certainly many descriptions of working-class homes stress grayness, grime and monotony, shabbiness at the least, filth and squalor in extreme cases. Nevertheless, I suggest that certain surface qualities achieved by maintenance were important, and that in the purchase of new goods there was also a delight in shiny and showy objects.

Many accounts of life in the poorer districts of London in the late nineteenth and early twentieth centuries include descriptions of the market streets that served each locality. These descriptions often describe the market in darkness (the peak shopping time was Saturday evening), lit by the flickering light of naphtha flares that picked out the bright colors and glossy surfaces of the heaped-up goods, from shiny fruit to furniture and decorative items for the home. The autobiography of Eileen Baillie includes one such description, of Chrisp Street in the East End:

> Pyramids of oranges, and russet apples polished to a startling degree—by spitting on them, we always understood—made patches of brilliant, warming

colour on the fruit–stalls ... There were bales of shoddy materials in the vivid shades so dear to East End hearts—blue, violet, magenta, carmine; and gaudy oleographs, both sacred and profane ...

Over the hardware stalls the brightest lights of all were reflected on the shining tin pots and pans, the cheap white china, the coloured and gilded vases set out so temptingly to divert a shilling or two from the housewife's purse. Indeed, you could furnish a home in Chrisp Street, for whole suites of rough deal furniture ... stood about on the pavement, together with rolls of carpet and shiny, beflowered oilcloth. (47–51)

Helen Bosanquet, an early social worker who wrote many accounts of her work in the East End of London, also described the market streets and the goods on sale there. She too emphasized the concurrence of poor quality and showy surface, in all sorts of goods: "something cheap and 'stylish' is what they aim at, and what is therefore provided" (130). She uses women's boots as an example: "the boots which sell here are cheap and showy goods, with pointed toes, high heels, and much adornment of stitching and glaze; they cost from five to ten shillings a pair, and are worn out in as many weeks" (130). Caution demands skepticism in the face of such accounts. Did the working classes really buy such cheap and showy goods, superficial in their attractions, lacking "depth" and quality? Or is Mrs Bosanquet's description exaggerated in order to provide support for a social and political analysis of working-class "character" which problematized it on the grounds of lack of foresight, of economic prudence, of commitment in family relationships and skill in consumption—in other words, on the grounds of a number of characteristics that might be associated with superficiality and shallow fecklessness? (Remember how Miller described criticisms of the "superficiality" of Trinidadian fashion?) I would argue that solid enough evidence exists of a taste for showy shiny goods, which functioned alongside techniques of maintenance that also emphasized the delights of the shiny, polished surface. The parallel with *rasquachismo*, as well as with Miller's Trinidadian case study, supports the validity of this aesthetic, which may be particularly meaningful in relatively poor communities where the social identity of women is expressed chiefly through family relations and the material objects that support them.

My final point here is that cheap yet showy goods did not patinate well—they did not age gracefully under the influence of simple hygiene-oriented cleaning techniques (Foakes 30). Thus the wealthy taste for elegantly worn antique goods made no sense in a community in which objects that showed their age did so in ways that undermined their value. Shoddy goods required skillful, assiduous and quite delicate maintenance that respected their rather fragile surfaces and kept them looking *new*, rather than attractively faded. It is perhaps not coincidental that the 1880s saw the advent of numerous branded polishes and cleansers, many of which seem to have sold particularly well to working-class consumers.[9]

*   *   *

This has been a brief foray into a large and complex subject, and one that invites further historical and theoretical analysis. In conclusion of this initial survey, I return to the museum object. The former British Art and Design Galleries of the Victoria and Albert Museum contained an eighteenth-century period room that I always found very surprising. Robert Adam's Glass Drawing Room from Northumberland House in 1770s London was dominated by walls paneled in glass, backed with a layer of intensely glittery ruby-red foil fragments (an improbable effect in an interior of this date, and to the lay eye more reminiscent of the casino than the drawing room). This very particular surface was barely acknowledged, let alone explained, in the accompanying museum label. Between 1998 and 2001 these galleries were redeveloped and transformed into the widely-praised British Galleries,[10] and a section of the room was reinstalled in this new setting (Victoria and Albert Museum Room 118). In this context it is supported both with written interpretation that discusses the foil-backed glass panels, and with a model of the complete room lit by candlelight that effectively evokes the impact of such a decorative scheme in contemporary lighting, rendering it much more intelligible.

Similar consideration of other, less dramatic, surface qualities might add to our understanding of the physical, aesthetic, social or symbolic properties of many other objects within these galleries. And what about process, the hard (but potentially rewarding) labor of maintenance? Some museums, mostly those that focus on the everyday life of ordinary people, do let us into such process. However, as Tony Bennett has noted, using the open air museum at Beamish in Country Durham, UK as an example, these museums sometimes sentimentalize their subject and in doing so risk offering somewhat parodied versions of everyday activities, demonstrated through replica objects and re-enactments that are a hybrid of the past and of a present-day mythology of the past (110–14). Thus I conclude with a question: how can museums of the decorative arts document in a scholarly manner both surface effects and surface processes, and thus enhance our understanding of historical objects and the people who owned, used and cared for them?

Works Cited

Adamson, Glenn, and Victoria Kelley (eds) *Surface Tensions: Surface, Finish and the Meaning of Objects*. Manchester: Manchester University Press, 2013. Print.

---

[9]   See Florence Bell 55–67; Kelley, *Soap and Water* 65–6.
[10]   For discussion of the new galleries, see Julius Bryant, and Christopher Wilk and Nick Humphrey.

Aynsley, Jeremy, and Francesca Berry. "Introduction: Publishing the Modern Home—Magazines and the Domestic Interior 1870–1965." *Journal of Design History* 18.1 (2005): 1–5. Print.

Baillie, Eileen. *The Shabby Paradise: The Autobiography of a Decade*. London: Hutchinson, 1958. Print.

Bell, Florence. *At the Works: A Study of a Manufacturing Town*. 1907. London: Virago, 1985. Print.

Bennett, Tony. *The Birth of the Museum: History, Theory, Politics*. London: Routledge, 1995. Print.

Bosanquet, Mrs Bernard [Helen Bosanquet, née Dendy]. *Rich and Poor*. London: Macmillan, 1896. Print.

British Galleries (Rooms 118, 118a). Victoria and Albert Museum, London.

Browne, Phillis. *Common-sense Housekeeping*. London: Cassell, Petter and Galpin, 1877. Print.

Browne, Phillis. "House-cleaning." *Our Homes and How to Make Them Healthy* (ed.) Shirley Forster Murphy. London: Cassell, 1883. 868–94. Print.

Bryant, Julius. "Curating the Georgian Interior: From Period Rooms to Marketplace?" *Journal of Design History* 20.4 (2007): 345–50. Print.

Bryson, Elizabeth. *Look Back in Wonder*. Dundee: David Winter, 1966. Print.

Burnett, John (ed.) *Useful Toil: Autobiographies of Working People from the 1820s to the 1920s*. 1974. London: Routledge, 1994. Print.

Clarke, Alison. "The Aesthetics of Social Aspiration." *Home Possessions: Material Culture Behind Closed Doors* (ed.) Daniel Miller. Oxford: Berg, 2001. Print.

Classen, Constance. "Touch in the Museum." *The Book of Touch* (ed.) Constance Classen. Oxford and NY: Berg, 2005. Print.

Cohen, Deborah. *Household Gods: The British and Their Possessions*. London: Yale University Press, 2006. Print.

Dickens, Charles. *Hard Times*. 1854. Harmondsworth: Penguin, 1969. Print.

Dickens, Charles. *Our Mutual Friend*. 1865. London: Penguin, 1997. Print.

Eastlake, Charles Locke. *Hints on Household Taste*. London: Longmans, Green, 1868. Print.

Edis, Robert. *Decoration and Furniture of Town Houses*. London: C. Kegan Paul, 1881. Print.

Edis, Robert. "Internal Decoration." *Our Homes and How to Make Them Healthy* (ed.) Shirley Forster Murphy. London: Cassell, 1883. 309–65. Print.

Edwards, Clive. *Victorian Furniture: Technology and Design*. Manchester: Manchester University Press, 1993. Print.

Foakes, Grace. *Between High Walls: A London Childhood*. London: Shepheard-Walwyn, 1972. Print.

Garrett, Rhoda, and Agnes Garrett. *Suggestions for House Decoration*. London: Macmillan, 1876. Print.

Girouard, Mark. *Life in the English Country House*. London: Yale University Press, 1978. Print.

Kelley, Victoria. "The Interpretation of Surface: Boundaries, Systems and Their Transgression in Clothing and Domestic Textiles, c.1880–1939." *Textile: The Journal of Cloth and Culture* 7.2 (2009): 216–35. Print.

Kelley, Victoria. *Soap and Water: Cleanliness, Dirt and the Working Classes in Victorian and Edwardian Britain.* London: I.B. Tauris, 2010. Print.

Leddy, Thomas. "Everyday Surface Aesthetic Qualities: 'Neat,' 'Messy,' 'Clean,' 'Dirty.'" *The Journal of Aesthetics and Art Criticism* 53.3 (1995): 259–68. Print.

Leddy, Thomas. "Sparkle and Shine." *British Journal of Aesthetics* 37.3 (1997): 259–73. Print.

Lees-Maffei, Grace. "Introduction: Professionalization as a Focus in Interior Design History." *Journal of Design History* 21.1 (2008): 1–18. Print.

Lees-Maffei, Grace. "Studying Advice: Historiography, Methodology, Commentary, Bibliography." *Journal of Design History* 16.1 (2003): 1–14. Print.

Loane, M.E. *From Their Point of View.* London: Edward Arnold, 1908. Print.

Logan, Thad. *The Victorian Parlour.* Cambridge: Cambridge University Press, 2001. Print.

Lubbock, Jules. *The Tyranny of Taste: The Politics of Architecture and Design in Britain 1550–1960.* London: Yale University Press, 1995. Print.

McCracken, Grant. *Culture and Consumption: New Approaches to the Symbolic Character of Consumer Goods and Activities.* Bloomington, IN: Indiana University Press, 1988. Print.

Miller, Daniel. "Style and Ontology." *Consumption and Identity* (ed.) Jonathan Friedman. London: Harwood, 1994. 71–96. Print.

Murphy, Shirley Forster (ed.) *Our Homes and How to Make Them Healthy.* London: Cassell, 1883. Print.

Muthesius, Hermann. *The English House.* Trans. Janet Seligman. London: Crosby, Lockwood, Staples, 1979. Print.

Muthesius, Stefan. *The English Terraced House.* New Haven and London: Yale University Press, 1982. Print.

Nead, Lynda. *Victorian Babylon: People, Streets and Images in Nineteenth-Century London.* New Haven and London: Yale University Press, 2000. Print.

Orrinsmith, Mrs [Lucy]. *The Drawing Room.* London: Macmillan, 1878. Print.

Pearce, Susan M. *On Collecting: An Investigation into Collecting in the European Tradition.* London: Routledge, 1995. Print.

Ponsonby, Margaret. *Stories from Home: English Domestic Interiors, 1750–1850.* Aldershot: Ashgate, 2007. Print.

Raverat, Gwen. *Period Piece.* 1952. London: Faber and Faber, 1977. Print.

Reeves, Maud Pember. *Round About a Pound a Week.* 1913. London: Virago, 1979. Print.

Richardson, Benjamin Ward. "Health in the Home." *Our Homes and How to Make Them Healthy* (ed.) Shirley Forster Murphy. London: Cassell, 1883. 1–32. Print.

Ruskin, John. Letter to the Editor. *The Times* (London). 25 May, 1854. *The Works of John Ruskin*. Vol. 12 (eds) E.T. Cook and Alexander Wedderburn. London: George Allen, 1904. 333–5. Web.

Stacpoole, Florence. *The Mother's Book: On the Rearing of Healthy Children*. London: Wells Gardner, Darton, 1912. Print.

Thornton, Peter. *Authentic Décor: The Domestic Interior, 1620–1920*. London: Weidenfeld and Nicolson, 1984. Print.

Vickery, Amanda. "Golden Age to Separate Spheres: A Review of the Categories and Chronology of English Women's History." *Historical Journal* 36.2 (1993): 383–414. Print.

Wilk, Christopher and Nick Humphrey (eds) *Creating the British Galleries at the V&A: A Study in Museology*. London: V&A, 2004. Print.

Woolf, Virginia. *Orlando*. 1928. London: Bloomsbury, 1993. Print.

Chapter 5

Kitchen Magic: Reforming the Victorian Kitchen with Alexis Soyer

Sumangala Bhattacharya

In "Characteristics" (1831), Thomas Carlyle famously compares the social disaffections of his time to the "constant grinding internal pain, or from time to time the mad spasmodic throes" of a dyspeptic patient (83). Just as the dyspeptic individual is constantly on the lookout for nostrums to cure his condition, the "dyspeptic" self-reflexive society is constantly on the lookout for new systems to cure its various symptoms.[1] Carlyle's satire targeted the spirit of political and social reform associated with the Whigs, which culminated in the passage of the Reform Acts of 1832 and 1834. Whig programs of reform in Carlyle's view were faddish novelties akin to the "patent Dinner Calefactor" or the latest pronouncements of "Dietetic Philosophy."[2] Carlyle's choice of extended metaphor illuminates the growing influence of another kind of reformism: the use of gastronomical discourses to infuse English culture with new ways of thinking and talking about the larger significance of food. In this line of thinking, new culinary techniques and technologies were necessary remedies for a nation in which bodies agitated by dyspepsia precipitated domestic discord.

Gastronomical reformism purported to improve domestic life by holding that an upset stomach was symptomatic of an upset in the domestic order. Through contrasting representations of the spontaneity and connoisseurship of male homosocial club and bachelor meals versus the banality and oppressive etiquettes of domestic dining, discourses of gastronomy constructed a gendered aesthetics

---

[1]   The metonymic relationship between the healthy individual body and the healthy social body in nineteenth-century social discourse about industrial capitalism is elaborated by a number of scholars, such as Catherine Gallagher and Bruce Haley.

[2]   Elaborating on his argument that "the healthy know not of their health, but only the sick" (67), Carlyle scathingly dismisses the "Dietetic Philosophy" or nutritional theories set forth by Dr William Kitchiner (1775–1827) in two bestselling volumes: *Apicius Redivivus, Or, the Cook's Oracle* (1817) and *Peptic Precepts* (1821). "If a Dr Kitchiner boast that his system is in high order," Carlyle writes, "Dietetic Philosophy may indeed take credit; but the true Peptician was that Countryman who answered that, 'for his part, he had no system'" (67). In a similar vein, Carlyle contrasts the ephemeral fame of culinary gadgetry against the enduring significance of important ideas: "The uses of some Patent Dinner Calefactor can be bruited abroad over the whole world in the course of the first winter; those of the Printing Press are not so well seen into for the first three centuries" (81).

of food and eating that was also a critique of bourgeois domesticity.[3] The critique centered on the allegation that dinners in a conventional domestic setting forced masculine appetites to conform to feminine habits of consumption. While men looked for sophisticated and well-cooked dishes, women supposedly valued the sumptuous appearance of table settings and the elaborate rituals of etiquette. Since women presided over the planning and execution of meals, domestic dinners satisfied the feminine fondness for superficialities, but were inimical to free-spirited masculinity and male models of consumption. The tension between these two modes raised a variety of questions: Could gastronomy and domesticity coexist? Could masculinity be accommodated within bourgeois domesticity? Could English tastes be elevated to rival the sophisticated tastes of the French, their Continental and imperial rivals, without sacrificing national character? Victorian celebrity chef Alexis Benôit Soyer (1810–1858), a transplanted Frenchman determined to infuse English life with gastronomic *savoir-faire*, helped address these questions with the design and marketing of two patent stoves that were implicitly presented as counterparts of each other: one a heavy-duty appliance intended as a kitchen fixture, and the other a lightweight, portable unit suitable for camping and travel. With these stoves, advertised in conjunction with *The Modern Housewife* (1849), a cookbook aimed at middle-class housewives, Soyer offered culinary reform with a built-in escape plan. Should even the improved domestic dinners his kitchen commodities made possible seem stifling or unsatisfying, the free-spirited, gastronomic (male) Briton had recourse to his portable stove, confident of making a tasty repast outside the confines of the domestic space.

Engravings of both stoves appear in *The Modern Housewife* in a section entitled "Conversations on Household Affairs" appended after the recipes. The Magic Stove, also called the Magic lamp-stove, receives the first mention (Figure 5.1). A light-weight, table-top appliance, this stove is a wick-less precursor of the kerosene camping stoves still in use today, operating in a manner similar to Bunsen burners. The engraving uses as a setting what might be a side-table or a small dining table, neatly covered with a white tablecloth. Three objects are arranged on this surface: a small frying pan with three chops, yet to be cooked, providing visual cues to the dimensions of the appliance as well as to its functionality; the cooking base of the stove; and the lamp-shaped fuel reservoir. The original caption below identifies the display as "Soyer's Magic Stove." However, without the accompanying textual explanations, the illustration is mystifying. The cylindrical cooking base, engraved with a delicate floral design and resting daintily on tiny, clawed feet, bears little resemblance to the coal-fired, sooty, massive ranges endemic to Victorian kitchens. The top rim, which comprises a cooking ring on which pans can be rested, resembles the lid of a hatbox. The flame is shown as an upright beam emerging from a smaller ring placed in the center of the lid as if it were the handle of a container. The adjacent fuel reservoir resembles a small table-

---

[3]   For an account of how upper-class men relied on clubs as a surrogate for domesticity, see Amy Milne-Smith.

SOYER'S MAGIC STOVE.

Figure 5.1   Soyer's Magic Stove
Source: Alexis Soyer. *The Modern Housewife or Ménagère.* 2nd edn, London: Simpkin, Marshall, 1849.

lamp with a conical shade and a hookah-like tube down its side. The illustration augments the "magical" associations of the stove by eliding the mechanism by which the stove works. The two burners situated in the lamp, one to heat the alcohol in the conical reservoir and the other to act as a pilot light for the alcohol fumes that are transferred through the tube, are invisible. Nor is it clear that the ignited vapor is transferred to the cooking base through the tubular attachment jutting between the two parts. The white tablecloth and uncluttered arrangement argues for the ease and convenience of cooking with the Magic Stove. The pan and the stove are pushed back from the front edge of the table to display enough open space to accommodate one or two place settings for a casual meal. The illustration thus conveys a sense of anticipation and spontaneity, with the chops waiting to be cooked suggesting that there are persons offstage simultaneously waiting to consume them.

In contrast, the illustration of the Kitchen Apparatus, mentioned several pages later in the cookbook, shows a hefty appliance with multiple components (Figure 5.2). The original caption identifies it as "Soyer's Modern Housewife's Kitchen Apparatus" and adds in small print a list of its functions and its dimensions. The accompanying text identifies it as a gas appliance, but this feature is not apparent in the illustration.[4] Although recognizable as a stove, the Kitchen Apparatus

---

[4]   Gas did not become widely available for cooking until the early twentieth century. However, several gas appliances were exhibited at the Great Exhibition in 1851 and Soyer received considerable publicity for roasting a whole ox by gas at Exeter for a banquet.

nonetheless seems a mystifying, and perhaps frightening, device. Taking up most of the space on the page, it looks more massive than its advertised dimensions: 2 feet 4 inches high, 2 feet wide, and 3 feet long. Unlike conventional Victorian ranges, it is not attached to a wall but instead is a free-standing device mounted on a low platform base. The dark shading, used to indicate its iron metalwork, adds to the appearance of stability and weight. However, drawn obliquely to show off the functionality of side components, the Kitchen Apparatus seems to be advancing out of the frame towards the reader. The concave supports in the front, framing the barred grate of the built-in oven and broiler, further augment this impression with the suggestion of a mechanical maw. A swinging spring-and-pulley arrangement with a metal hook hangs down in front of the oven. Intended presumably to attach onto a latch designed to hold open the heavy oven door, the sharp point of the hook seems liable instead to puncture an unwary or novice cook. The top surface of the appliance is the hot plate, on which are placed four pots of varying sizes, whose protruding handles might be mistaken for levers to additional components. A large toasting rack is set against the side of the appliance, hanging from a knob designed for that purpose. Several other handles, knobs, panels, and decorative elements give the impression of additional unperceived capabilities or compartments.

While the illustration of the Magic Stove conveys casual spontaneity, the illustration of the Kitchen Apparatus evokes the mechanical uncanny. Through technological transformation, the familiar kitchen range seems to have acquired an unfamiliar and vaguely menacing presence. Although intended for human convenience, the stove appears to exist independent of human needs or attendants. There are no chops waiting to be cooked, or other signs of ordinary kitchen activity around it. The gas line is not visible in the picture to indicate its source of fuel, and since the cooking would be done either in the closed oven and broiler, or on the hot plate, no open flames signal the function of the device. For all the practical features and conveniences of the stove, the illustration renders it as a sculptural, industrial artifact rather than an object of everyday use.

While the illustrations of these two Soyer stoves point to contrasting attitudes about food and cooking, both speak to a growing cultural investment in the culinary that even contemporaries found remarkable.[5] In *Essays, Moral, Philosophical, and Stomachical on the Important Science of Good-Living* (1822), the pseudonymous Launcelot Sturgeon advises: "It was formerly considered well-bred to affect a certain indifference for the fare before you; but fashion has acquired more candour; and there is now no road to the reputation of a man of ton, so sure as that of descanting learnedly on the composition of every dish" (41). Nineteenth-century Britain saw significant improvements in the access of the middle classes to a

---

For more on the development of cooking ranges during the nineteenth century, see Alison Ravetz (455–8).

[5]   Jules Prown, noted art historian and material culture theorist, alerts us to the fact that the design of everyday objects reveals "concretions of the realities of belief of other people in other times and places" (16).

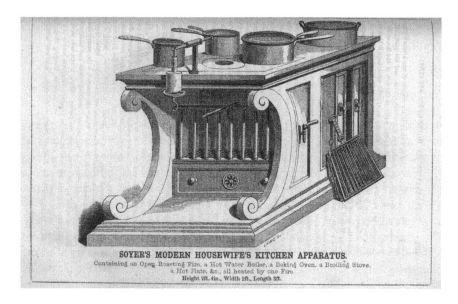

Figure 5.2   Soyer's Modern Housewife's Kitchen Apparatus
Source: Alexis Soyer, *The Modern Housewife or Ménagère*. 2nd edn, London: Simpkin, Marshall, 1849.

consumer culture based on the conspicuous consumption of items of fashion, food, home furnishings, and so on.[6] Middle-class consumerism fueled the popularization of a gastronomical press in Britain, which ranged from translations of French texts to original works in English. The British literary market for gastronomical writing was also a response shaped by British experiences with the booming restaurant culture of post-revolutionary France. British travelers to France, having had a taste of the restaurant culture, returned home with novel notions which loosened the association of dining with domestic life and interjected a gastronomic sensibility that transmuted the material culture of food and eating into an intellectual and discursive experience. Dinners at home thereby became the contested ground where these new tastes impinged on the middle-class domestic ideal, demanding

---

[6]   In *Theory of the Leisure Class* (1899), Thorstein Veblen coined the term "conspicuous consumption" to refer to the lavish expenditures made by the rising middle class on leisure activities and services. Veblen argued that as the industrial economy produced a leisure class whose chief role in the economy was to appropriate through consumption the surplus produced by the working class, such individuals would imitate the consumption patterns of individuals of a higher rank in the effort to transform wealth into status.

the transformation of everyday cookery and food practices into something less familiar and more *French.*[7]

National Fare

According to Stephen Mennell, the French Revolution was a culinary "landmark" that saw the emergence of French *haute cuisine* from the private domains of aristocratic households into the bourgeois public space of gourmet restaurants (134). Under the *Ancien Régime,* elite cuisine developed through the feudal relations between the chef and his aristocratic or royal master. In post-revolutionary France, a wide range of cuisines was sustained through market competition defined by the relations between professional chefs and increasingly sophisticated customers. The emergence of gastronomical discourses during a period of volatile political and cultural changes contributed powerfully to a sense of national unity at a time of deep regional and political divisions. French identity accreted around the notion of an innate love of good food. As Priscilla Ferguson argues, nineteenth-century France saw the development of the cultural construct of a national cuisine which "encouraged the French to see themselves through this distinctive lens as both different and superior" (5). Mennell and Ferguson agree that this shift helped greatly to establish the hegemony of French cuisine over that of Britain and the rest of Europe in the nineteenth century.

British gastronomy, less concerned with contesting French culinary prowess than with imitating it, positioned itself in an uneasy relationship with the culinary arena of bourgeois domesticity, offering both to correct domestic dining and to supplement it. Class and gender snobbery were marshaled around food snobbery. The ambivalent relation between gastronomy and domesticity reflected a wider cultural ambivalence about the rise of the middle classes. While the economic power of the British middle classes was a source of national pride, it was also a cause for concern for those who feared it portended the spread of materialistic and vulgar tastes that would mark Britain as a nation of shopkeepers. Furthermore, as many scholars have observed, middle-class tastes and habits were arranged in relation to the private and feminized ethos of the bourgeois domestic ideal.[8] While professing to wean middle-class households from their putatively preferred everyday diet of roast, boiled, or fried meats washed down with ale, British gastronomy redefined sophisticated dining as an activity belonging to the public

---

[7]   The exoticism of French cuisine had more to do with its class connotations than its foreignness. While colonial culture had an influence on British cookery, most clearly visible in mid-century household manuals such as Isabella Beeton's *Book of Household Management* (1861), colonial fare such as curries and kedgerees were regarded as novelties and did not have the social status of French *haute cuisine.*

[8]   For more on the development of the middle-class ideal of domesticity, see Leonore Davidoff and Catherine Hall.

sphere and characterized by rules of taste as intricate as rules of social etiquette. To be counted a sophisticated diner, one needed to dine out, away from the sway of feminine tastes. In addition to consuming diverse foods, one was required to analyze, evaluate, and critique what one ate in conformity with expert opinion. This redefinition of what it meant to be a gourmand demarcated a division of rival culinary spaces mapped onto the conventional nineteenth-century gendering of the private and public spheres. Dining at home was associated with traditional cookery, everyday meals, and affective relations. Dining out was associated with professional cooking, elite cuisine, and, since "proper" women did not move in gastronomic circles, male homosocial relations.[9]

Hence, along with the proliferation of restaurants open to the middle-class diner, there was a parallel rise of the expert diner, a figure Mennell labels the "bourgeois gastronome" (134). Analogous to the modern-day food critic, the gastronome bridged the literary and the culinary by writing and discoursing about food, offering opinions that were supposedly the evaluative judgments of a trained palate. A culinary flâneur wandering the city in search of the pleasures of the table, the gastronome reconstituted dining as urban adventure and aesthetic experimentation. The gastronome's freedom to roam the city in search of culinary thrills meant that this was an identity available only to men. Furthermore, since restaurants likely to attract gastronomic diners were also likely to be expensive and exclusive, only men with sufficient leisure and wherewithal could pursue this interest. Reporting back from his food encounters in texts addressed to other men of wealth and leisure, the gastronome diffused an aesthetic sensibility that converted the pleasures of eating into the intellectual pleasures of talking or reading about food with like-minded fellows. Not only an arbiter of food taste, but also a public educator and theorist on matters of food and dining practices, the gastronome ameliorated anxieties about *arriviste* consumption habits while offering valuable insider advice to the newly affluent about elite consumption. He thus fulfilled a vital function in a culture where the practices of leisure and pleasure were undergoing reinvention in response to the growing economic and cultural clout of the middle classes.

Nevertheless, in his self-presentation as a Man of Taste, the gastronome was the antithesis of the bourgeois man of business. The man of business, or the economic man as producer, was defined by qualities such as seriousness, dedication to work,

---

[9] Restaurant dining opportunities were for the most part limited to men. Although metropolitan centers boasted a range of options for middle-class eating out, from coaching inns, taverns and chop-houses to high-end spas, hotels and clubs, these were mostly male establishments, with some limited accommodations for women who were traveling. A few establishments in mid-century provided separate dining rooms where women could be entertained by gentlemen. However, the respectability of this practice continued to be suspect until the end of the century, when London establishments such as the Savoy and Claridge's became popular among upper-class women. For more on the culture of eating out in the nineteenth century, see John Burnett (66–102).

respectability, moderation, and fiscal stability. Furthermore, the middle-class man of business was defined by his commitment to domestic life and his enjoyment of family activities. As Victorian ideals of manliness coalesced around these traits, the middle-class man of business came to represent a masculine norm.[10] Nonetheless, the gastronome continued to offer an alluring alternative to the idea of normative masculinity structured around the duties and responsibilities of home, work, and family. Representing the economic man as consumer, the gastronome was a creature driven by pleasure. Whereas the man of business emphasized utilitarian and frugal habits of consumption, the gastronome emphasized aesthetic pleasure, extravagance, and the ability to draw ever finer distinctions between flavors and varieties of food. For the gastronome, food provided the occasion for exercising intellectual powers in bravura displays of aesthetic judgment. To the extent that his activities demonstrated that the pursuit of taste was a rational pleasure available to all, the gastronome helped disseminate to the culture at large knowledge of food practices formerly available only within elite circles. However, to the extent that these activities contributed to a culture of food snobbery, the gastronome, as Mennell points out, served "the function of elite demarcation" (274–5). Denise Gigante draws a compelling comparison between the gastronome and the dandy, in that both figures invested the consumption of everyday objects with immense significance: "There was a connection between gourmands and dandies as modern Men of Taste at this time. The gourmand treated food with philosophical consequence" (*Taste* 173). What is especially telling about the analogy between the gastronome and the dandy is that the dandy is a figure defined by his rejection of bourgeois values. The gastronome as food dandy encodes in his food aestheticism a subversive set of ideas about pleasure, productive labor, and conventional morality. In a sense, gastronomy offers up a model of masculinity that is on the run from the sticky messes of bourgeois domestic life.

Not surprisingly, gastronomy revolved around the cult of the male, and usually foreign, celebrity chef surrounded by knowledgeable male patrons. The renowned Antonin Carême (1784–1833) was regarded as a cosmopolitan genius on par with celebrated painters and writers. During a stunning culinary career, Carême served as chef to Napoleon Bonaparte, the Prince Regent of Britain, Tsar Nicholas of Russia, and the Baron de Rothschild. He also freelanced with a number of wealthy and aristocratic patrons. While the cult was slower to take hold in Britain, mid-century gastronomical circles were familiar with the names of a number of notable chefs, the most famous among them being Alexis Soyer. These personages concocted for the trained palates and deep purses of select patrons complex and expensive recipes with French names. Soyer's *Gastronomic Regenerator* (1846), a gourmet cookbook that compiled many of his signature dishes, featured such items as *Salade de Grouse à la Soyer*, *Potage Velouté d'Asperges au pois verts*, and *Côtelettes de Mouton à la Reform*.

---

[10] For more on the significance of domesticity for Victorian ideas of manliness, see John Tosh.

Of course, a cook at home might also serve up a home dinner of salad, pea soup, and lamb chops, but its status would be entirely different. As not only a domain of feminine knowledge and praxis, but also in its associations with bourgeois living and economy, domestic cookery by definition was déclassé. Cooks in ordinary households tended to be working-class women under the direction of middle-class housewives. They worked under the constraints of tight household budgets, inconvenient working conditions, and the necessity of accommodating different dietary needs, such as those of children and the elderly. The everyday concerns of these domestic practitioners were addressed by a thriving market in instructional cookbooks which eschewed the gastronomic imperative of novelty and complexity. The most successful of these texts were written by women speaking to other women as a means of disseminating a uniquely feminine area of knowledge. The authors emphasized practicality and tradition, which led to some books becoming household standbys. Hannah Glasse's *The Art of Cookery, Made Plain and Easy* (1747) remained in print well into the nineteenth century. Other commercial successes included Maria Rundell's *New System of Domestic Cookery* (1806), Eliza Acton's *Modern Cookery for Private Families* (1845), and, most famously, Isabella Beeton's *Book of Household Management* (1861). These texts relied on terms that resonated with their readership of middle-class housewives: plain, easy, modern, private families, domestic cookery, and so on. While the gourmet cookbooks of celebrity chefs offered up economic and aesthetic extravagance, domestic cookbooks emphasized frugality. Indeed, domestic cookbooks sought to convince the reader that being attentive to cost did not preclude serving up appealing meals. Even Beeton's ambitious text, whose scope included large and small households, emphasized the conflation of economy and good living: "The object, then, is not only to *live*, but to live economically, agreeably, tastefully, and well" (57). Domestic cookbooks thus implicitly criticized gastronomical theory as needless mystification, and presented "plain cookery" as the commonsense practice more suited to everyday living and health.

Yet there is an additional register of contrast implied in these texts: plain cooking is implicitly identified as *English*, while gourmet cooking, decried as faddish, extravagant, and unhealthy, is also identified as foreign.[11] Even noted gastronomes sometimes concurred with this characterization. Thomas Walker, a barrister and gastronomical writer who lived as a bachelor in London, wrote in *Aristology, or the Art of Dining* (1835): "I do not think, from my own experience and observation, that the French mode of cookery is so favourable to physical power as the English. If I might have my choice, I should adopt the simple English style for my regular diet" (213). Nevertheless, Walker enjoins the inclusion of French dishes in a sophisticated menu: "when composed of variety, the dishes should

---

[11] Although aimed at a general national readership, most domestic cookbooks featured the traditional food of England (principally manor house cooking) with a handful of stereotypical dishes drawn from the culinary traditions of other British ethnicities, such as Scotch woodcock, Welsh rarebit (or rabbit), or Irish stew.

be lighter in nature, and in the French style. It must be confessed that a French dinner, when well dressed, is extremely attractive" (213). He never seems able to fulfill his wish to live on simple English fare alone, and instead seems always to be drawn back to the complex attractions of French dinners. And so the battle lines were drawn between male, professional, gourmet cuisine and female, domestic, plain cookery. However, as Walker's ambivalence demonstrates, gourmet taste militated against nationalist spirit. If English plain cookery was better for physical power, then the gourmet's preference for and promotion of fancy fare put English (masculine) hardihood in jeopardy.

Dining as Domestic Display

Middle-class formal dinner parties bridged the divide between gastronomic dining out and home meals, offering bourgeois women a chance to participate in the sophisticated culinary culture without trespassing on the male homosociality of gastronomic circles. However, as dinner parties were also sites at which families could display and consolidate class status, women had the obligation of ensuring as magnificent a spectacle as the family finances and the social experience of the lady of the house would allow. All arrangements for a successful occasion devolved upon the wife, who was responsible for choosing the menu, budgeting for the expense, managing the staff, and directing the cook if necessary. Furthermore, she was responsible for observing the intricate rules of etiquette governing every aspect of such parties. As such, hostesses confronted numerous challenges to success. Whatever might be the everyday cooking practices of the household, the menu for the dinner party was likely to feature complex French dishes intended to demonstrate the upper-class aspirations of the family. Even if a family was affluent enough to boast a male cook, these unfamiliar dishes would test his mettle and the capabilities of his staff. For smaller, less affluent households, formal dinners entailed hiring temporary staff, renting plates and cutlery, and ordering in pre-cooked items. Given the vagaries of such arrangements, these occasions involved enormous labor and anxiety for the lady of the house—all the more so since she could not allow herself to be seen as actively supervising any of the arrangements.

Dinner parties were reflections of feminine tastes and social education, and even gastronomes bowed to the rules of politesse that placed greater importance on the conventions than the meal. Not that they were happy about it. One of Sturgeon's moral maxims on dining states: "As every one's attention should be entirely given up to what is *on* the table, and not to what *surrounds it*—ladies should not expect particular notice until the dessert is served" (15). Yet few guests would be so bold as to ignore the ladies in order to concentrate on the food alone. Unlike bachelor gastronomic dinners, social manners had to be observed at these events (especially if a guest did not want to risk being blacklisted). In his chapter on dinner etiquette for gentlemen, Sturgeon warns that only when the ladies have left the table can gentlemen allow themselves to relax: "when the ladies have retired, and you are *at length relieved from all etiquette*, clap both your hands into your breeches pockets, and stretch yourself out in your chair, as if you had just awoke from a long nap" (43; emphasis added). The allusion to napping hints at Walker's complaint that such formal dinners are wearisome: "The legitimate objects of dinner are to refresh the body, to please the palate, and to raise the social humour to the highest point; but these objects, so far from being studied, in general are not even thought of, and display and an adherence to fashion are their meager substitutes" (212). He has no doubts about who is responsible for this state of affairs: "Hence it is, that gentlemen ordinarily understand what pertains to dinner-giving so much better than ladies, and that bachelors' feasts are so popular. Gentlemen keep more in view the real ends, whereas ladies think principally of display and ornament, of form and ceremony" (212). For a bachelor and borderline misogynist, Walker shows himself surprisingly percipient in speculating that women's misinformed notions about dinner arrangements may signal a buried resentment of male pleasure: "Ladies are very apt to suppose that men enjoy themselves the most when they are not present. They are in measure right, but for a wrong reason" (217). Walker insinuates that women see middle-class dinner parties as opportunities for getting even with men by arranging Barmecidal feasts that titillate the appetite but are ultimately disappointing: "It is not that men prefer their own to a mixture of female society, but that females delight in a number of observances, and in forms … and upon a certain display and undeviating order, which conspire to destroy that enjoyment, which they seem to think they are debarred from … In their management of dinners, let them think only of what contributes to real enjoyment" (217). "Real enjoyment," of course, means the satisfaction of masculine tastes and habits.

Such allegations expose the discomfiture with the increasing social power of bourgeois women, and especially with women's appropriation of the hitherto masculine practice of dining out. Middle-class dinner parties, which blurred the distinction between dining at home and dining out, subverted the gendered division of spaces that gastronomy attempted to sustain. These occasions allowed women to make their presence felt in the public sphere of social interactions, and to solicit recognition for their vital role in the rise of family fortunes. Instead of dining out with male friends at restaurants and clubs, gentlemen increasingly attended or hosted dinner parties supposedly dominated by the sensibilities and tastes of women. Gastronomical writers acknowledged (perhaps even exaggerated) the social and political importance of giving and attending dinners. However, they imagined the dinner table as a site for bonding experiences among men of similar interests and social status.[12] They opined that the presence of women at the table

---

[12]   William Thackeray is especially saturnine in his criticism of the practice of giving dinner parties as a means of advancing family fortunes. In the satirical "The Book of Snobs" he devotes a section to the pretensions of two groups of people he labels the "Dining-Out Snobs" and the "Dinner-Giving Snobs": "For instance, suppose you, in the middle rank of life … with small means and a small establishment, choose to waste the former and set the

kept the gathering focused on trivialities, and all substantive conversations about intellectual, political, commercial, or even gastronomical matters had to be postponed until they retired, leaving the men to their brandy, port, and cigars. As Mark Girouard notes, the separation of spaces by gender and class was a hallmark of respectability for affluent Victorian households. Drawing rooms, furnished with feminine designs and delicate furniture, were distinctively feminine spaces in which women exercised the crucial social function of receiving guests and visiting. For gentlemen, there were spaces suited to masculine sociability, such as smoking rooms, billiard rooms, and the library, which tended to be furnished with heavy pieces and dark colors. While the décor of the feminine spaces connoted being *au courant* with fashionable tastes, the décor of the masculine spaces connoted financial solidity and the weight of tradition. The dining room, however, was a place of contestation. While the furnishings of the dining room tended to be solid and formal, it was also a place where the lady of the household reigned alongside her husband, and jointly shared the duties of sociability. For Walker and other gastronomes, this joint sociability rendered dinner parties stultifying exercises in fashionable pretensions from which "most people retire … rather wearied than repaid" (212).

Kitchen Efficiency

Regarded as a Victorian notable for his virtuoso culinary performances (which received sufficient mention in the periodical press to make him known even outside gastronomical circles), Alexis Soyer attracted considerable attention when he chose to intervene in these culinary discussions.[13] Furthermore, unlike Walker and other gastronomes who could speak only as disgruntled consumers, Soyer's practical experience as a chef enabled him to consider the production end of such matters. Soyer had been employed privately as master-chef by a number of gastronomical gentlemen. However, his most significant professional accolade came with his engagement as the *chef de cuisine* of the newly constructed Reform Club, a London club for wealthy Whig gentlemen who wanted an establishment rivaling the grandeur and prestige of existing clubs (especially Tory ones such as White's and the Carlton).[14] Soyer was entrusted with supervising the design and planning of the club kitchen, a unique opportunity that enabled him to realize the foundational principles of his culinary theory. He worked with architect Charles Barry to design a unique, state-of-the-art kitchen in which efficiency, discipline,

---

latter topsy-turvy by giving entertainments unnaturally costly—you come into the Dinner-giving Snob class at once" (225).

[13] See Michael Garval's analysis of Soyer as a public figure. Helen Morris's biography of Soyer also elaborates on the flamboyant personality Soyer used in public life, as does Elizabeth Ray's biography.

[14] For more on the establishment of the Reform Club, see Ray (21–5).

and technology were the reigning principles. The Reform Club kitchen became a showplace for its use of gas ovens, its emphasis on cleanliness, and its panoptical design that enabled the *chef de cuisine* to keep an eye on the entire operation. Many periodical press reports on the club's opening focused on the design of the kitchen (giving the magnificent members' rooms considerably less attention).[15] This experience allowed Soyer to develop his inventive culinary and managerial talents and to think about the broader social applicability of his ideas.

For Soyer, the failings of middle-class kitchens conspired with middle-class women's ignorance of the scientific principles of cookery to produce the disappointments of domestic dinners. Soyer invented numerous new culinary gadgets (or designed refinements of existing ones) that would make home cooking more convenient and reliable. However, he was especially interested in how the gas stove might revolutionize society, one household at a time. Victorian kitchens generally featured a large iron range, set into the masonry below a wide chimney, burning charcoal or wood in an open fire. The range was designed primarily for roasting joints, with ingenious attachments for mechanical turnspits. Broiling was done by holding a gridiron over the open flames. Iron hooks suspended above the fire could hold pots or kettles for boiling. In more affluent households, the range was flanked by an oven and a water boiler, both set into the masonry and heated by the same open fire.[16] Kitchens were thus hot, smoky, and steamy places which discouraged precision cookery. Gas stoves, on the other hand, would burn more cleanly, efficiently, and predictably, and would create an environment in which more complex cooking procedures, requiring the manipulation of temperatures, could be conducted. Culinary reform had to begin with the range. Changing the range would not only substitute a new technology for an old one, but would institute a new kitchen ethos in response to that technology.

Soyer's Kitchen Apparatus, intended to remedy the inefficiencies and inconveniences of the conventional coal-fired range, was a scaled-down version of Soyer's gas-fueled *batterie de cuisine* at the Reform Club. Soyer had marketed a version of this appliance, a kitchen range labeled Phidomageireion (i.e., "Thrifty Kitchen") and expensively priced at £22, with the firm of Smith & Phillips. He registered a patent for the design of the version called "Modern Housewife's Kitchen Apparatus" in 1850. Bramah, Prestage, and Ball licensed the design for two versions of the kitchen apparatus: the "Cottager's Stove" and the "Deluxe Kitchen Range." There was even a version adapted to a ship's galley (with special fittings suitable for shipboard cooking) installed on the merchant steamship called the *Guadalquiver*.[17] However, Soyer believed the appliance worked best when

---

[15]   For a detailed description of Soyer's role in building the kitchens, see Ruth Cowen (31–51).

[16]   See Ravetz (435–8).

[17]   Ray notes that the *Guadalquiver* was a steam merchant vessel owned by a cigar merchant and carried goods and passengers to Cuba. The galley kitchen was equipped with several innovations designed to compensate for motion, and Soyer even received a write-up

installed in a kitchen modeled after the renowned Reform Club kitchen. Described by a gushing *Illustrated London News* write-up as a "temple" for the "worship of the culinary art upon a scale of magnificence and rapidity only commensurate with the progress of steam itself" ("Kitchen Department" 477), the Reform Club kitchen proved to be a remarkably versatile template that Soyer believed could be adapted to different domestic environments, as well as to taverns, restaurants, inns, and ships. The key principle of the design centered on the economical use of space (whether the available space was the enormous expanse of the Club kitchen, the compact galley of a ship, or the cramped quarters of a middle-class "below-stairs" kitchen) so that cooking equipment and ingredients could be arranged in a methodical fashion and work surfaces could be clean, uncluttered, and convenient to use.

Soyer ensured that the Kitchen Apparatus would be accompanied by his vision of the new domestic kitchen by marketing the appliance in conjunction with his cookbook aimed at middle-class women, the putative "modern housewives" interested in reforming the domestic space. Inspired by the commercial success of Acton's *Modern Cookery for Private Families* (1845), which presented English manor and farm cookery for the urban middle classes, Soyer set out to adapt his previous success, the *Gastronomic Regenerator*, for a middle-class audience. His new book, *The Modern Housewife*, takes an oddly coy form: it is written as a series of letters (interspersed with dialogues) from an experienced and thrifty housewife, Mrs Hortense B., to an admiring friend, Mrs Eloise L., who hopes to learn the tips and secrets of Mrs B.'s household management. Soyer's cookbook yokes material and psychological rewards to expert housewifery, hinting that a wife can gain renown, gifts, and the attentions of her husband, if only she runs her kitchen wisely. In the introductory dialogue, Hortense reveals with becoming modesty how her housekeeping has made Mr B.'s associates envy him. Labeled a "Model Housekeeper" by guests for the comforts of her domestic arrangements, Hortense is also believed by these same guests to be "the most extravagant of wives" (ix). Both Hortense and her husband enjoy this little deception. Mr B. is both envied and pitied for having such a remarkable wife: a woman with superior domestic skills, and a seductress capable of inveigling enough money from her husband, a mere grocer, to maintain a fine household beyond his means. However, Mr B. takes great pride in Hortense's prowess at managing to provide comfort with economy, and enjoys occasionally disabusing his guests by showing them her household accounts. He also boasts of how Hortense's frugality enables him to show his appreciation with gifts: "this year, Mrs B. with the two children had a pretty little house at Ramsgate for two months" (xii).

After a fortnight's stay at Hortense's house, Eloise is convinced. When she returns to her home, she immediately writes back to Hortense pleading for instruction: "This style is now quite unbearable, and I mean to have quite a reform

---

in the *Illustrated London News* about its design. However, the *Guadalquiver* was lost at sea two years later in 1850 (Ray 55). For more on Soyer as an inventor, see Cowen (15–75).

in my little establishment ... I have come to the determination of adopting your system of management as closely as possible; but, first, you must know, that, without your scientific advice, it will be totally impossible" (xv–xvi). Needless to say, the advice and recipes detailed in the letters demonstrate the clever and frugal ways in which Hortense is able to achieve the effect of luxury. However, these are not common household tips, but adaptations of Soyer's own methods. The cookbook even includes a correspondence between Hortense and Soyer, in which the chef, writing from the Reform Club, gallantly agrees to allow Hortense to include in *her* book the section entitled "My Kitchen at Home" from the *Gastronomic Regenerator* (67). Despite the arch tone of Hortense's letters, the systematic approach to housekeeping laid out in *The Modern Housewife* derived from Soyer's experience of managing large-scale dining halls and public banquets, marked the cookbook as being informed by industrial values of efficiency and standardized production methods. Furthermore, unlike the usual run of domestic cookbooks, Soyer incorporates French culinary concepts and terms into his instructions, accompanied by detailed explanations for novice cooks.

The Kitchen Apparatus, Hortense's (that is Soyer's) favored appliance, would replace the vagaries of experiential knowledge in one area of domestic labor with "modern" values that mirrored the industrial economy. A family choosing to invest in a Kitchen Apparatus would be making not only a financial but also an ideological decision. The Kitchen Apparatus promised to institute a minimum standard in domestic cookery, whether by minimizing the impact on the household of a temperamental or unskilled cook or of an ornamental housewife ignorant of household management. It also promised to bring to quotidian domestic labor a professional and industrial ethos by encouraging households to conceptualize the kitchen in terms of a workplace whose productivity depended on the efficiency of its workers. Ordinary households depended on "plain cooks" whose knowledge of the science behind various modes of cooking would be haphazard and limited. Furthermore, ordinary housewives would be ignorant of the "scientific" management style that contributes to Hortense's success. Not only is Hortense immensely knowledgeable about all aspects of housekeeping, but she is also a skilled accountant and an excellent supervisor of her staff (which grows as the family's finances and status improve, in part due to her superb housekeeping). Although she sits demurely at the head of the table during dinner parties, she works actively at all other times to ensure the smooth operation of the household. In other words, Hortense is the domestic counterpart of her husband, applying similar principles of economy and discipline at home as her husband does at the shop. This is the paradoxical insight Hortense offers in her letters: the home can be a Ruskinian refuge only when it is run along the lines of a commercial enterprise. Elevating the standards of domestic cookery thus entailed restructuring the domestic space in keeping with the values of industrial modernity. Despite Soyer's emphasis on taste and variety in his recipes, the systematic approach of the cookbook and the efficient design of the Kitchen Apparatus emphasize discipline, organization, and economy, thereby revealing how a reformed kitchen brought the gendered values of supposedly separate spheres into closer proximity.

Portable Cookery

The Kitchen Apparatus promised to enhance the daily comforts of the home, but only by imposing the values of industrial modernity on the domestic space. It required installation, maintenance, and a trained staff. It also called for planning and oversight from the lady of the house (or a surrogate) for optimal performance. In contrast, the Magic Stove rejected the professional and industrial spirit of the Kitchen Apparatus in favor of spontaneity, intimacy, and playfulness. More significantly, however, the portable design of the stove crossed gender lines to signal an appeal to middle-class men to acquire sufficient skills for basic cookery. Soyer registered a patent for the design in 1850. The stove was manufactured by a lamp-making firm called Gardner's, and was heavily advertised and promoted. The design was versatile: there was an expensive model for upper-class households, and a small, cheap version for low-income households. A travel version, called Soyer's "Magic Kitchen" (or "Camp Kitchen"), was sold as a complete kit. The kit consisted of the stove, small pots and pans, cooking utensils, dishes, coffee-pot, spice-box, and a tray, all contained in a lightweight tin chest capable of fitting under a carriage seat (Cowen 162–3). Since the freedom to travel widely and at their own pleasure was principally a masculine privilege, these design features would be less salient for female customers. Additionally, the self-contained design, which emphasized the ease with which culinary self-sufficiency could be achieved, supported the notion of masculine escape from the tyranny of domestic fuss, a desire that was evident in the previously discussed critiques of middle-class dinner parties.

While the Kitchen Apparatus was intended to appeal to "modern" middle-class women, the Magic Stove was designed for their male counterparts. The advertising and promotions for the Magic Stove suggested that anyone—that is, middle-class men unaccustomed to cookery—could use it to dish up delicious meals with minimal fuss and labor. A write-up in the *Morning Post* proclaimed its indispensability for bachelors and travelers, while a *Morning Chronicle* article conducted a test in a railway carriage and promoted its utility to anglers and sportsmen (qtd in Cowen 162–3). An endorsement in *The Modern Housewife* states that "it will cook cutlets or boil water in as short a time as the best of charcoal, and to the sportsman on the moors must be of great utility; with the sautépan everything can be cooked as on a charcoal fire" (400). Soyer conducted live demonstrations of the stove's capabilities by inviting a select audience of journalists, aristocratic acquaintants, and members of the public to his small London office, where he would cook and serve a gourmet meal as they conversed. A review in the *Sun* recommended the stove for "soldiers, sailors, and sportsmen" and announced that it would "emancipate the bachelor living in chambers from the thralldom of his laundress" (qtd in Morris 61).

Eliding the feminine labor of domestic cookery and the rituals of family dining, such promotions invited men to imagine themselves "emancipated" from the domestic space by the convenience of this stove. Yet even in domestic settings, the stove represented fun and freedom. When used at home, it offered the opportunity for private, intimate moments. In *The Modern Housewife*, Hortense uses the Magic Stove for intimate breakfasts with her husband: "In addition to the eggs we often have cold meat, and sometimes Mr B. has a cutlet or any other nick-nack [sic], which I always cook myself on the breakfast table with my newly-invented Magic lamp-stove" (399). However, the liberatory potential of the stove is especially apparent when used by men outside the home. Indeed, men appreciate the stove so thoroughly that women find themselves unable to obtain one for home use. A letter from Hortense in the frontispiece of *The Modern Housewife* notes that she had intended to send Eloise one of these gadgets, but that the device intended for her friend was "taken by the Marquis of N. and party to Egypt, with the view of having a dinner cooked on the top of the Pyramids" (vi).

For middle-class women, then, the stove is a novelty item that allows the occasional demonstration of housewifely skills to an admiring husband, suitable for cooking up "nick-nacks" but not for the everyday demands of a household. For their male counterparts, however, the stove is a necessary adjunct to adventure away from the home. While Hortense's testimony emphasizes the convenient, if limited, domestic uses of the stove, various illustrations depicting masculine uses of the stove emphasize its ruggedness. The stove can be relied upon anywhere the hardy Englishman chooses to venture. One illustration shows figures of a number of gentlemen (supposedly the Marquis of Normanby, a public figure and member of the Reform Club) cooking on top of an Egyptian pyramid.[18] Some figures in local attire and several camels roam at the base of the pyramid. A detail illustration shows the scene at the top of the pyramid: three English gentlemen, accompanied by two Arab guides, cluster around a Magic Stove, one of them gingerly handling a frying pan set on it while the other men watch with interest. Another illustration shows the stove in use among the ruined pillars of the Acropolis, with Soyer cooking up breakfast for a number of military officers (Figure 5.3). A small basket of provisions and another of wine sit near Soyer's feet. Some men stand watching the cooking, while others lounge on the fallen stones and talk among themselves.[19] The context of this latter illustration is Soyer's voluntary service in the Crimean War in 1855–1856. Having read newspaper reports of the horrifying barrack conditions in Scutari, and inspired by Florence Nightingale's intervention

---

[18] The illustrations are also reproduced in Morris (60–61).

[19] The illustration was part of a dispatch sent to the *Illustrated London News* during Soyer's journey to Crimea in 1855. Soyer had volunteered his services to reform the terrible conditions of the barrack kitchens. The full plate appears in Cowen, Section Two. A detailed version appeared in *Harper's New Monthly Magazine* (1857–8).

in the hospital, Soyer contacted Lord Panmure, the newly-appointed war secretary, to offer his services in reforming the barrack kitchens (Cowen 258–62). The illustration records an occasion on his journey to Scutari, when he stopped at Athens on the way to Constantinople (now Istanbul). The Magic Stove is perched on the flat top of a broken acropolis pillar—an apt symbol of Britain's eminence as a political and cultural force in the region. The Magic Stove restores civilization to the ruins of the Acropolis, and promotes masculine camaraderie even in the face of death. For all its suggestion of an impromptu picnic in an exotic setting, the image of uniformed officers in Athens in 1855 would have been a reminder to contemporary readers of Balaclava and Inkerman.

The Magic Stove offered a vision of cookery as a means of fostering male bonding, outdoors or in bachelor households, where the values of gastronomy, spontaneity, and fellowship could be celebrated without feminine interference. The stove appears magical in its genie-like ability to conjure up feasts out of thin air. Soyer's memoirs recount an anecdote about a promotional event presenting cooking on the stove as a kind of magic trick:

> Soyer had once promised to supply food for a picnic, but when the food was unpacked in the middle of a field, miles from anywhere, the party discovered with horror that it was all uncooked. Soyer, says his secretary, 'called the "spirits" of his stove ... from the "vasty deep," and they did "come when he did call them."' The meal was a grand success. (Morris 62)

In a similar promotional demonstration, Soyer performed as an attraction at a farewell ball for Queen Victoria at Castle Howard, where she had been staying as a guest. A report in *The Times* for September 7, 1850 notes that "one of the greatest attractions was afforded by M Soyer's cooking various dishes on the supper-table with his Lilliputian magic stove ... The favourite dish amongst the ladies present was *les oeufs au mirroir* [sic], half a dozen of which seem to have been done every two minutes with the greatest ease and expedition" ("M. Soyer at Castle Howard" 5). Despite the popularity of the show with the ladies at the ball, this demonstration proclaimed the stove to be an instrument of masculine culinary prowess. In this scene, the male chef composedly and expertly carries out his tasks while an admiring crowd of ladies gathers around him to watch a feat of culinary showmanship that emphasizes its physical and aesthetic distance from the harried routines of domestic cookery.

Through the complementary design of his two stoves, Soyer expresses a culinary dialectic centering on the Victorian ambivalence about the iconic status of the middle-class British home as simultaneously a refuge from and a reflection of Britain's commercial, industrial, and imperial prowess. This culinary dialectic is mapped onto a gendered dynamic of culinary taste in which supposedly men sought to gratify the palate but women sought to gratify the eyes. In this view, men prioritize the need for home dinners to be tastefully prepared (thus refreshing the wearied body and spirit), while women prioritize the need for meals to be

COOKING ON THE MAGIC STOVE IN THE ACROPOLIS AT ATHENS.   P. 69.

Figure 5.3   Cooking on the Magic Stove in the Acropolis at Athens
Source: Alexis Soyer. *Soyer's Culinary Campaign; Being Historical Reminiscences of the Late War.* London: G. Routledge and Co., 1857.

tastefully served (thus demonstrating the family's social standing). For men, a pleasing meal derives from following gastronomic dicta; for women, a pleasing meal entails following social etiquette. Furthermore, women needed to ensure that the aesthetics of home dinners were accomplished within the constraints of the household budget. Soyer targets the disjuncture of these two modalities not through synthesis but by offering a gadget for each modality. Whether in a grand ballroom or in the outdoors under an open sky, the Magic Stove appears to empower men to realize their gastronomic visions without needing to mediate with women, the conventional guardians of culinary expertise, and hence to resist the constraints of industrial domesticity. The Kitchen Apparatus, on the other hand, appears to empower women by educating them in the principles of industrial modernity and by offering the efficiency and convenience of a labor-saving appliance. However, while the Magic Stove enables middle-class men to flee the home when it becomes too oppressive, the Kitchen Apparatus necessitates middle-class women's return to the kitchen, not as expert cooks, but as mere technicians and attendants of the machine. Like the gendered tensions raised by the practice of middle-class dinner parties, gastronomical reformism of bourgeois domesticity, as illuminated by the design of Soyer's stoves, reveals an anxiety about middle-class women's resistance to the separation of spheres. Soyer's "modern housewife" is a "domesticated wife" who has learned the "keys of the store-room before those of the piano" (xiii). As women began to claim a greater share of the public space through dinner parties and social events, and thereby blurred the boundaries between the private and public, gastronomical reformism called for women to return to more traditional duties within the home. The Kitchen Apparatus, for all its modern conveniences, reinstated women in the kitchen.

It is not surprising, then, that Soyer's model housekeeper, Hortense, exhorts her readers in her parting letter: "let every housekeeper devote more time to the study of domestic and practical economy; and in many instances it will increase their incomes as well as their daily comforts" (416). In contrast, the Magic Stove sustained the idea of a rugged, free-spirited British masculinity, ready to forgo such comforts for the further reaches of the empire. Thus the Magic Stove served an apotropaic function against the enervating influence of excessive domestic comfort. It accompanied middle-class men to the furthest reaches of the empire as a civilizing artifact, reforming the world even as its counterpart reformed the Victorian domestic space. Working in tandem, the two gadgets achieved the acme of gastronomic reformism, enabling the transformation of a nation of shopkeepers into a nation of empire builders.[20]

Works Cited

Acton, Eliza. *Modern Cookery for Private Families*. 1845. London: Longman, Green, Longman, and Roberts, 1860. Print.

Beeton, Isabella. *Mrs Beeton's Book of Household Management*. Oxford: Oxford University Press, 2000. Print.

Burnett, John. *England Eats Out: A Social History of Eating Out in England from 1830 to the Present*. NY: Longman, 2004. Print.

Carlyle, Thomas. "Characteristics." *A Carlyle Reader: Selections from the Writings of Thomas Carlyle* (ed.) G.B. Tennyson. NY: Modern Library, 1969. 71–93. Print.

Cowen, Ruth. *Relish: The Extraordinary Life of Alexis Soyer, Victorian Celebrity Chef*. London: Phoenix, 2006. Print.

Davidoff, Leonore and Catherine Hall. *Family Fortunes: Men and Women of the English Middle Classes, 1780–1850*. Chicago: University of Chicago Press, 1987. Print.

Ferguson, Priscilla Parkhurst. *Accounting for Taste: The Triumph of French Cuisine*. Chicago: University of Chicago Press, 2004. Print.

---

[20] I wish to express my thanks to the editors for their helpful and insightful comments, and to Dr Sharilyn Nakata for her encouragement and critical insights. As in all my scholarly endeavors, I would like to acknowledge my parents, the late Professor Sushil Kumar Bhattacharya and Mrs Gitanjali Bhattacharya, and my family elders, Ms Gayatri Bhattacharya and Mr Bishwanath Bhattacharya, for their support of my pursuit of intellectual pleasure.

Gallagher, Catherine. "The Body versus the Social Body in Thomas Malthus and Henry Mayhew." *Representations* 14 (1986): 83–106. Web.

Garval, Michael. "Alexis Soyer and the Rise of the Celebrity Chef." *Romantic Circles* (January 2007): n.p. Web.

Gigante, Denise (ed.) *Gusto: Essential Writings in Nineteenth-Century Gastronomy.* NY: Routledge, 2005. Print.

Gigante, Denise. *Taste: A Literary History.* New Haven: Yale University Press, 2005. Print.

Girouard, Mark. *The Victorian Country House.* New Haven: Yale University Press, 1979. Print.

Haley, Bruce. *The Healthy Body and Victorian Culture.* Cambridge, MA: Harvard University Press, 1978. Print.

"Kitchen Department of the Reform Club House." *Illustrated London News* 3 December, 1842: 477–8. Web.

"M. Soyer at Castle Howard." *The Times* 7 September, 1850: 5. Web.

Mennell, Stephen. *All Manners of Food: Eating and Taste in England and France from the Middle Ages to the Present.* 2nd edn, Urbana and Chicago: University of Illinois Press, 1996. Print.

Milne-Smith, Amy. "A Flight to Domesticity? Making a Home in the Gentlemen's Clubs of London, 1880–1914." *Journal of British Studies* 45 (2006): 796–818. Web.

Morris, Helen. *Portrait of a Chef: The Life of Alexis Soyer, Sometime Chef to the Reform Club.* NY: Macmillan, 1938. Print.

Prown, Jules David. "Mind in Matter: An Introduction to Material Culture Theory and Methods." *Winterthur Portfolio* 17 (1982): 1–19. Web.

Ravetz, Alison. "The Victorian Coal Kitchen and its Reformers." *Victorian Studies* 11 (1968): 435–60. Web.

Ray, Elizabeth. *Alexis Soyer: Cook Extraordinary.* Lewes, UK: Southover Press, 1991. Print.

Soyer, Alexis. *The Gastronomic Regenerator.* London: Simpkin, Marshall and Co., 1847. Web.

Soyer, Alexis. *The Modern Housewife or Ménagère.* 2nd edn, London: Simpkin, Marshall, and Co., 1849. Print.

Soyer, Alexis. *Soyer's Culinary Campaign; Being Historical Reminiscences of the Late War.* London: G. Routledge and Co., 1857. Print.

Sturgeon, Launcelot. *Essays, Moral, Philosophical, and Stomachical on the Important Science of Good-Living.* 2nd edn, London: G. and W.B. Whittaker, 1823. Print.

Thackeray, William Makepeace. "The Book of Snobs." *Gusto* (ed.) D. Gigante. NY: Routledge, 2005. 224–31. Print.

Tosh, John. *A Man's Place: Masculinity and the Middle-Class Home in Victorian England.* New Haven, CT: Yale University Press, 1999. Print.

Veblen, Thorstein. *The Theory of the Leisure Class: An Economic Study of Institutions.* NY: Modern Library, 1934. Print.

Walker, Thomas. "Aristology, or the Art of Dining." *Gusto* (ed.) D. Gigante. NY: Routledge, 2005. 207–22. Print.

Chapter 6
Tea, Gender, and Middle-Class Taste

Deirdre H. McMahon

Any history of tea, of the good English "cuppa," is a primer of empire. Tea is not produced in the United Kingdom, and in sharp distinction to ale or beer, non-medicinal steeped beverages were not widely enjoyed in pre-industrial Britain. By the mid-nineteenth century, however, little seemed more British than tea, brewed strong, usually mixed with milk and sugar, prepared according to individual preference but imbued with national significance, as if the rituals of the teapot constituted a collective identity, a mode of being or habitus made all the more important for its quotidian and unassuming nature. Britons may have exulted in their predilection for beef, but the true backbone of the national cuisine remained liquid, as an anonymous 1868 paean in Charles Dickens's *All The Year Round* attests: "A cup of tea! Blessings on the words, for they convey a sense of English home comfort of which the proud Gaul, with all his boulevards and battalions, is as ignorant as a turbot is of the piano!" (153).

Despite France's long history of culinary prowess or the superiority of French urban and military display, the "proud Gaul" has no claim to the simple and profoundly domestic cup of tea. Extending the logic of the piece in *All The Year Round*, each cottage and castle in England is linked by the "home comfort" of the kettle, so that—at least in popular myth—vagaries of class, region, and station are smoothed away by the tea table and the presence of those assumed to be gathered around it. Individual tea consumption thus takes place within a highly scripted and socially codified ritual in which making and serving this staple of Asian culture helps to establish the sanctity and reliability of the English home. Despite its ubiquity, tea remained an imperial product, one that could not be grown in England, and so the national taste for tea links the gustatory to the ideological: idealized visions of both successful domestic order and imperial rule merge in the swirling dampened leaves. To this day, tea as a *product* stands as a mainstay of grocer's and kitchen shelves across the country, but when considering the role of tea in the nineteenth century, the actual contents of tin or cup are less important than the related *practices* that emerge from the leaves' harvesting, trade, preparation, and consumption. As part of a ritual affirmation of the collective as well as an everyday yet prized product, tea accrues immense cultural clout in that Englishness itself is reaffirmed with every cup consumed.

By charting how tea was continually tamed and domesticated through reference to the familial and to women in particular, while also representing a significant and pervasive disruption to central tenets of nineteenth-century British national identity, my argument focuses on tea as an exemplary site in British cultural history in which products and practices form a kind of material wheel, in this case with tea itself at its hub. Exactly because it is foreign in origin yet integrated into the British body, tea as a substance threatened normative British identity. Critics ranged from eighteenth-century pundits such as the author "South Briton," who claims in a letter to *The Gentleman's Magazine* (1737) that "If we consider the Nature of Tea with the nature of the English diet, as mentioned before, no one could think it a proper vegetable for our diet … Tea is utterly improper for food, hitherto useless in physic, and therefore to be ranged among the poysonous vegetables" (213), to well-known nineteenth-century scientists and physicians such as Edward Smith and Charles Browne, who warned against the growing addiction—especially of women and the lower classes—to this Eastern beverage, which they saw as undermining individual health as well as the body social.[1] Even Thomas De Quincey, who championed tea for its salubrious benefits, stressed England's midcentury vulnerability to the Chinese control of the trade: "Without tea … Great Britain, no longer great, would collapse into an anomalous sort of second-rate power" (25).[2] Although tea's perceived threats arose at least in part from Britain's increasing consumption rates coupled with its inability to produce the actual substance, the varied outlines of tea-related anxieties suggest that the British public focused not only on tea's external dangers to individual constitutions as well as Britain's geopolitical standing, but also on how the addiction to, reuse, reselling, or adulteration of tea might destabilize the status quo of internal economic divisions. None of these threats, however, were sufficient to deter tea-drinking as a national pastime. As illustrated by headmaster of Rugby and Oxford professor Thomas Arnold, who explained in his *Lectures on Modern History* (1843) that it is a "physiological fact that the tea-plant is become so necessary to our daily life," Britons were anxious both to secure the tea-trade and to cleanse it of potentially volatile associations with contamination from afar or within (149).

---

[1]   Such debates followed from the start of British importation of tea. For more on the threats against the body politic associated with British tea drinking in the eighteenth century, see Elizabeth Kowaleski-Wallace's path-breaking chapter on tea in *Consuming Subjects: Women, Shopping and Business in the Eighteenth Century* (1997). For more on the "revolutionary" health threats associated specifically with working-class tea consumption in the latter nineteenth century, see Ian Miller.

[2]   In his essay "The English in China," De Quincey adds "It is certainly a phenomenon without a parallel in the history of social man—that a great nation, numbering twenty-five millions, after making an allowance for the very poorest of the Irish who do not use tea, should within one hundred years have found themselves able so absolutely to revolutionise their diet, as to substitute for the gross stimulation of ale and wine the most refined, elegant, and intellectual mode of stimulation that human research has succeeded in discovering. But the material basis of this stimulation unhappily we draw from the soil of one sole nation—and that nation (are we ever allowed to forget?) capricious and silly beyond all that human experience could else have suggested as possible" (26).

Looking at tea as the visible trace of a larger cycle, we can see how a series of related practices, emerging from the exchange and use of tea as a product, mediate the potential threat of tea as a substance by reaffirming its connections to foundational discourses of Britishness, central among them being the power of domesticity. As tea gained its ascendancy during the nineteenth century, discussion of the rituals surrounding its daily preparation became a discursive shortcut for talking about hospitality, family nurturance, stoicism under pressure, middle-class taste, imperial control, and other quintessential British character traits. Above all, tea's connection to "English home comfort" invoked the familiar image of the woman as the heart of the home, tending carefully to the needs of her family and guests via her kettle. Tea became the national drink not just for its eupeptic pleasure or caffeine content, but because of the conservative ideological work performed with each cup. The hazards of physical degeneration, foreign corruption, and social upheaval linked to the consumption of tea were displaced onto the woman of the house, who functioned as the guarantor of the domestic success of the household just as the middle-class home acted as the guarantor of British moral and economic stability.

With or without a cup in their hands, women became increasingly associated with tea as both a commodity and a practice. Mary Elizabeth Braddon's *Lady Audley's Secret* (1861), for example, suggests that as a substance tea, ubiquitous in consumption and exotic in origin, enables the daily performance of femininity, at once prosaic and mysterious:

> Surely a pretty woman never looks prettier than when making tea. The most feminine and most domestic of all occupations imparts a magic harmony to her every movement, a witchery to her every glance. The floating mists from the boiling liquid in which she infuses the soothing herbs, whose scents are known to her alone, envelop her in a cloud of scented vapour, through which she seems a social fairy, weaving potent spells with Gunpowder and Bohea. At the tea-table she reigns omnipotent, unapproachable ... To do away with the tea-table is to rob woman of her legitimate empire. (222)

Here tea leaves are important only as far as they allow the woman of the house to reign supreme and almost supernatural in her hearth and home, her powers "weaving potent spells" over cups and diners, creating the perfect elixir to nourish individual bodies and collective social bonds. Woman's place remains within the home, constrained to the tea table, a physical and ideological restriction at odds with the agency promised by Braddon's rhetoric of "magic" and "witchery."

The above midcentury descriptions of tea reinforce the utility of this imperial product as emblematic of both *English* home comfort and *woman's* "legitimate empire." Overlapping and mutually constitutive, the practices and discourses associated with tea as a substance worked to bind the English home and British imperial success, so that any number of concerns about the sanctity of the household, nation or empire could be mediated through the kettle. When examined through this lens, tea's role as a substance and ideological juggernaut seems deliberately naturalized, as if it were a given that these leaves would be found in every Englishman's cup and kitchen. The following history of Britain's association with tea suggests that these naturalizing imperatives arise from and reinforce disciplinary consequences of conventional domesticity, so that the ongoing control of women, and particularly of women's labor, becomes central to broader cultural dictates that linked the Englishness of individual homes to the Britishness undergirding ideas of the nation and its imperial right to rule.

Empire in a Cup

Tea was introduced to Britain in the mid-seventeenth century, with the first written record of English tea making at home coming from Samuel Pepys, whose wife carefully infused two very expensive cups of tea in 1667. Rather than remaining a fad among the elite, tea soon became very popular, so popular and profitable in fact, that it created a trade imbalance between Great Britain and China, the sole exporter of the commodity for the first century and a half of the tea trade. Great Britain wanted more and more tea, but Chinese markets were not interested in English woolens, cottons, or manufactured goods. The government of China demanded all payments in silver, but given the increasing demand for tea as well as the need to buy silver from Germany to appease Chinese trade stipulations, the British government feared that the growing taste for tea would come at the expense of the devaluation of the pound.[3] To offset this imbalance, the East India Company, which held a monopoly on all imported Chinese tea until 1833, began a campaign to cultivate poppies in India and distribute their addictive products in China, an effort that culminated with the Opium Wars of the early nineteenth century. In short, as historian Brian Inglis notes, the First Opium War (1839–42) was "in a sense really the Tea War" (198).

British taste in tea merged with their hunger for sugar, another product of empire. Sidney Mintz's germinal study *Sweetness and Power: The Place of Sugar in Modern History* (1986) argues that cross-class consumer desires for exotic, imperial products like chocolate, coffee, and above all, tea and sugar, reinforced one another and changed the ways the metropole saw itself:

> On the one hand, [the steps by which England shifted from buying modest quantities of sugar from Mediterranean shippers … to establishing her own sugar colonies] represent an extension of empire outward, but on the other, they mark an absorption, a kind of swallowing up, of sugar consumption as a national habit. Like tea, sugar came to define English 'character.' (39)

---

[3]   See Roy Moxham, Julie E. Fromer, Erika Rappaport, and Alec Waugh. For more details about the history of the Sino–British tea trade, see Brian Inglis and Cannon Schmitt.

In an imperial sleight of hand, "an absorption" that happens gradually and almost imperceptibly, products from disparate parts of the realm—tea from the East, sugar from the Caribbean—become sufficiently naturalized in the British diet that their colonial origins either fade away or are seen as proof positive of the necessity of British rule. Politician Edward Gibbon Wakefield, apologist for both British colonization and American slavery, asserts in 1833 that "It is not because an English washerwoman cannot sit down to breakfast without tea and sugar, that the world has been circumnavigated; but it is because the world has been circumnavigated that the English washerwomen *requires* tea and sugar for breakfast" (84, emphasis added). For Wakefield and many other nineteenth-century capitalist thinkers, empire was progressive in that global trade spurred laborers at home to greater consumer desires and hence to greater productivity, which in turn contributed to both imperial zeal and the empire's economic prowess.[4] The washerwoman's breakfast tea remains a symbol of how average Britons through their consumption practices could define themselves as participants in and heirs to the empire. At the same time, however, it is possible to see the washerwoman as absorbing, without much thought or agency, messages about her rightful place in both empire (as a consumer of imperial goods) and the workforce at home, where her efforts will gain her morning tea rather than upward mobility. In each case, laborers in England are positioned as the final beneficiaries of the imperial refashioning of India's agriculture, even as such assumptions align workers in the metropole with imperialism writ large rather than with workers in the colonial sugar and tea fields, further distancing all Britons from those they purportedly controlled.

Just as imperialism brought sugar to the West Indies, where it had never before been grown, Great Britain and the East India Company brought tea cultivation to India. As early as 1822 the Royal Society of the Arts promised 50 guineas to anyone who could cultivate tea in a British colony. Seeing great commercial potential, botanist Charles (C.A.) Bruce imported and cross-bred Chinese seeds with local plants in the Assam region. Some sources suggest he thereby *created* Assam tea. Other sources insist that Bruce's cultivation failed, but that he deserves credit for *identifying* the indigenous tea plants of the region.[5] Whether or not tea was indigenous to the subcontinent became a political lightning rod, inasmuch as

---

[4] Mintz notes that Wakefield was roundly criticized by Marx in *Das Kapital,* exactly because Wakefield's view of imperial economics holds that the extension of markets through colonization benefitted workers at home (253, n. 14). In contrast, Marx held that Wakefield's theories are based on the expropriatory effects of capitalism at home and abroad, so that workers are routinely and necessarily barred from ownership of any real property: "It is the great merit of E.G. Wakefield to have discovered, not anything new about the Colonies, but to have discovered in the Colonies the truth as to the conditions of capitalist production in the mother-country" (839). According to Marx, the truth about the social relations inherent to capitalism is that capitalism depends upon and thus reproduces a surplus of property-less wage laborers, whether in the Colonies or in Britain.

[5] For discussion of Bruce's "discovery" of tea plants in India, see Fromer, 48–51; John Griffiths, 36–45; Moxham, 94–8; and Anandi Ramamurthy, 96.

Britain's Jewel in the Crown provided both a "British" locale for the production of the highly prized cash crop and a rationale for breaking the Chinese monopoly on the global tea trade. According to George Gabriel Sigmond's *Tea: Its Effects, Medicinal and Moral* (1839):

> A discovery has been made ... that the hand of Nature has planted the shrub [the tea plant] within the bounds of the wide dominion of Great Britain: a discovery which must materially influence the destinies of nations; it must change the employment of a vast number of individuals; it must divert the tide of commerce, and awaken to agricultural industry the dormant energies of a mighty country, whose well being must be the great aim of a paternal government. ... The resources of a magnificent empire are yet to be developed. India has, within her bosom, the richest vegetable and mineral treasures, which are to be given to the rest of the world, to unite together in closer bonds of harmony two great nations, the one capable, by the energies of her people, of governing, the other, by her climate, evidently destined to be the not unwilling vassals of foreigners; for such has been her lot from the earliest records of mankind; and to possess her wealthy domain has been, and will be, the ambition of the conquerors of the world. (3–4)

It seems important for Sigmond that tea be a natural product of India, presumably because its presence within British-controlled territory removed China's economic and geopolitical threat as well as any hint of national addiction to a "foreign" or exotic substance.[6] According to this argument, tea stands as an exemplar of the vast natural resources that India cannot deliver to the rest of the world without imperial intervention. In fact, tea cultivation would facilitate India's "dormant energies" and "well being," so British consumers of tea could see their purchasing and consumption practices as part of a larger civilizing mission that bettered Indian natives, the "not unwilling vassals," even while strengthening the Empire. Assam tea made its British debut in January 1839, when 350 pounds were sold in a single day from India House in London; by 1879, more tea was imported into the UK from India than from China. And by 1897, according to David Crole's *Tea: A Text Book of Tea Planting and Manufacture,* "80,000,000 cups of tea are *daily* imbibed in England" alone (1, emphasis added).[7]

---

   [6]   Fromer makes a similar point in *A Necessary Luxury: Tea in Victorian England* that according to Sigmond's enthusiastic claim to the "discovery" of tea within Great Britain's "dominion," "nature authorized British expansion into that region, reaffirming the rights and responsibilities of a "paternal government" as Sigmond puts it, to rule Indian territories and to reap the benefits of Indian resources ... . [F]inding tea growing wild ... appeared to be divine intervention, providing both the company and the nation with a new source of tea" (51).

   [7]   According to House of Commons records, tea consumption in the United Kingdom increased significantly toward the end of the nineteenth century: in 1898, 5.86 lbs of tea

The bare facts of the tea trade—the site-specific and global repercussions of tea's imbrication with sugar cultivation in the West Indies, for example, or the execution of Assamese nobleman Maniram Datta Barua, early ally of the British who became the first native owner of Assam's many tea plantations, for charges that he participated in the Indian Mutiny—illuminate political and economic complexities of British imperial history.[8] Given how thoroughly domesticated this imperial product became, however, it remains important to note how tea's relation to empire gradually disappeared into the fabric of everyday British experience during the period, while losing none of its ideological power. Rather than being a product imported through empire, tea became a staple whose imperial origins were less important than its presence throughout the kingdom. Put another way, tea's ubiquity made the bodily incorporation or absorption of empire into Britons a bygone conclusion. Far from a foreign threat, tea made manifest the benefits of empire, even as its status signified the cultural hegemony of a nation that could appreciate and control the best material resources of the globe. Thus in the midcentury imagination, tea makes the British more British, just as it allows Indian tea coolies the potential to improve their individual lot through carefully supervised agriculture and exportation.[9] Any parallel exploitation of the lower classes at home necessary to support this image of the imperial Briton remains obscured; the washerwoman may participate in empire by enjoying her morning cuppa, but she'll pay for it with the further straitening of her limited means or with her health.

---

were consumed per capita in the United Kingdom; in 1899, 5.98 lbs; and in 1900, 6.10 lbs, quantities far exceeding that consumed per capita by all other European countries and the United States combined ("Tea and Coffee, 1900"). It is probable that daily consumption rose beyond the 80,000,000 cups noted by Crole.

[8] For a nuanced discussion of workers' exodus from his plantations as cross-class solidarity with Maniram Barua (Maniram Dewan) in response to his execution, see Piya Chatterjee's *A Time for Tea*. Maniram Dewan was disturbed by exploitative plantation conditions and the rise of opium use among workers. See Jayeeta Sharma on Maniram Barua's frustrated attempts in 1853 to expose and critique British rule of Assam through official British channels.

[9] The racial and economic dynamics of the tea trade find parallels in other nineteenth-century geopolitical contexts. In *Occasional Discourses on the Nigger Question* (1849), for example, Carlyle makes a similar argument about the natural function of black field hands in the West Indies: "Yet this is the eternal law of Nature for a man, my beneficent Exeter-Hall friends; that is, that he shall be permitted, encouraged, and if need be *compelled* to do what work the maker of him was intended by the making of him for this World!" (469, emphasis added). Carlyle suggests that black workers in particular gain moral and physical benefits from agricultural labor, and it is natural that such labor should in turn benefit the "real proprietors" of the land, i.e., white owners and those back in Britain.

Adulteration and Threats from Within

People of all classes drank copious tea in Britain, but until tea was branded in the 1880s, the poor often did so in an adulterated or very weak state. Henry Mayhew claimed in 1851 that "exhausted leaves of the tea-pot are purchased of servants or of poor women, and they are made into 'new' tea" (455). To do so, the used leaves were dried on hot plates and then dyed darker or greener with infusions of copper, Prussian blue (a stable synthetic pigment), lead, sulphate of lime, and other potentially toxic substances. According to Mayhew, "[I]t would be fair to reckon that in London 1500 pounds of tea-leaves were weekly converted into new tea, or 78,000 lbs in the year!" (509). Robert Warrington, a Fellow of the Chemical Society also writing in 1851, estimated that some 750,000 pounds of adulterated tea had been distributed in Britain the past 18 months (360). In its least expensive forms, such as "bohea," the leaves were ground into a dust that could easily include many forms of adulteration. "Lye tea" (also known as "lie tea"), a compound of "sand, dirt, tea-dust, and broken down portions of other leaves" was particularly common ("Food, and Its Adulterations," 242).[10] Because tea was sold in bulk, distributed by tallymen who knocked on doors as well as by grocers, there was little quality control before branding became the norm.[11] Grocers would mix their own blends, whereas tallymen tended to distribute tea from wholesalers who may or may not have adulterated their product with recycled tea. Labor concerns about those who picked tea leaves gained no traction in the face of fears about the undue exotic influence and possible adulteration of Chinese tea; as the tea trade turned toward the subcontinent and stock was reliably under British control throughout its production, localized class-derived anxieties arose about adulteration by unscrupulous purveyors and servants back in England, whose efforts to reuse or extend leaves left millions of Britons vulnerable to contamination.[12]

Women of the middle class and above were urged by such experts in domestic management as Eliza Warren and Mary Eliza Haweis to monitor carefully the use and disposal of such consumables as candles, tea leaves, etc., lest servants

---

[10]   Crole explains that, "Many years ago a cry was started about the impurities of some of the Chinese teas and the epithet 'lie' tea was sufficient to damn a certain class of teas, hailing from that country in our market … On the other hands, no charge of the admixture of any dye, or other and more repulsive impurities could be cast upon British-grown teas" (40).

[11]   See "The Scotch Tally-Trade" for an overview of how 10 to 12,000 born "north of the Tweed" sold tea and then garments door to door in England (214).

[12]   Servants ranging from the parlour-maid to housekeeper would have had access to recently used tea leaves, as they were regularly scattered over carpets before sweeping in an effort to capture dust and impart a clean odor to the room (see Beeton 990). The temptation to sell such castoffs may have been great, given the long hours and low wages of most domestics.

profit from household goods reserved for the family.[13] Erika Rappaport cites an 1843 Inland Revenue Office Report that lists how "at least eight manufacturers in London revived tea used by hotels, coffee houses and other public places" (131). The possibility of refuse such as used tea leaves re-entering the family's teapot went hand in hand with potential betrayal by the servant class. Whether one's own servants sold used household goods, or whether newly purchased tea was contaminated by another household's spent leaves, the domestic ideal fractured under the implicit conflict of interests associated with differing factions within a household. In short, tea's popularity raised incentives to game the industry, which in turn raised popular anxieties about the purity of both the product and its consumers. Given the broad range of tea for sale and the high risks of adulteration, it became a feminine accomplishment for women of all ranks to know from whom to buy good tea, what good tea should taste like, and how much it should cost. A woman's "taste" thus functions literally to safeguard the family's interests.

As middle-class identity became increasingly associated with conformity in housekeeping over the first half of the nineteenth century, access to good tea, made full strength and without reusing leaves, was a basic claim to bourgeois respectability. This is especially true in contrast to the growing importance of "tea" as a reward and nutritive mainstay of working families, for whom tea as a meal became part of the national diet. According to the social historian John Burnett, at midcentury working-class families consumed half a pound of tea per week at an estimated annual cost of £5 4s, "almost as much as they spent on meat and half the cost of rent" (59). The cost for tea was a necessary expense, as protein was typically reserved for the man of the house and then doled out to children. The late afternoon "tea" was the heaviest meal of the day, but in many laboring-class households, mothers would drink tea while distributing any portions of sausage, fish or bacon available to the rest of family. Andrea Broomfield explains in *Food and Cooking in Victorian England* that tea followed a strictly gendered division: "Most working-class wives, even if they too were employed, reserved the meat

---

[13]   See Warren's *Cookery for Maids of All Work* (1856) and *Comfort for Small Incomes* (1866) as well as Haweis's *The Art of Housekeeping* (1889). In her 1882 treatise, *Our Servants: Their Duties to Us and Ours to Them*, Mrs Eliot James explained that in contradiction to the prevailing view "I always give the servants the same tea as I drink myself. People may exclaim at the extravagance of this plan, but I do not look on it as the least extravagant, for I do not believe in the short-sighted economy of giving your servants a mixture you would not drink yourself" (172). While James is rare in advocating that the same tea be provided for all members of her household, her phrasing suggests that her role as lady of the house is overtly managerial, and that part of her duty is to maintain control of servants through the wise distribution of tea. Anne Brontë's portrait of domestic success via the Markham house in *The Tenant of Wildfell Hall* (1848) suggests that keeping a tight rein on servants was not simply a late-century concern: each afternoon a maid brings the tea tray into the parlour, but Gilbert Markham's sister Rose retrieves the tea and sugar from a locked cabinet and then prepares tea for the family and guests (9). Brontë clearly approves of the daughter of the house, and not the servant, controlling these high-ticket comestibles.

for their husbands; they also ensured that no matter what their tea might consist of food-wise, their husbands received the biggest portion of it" (86). As an unsigned October 8, 1864 article in Dickens's *All The Year Round* explains,

> The household faith is that 'the husband wins the bread and must have the best food.' His physical well-being is the prop of the house. If he has eaten up his remainder of meat or bacon by the middle of the week, and there be butter or cheese, he takes that for his dinner at the close of the week, and the wife and children at home are then reduced to dry bread, which is converted into a hot meal by the use of tea. (203)

In terms of quantity and sheer caloric input, men received the lion's share of the family's food, so sugared tea remained all the more central to most women's sustenance. As the national beverage, and especially given its role in the temperance movement, which saw its consumption as a saving grace for the working classes, tea became another site and mechanism through which existing economic and gender imbalances were reaffirmed. Because middle-class women embody the largesse and hospitality of the tea table, providing and serving tea acts as proof of the family's economic status and allegiance to bourgeois domesticity. Working-class women, on the other hand, follow the unstated expectation of self-denial, so that keeping a proper home becomes attached to a distribution of resources in which they rank themselves lowest.

Tea as Women's Work

Julie E. Fromer, in her fascinating study *A Necessary Luxury: Tea in Victorian England* (2008), describes the democratizing potential of the tea trade, exactly because everyone drank tea. Fromer cites an extraordinary passage from Samuel Day's *Tea: Its Mystery and History* (1878) as proof of her contentions:

> That all classes of the community in this country have derived much benefit from the persistent use of Tea, is placed beyond dispute. It has proved, and still proves, a highly prized boon to millions. The artist at his easel, the author at his desk, the statesman fresh from an exhaustive oration, the actor from the stage after fulfilling an arduous *role*, the orator from the platform, the preacher from the pulpit, the toiling mechanic, the weary labourer, the poor governess, the tired laundress, the humble cottage housewife, the votary of pleasure, even, upon escaping from the scene of revelry, nay, the Queen on her throne have, one and all, to acknowledge and express gratitude for the grateful and invigorating infusion. (63; qtd in Fromer 72)

Tea, it seems, can help and has helped everyone, and has become a uniquely British phenomenon, a national drink that fortifies the entire social structure from weary laborer, to governess, to statesman, to Queen. Any democratizing potential of the beverage, however, is belied by the class and gender specific ways in which tea was bought, used, controlled and consumed.

Paradoxically, though a favorite by all classes, tea was at its heart a bourgeois product. On the levels of aesthetics and etiquette, the way tea was served—the everyday versus good porcelain teapot; the quality of the silver; the sweets or savories that were provided; the time given to sit, chat, and sip, etc.—was revelatory about one's economic standing and claims to middle-class respectability. *Cranford* (1853) suggests as much when Mrs Jamieson's dog—but not her guests—rates cream for tea:

> Mrs Jamieson said she was certain we would excuse her if she gave her poor dumb Carlo his tea first … [A]nd then she told us how intelligent and sensible the dear little fellow was; he knew cream quite well, and constantly refused tea with only milk in it: so the milk was left for us; but we silently thought we were quite as intelligent and sensible as Carlo, and felt as if insult were added to injury when we were called upon to admire the gratitude evinced by his wagging his tail for the cream which should have been ours. (77–8)

Because their small community's economic pecking order privileges the more financially secure Mrs Jamieson, the unmarried women of Cranford remain silent about their hostess's breach of etiquette, though readers are invited to share their dismay at her abuse of station.

In sketching the intricacies of the daily lives of genteel but impoverished spinster ladies, Elizabeth Gaskell moves beyond wry humor in her invocation of the cultural clout of tea. Due to their age, gender, unmarried status, and small incomes, the ladies of Cranford are especially vulnerable to financial upset and slippage in class status, as any attempt to make money commercially would signal a significant break from the conventions upon which claims to gentility would be based. Despite the relentless scrutiny of their small and rigidly proscribed circle, however, the ladies endorse specific dispensations against the lowering effects of certain entrees into trade. Exactly because it is seen as feminine, tea in particular affords the opportunity for a woman above reproach to engage in commerce.[14] The socially coded rituals that surround the purchase and preparation of tea enable Matilda Jenkyns, the past middle-aged daughter of the former rector, who has been left alone and destitute by the deaths of her parents and sister and the failure of the Town and Country Bank, to establish herself as a tea purveyor. Because Miss Matty "did not think men ever bought tea" (142), the tea trade retains a gender-specific respectability that elevates it above simple buying and selling. Still Miss Matty begins her career in trade only after receiving Mrs Jamieson's approval,

---

[14] Gaskell's association of tea with femininity in early nineteenth-century culture is supported by an April 1888 report in the *British Medical Journal* on "Tea-Drinking" which asserts: "Eighty years ago, the practice was looked upon as a sign of effeminacy" (812).

for as the narrator Mary Smith reports: "whereas a married woman takes her husband's rank by the strict laws of precedence, an unmarried woman retains the station her father occupied" (143). Miss Matty cannot proceed without sanction, as her actions reflect upon her late father's claim to gentility as well as her own. Always the rector's daughter, Miss Matty also visits the other shopkeeper who stocks tea in Cranford to inquire whether her sales would harm his business; in contrast to the principles of capitalist competition, he sends customers her way for a higher grade of tea. *Cranford* makes clear that because of its associations with genteel femininity, the tea trade, especially of the more expensive teas that Miss Matty stocks, is less sullying than marketing many other commodities might be. Moreover, Miss Matty's reputation as a woman of "elegant economy" (3) who would never stoop to selling a compromised product confers additional respectability to her decision to open her home to the public via the small shop she sets up in her former dining room.

Miss Matty supports herself for over a year by selling more luxurious tea than is available in any other shop in town. When her long-lost brother Peter returns from his career in India and rescues Miss Matty from trade, the novel subtly emphasizes the tea trade's colonial origins: both tea and Peter derive their economic power from empire, and so when substituting for tea, Peter reiterates its colonial connections even while simultaneously reasserting the bread-winning role of the man of the house within conventional British domesticity. Whether traded from her former dining room or made manifest by the sudden reappearance of her brother, the spoils of colonialism support Miss Matty, who quickly closes shop and distributes her stock of sweets to the children and fine tea to the aged folks of Cranford.

Tea retained its bourgeois and gendered connotations from the midcentury onward, in that whether sold, bought, prepared, given away in bulk, or dispensed by the exquisite china cupful, tea was seen as women's work.[15] Examples from fiction of the period—in Charlotte Brontë (Miss Temple's tea party which comforts Helen and Jane), Elizabeth Gaskell (tea abounds in *Mary Barton* and *North and South* as well as in *Cranford*), or Henry James (Pansy's obsession with tea in *Portrait of a Lady*)—suggest that tea functioned as a material and consumable marker of propriety inextricable from the gender politics that situated bourgeois women's work within the home. Moreover, these texts rely on the unstated assumption that the woman of the middle-class house would serve tea, even if the tea was prepared by young daughters or servants.[16] Adopting the role of hostess

---

[15]   Kowaleski-Wallace and David Porter concur that the feminization of tea in the British imagination was an eighteenth-century phenomenon. In *The Chinese Taste in Eighteenth-Century England* (2010), Porter argues that by the 1720s the tea party functioned as "the preeminent site for the conspicuous display of a woman's taste and social status" (83).

[16]   Tea became associated with appropriate middle-class femininity and nurturing to such an extent that the phrase "to be mother" remains in use today to refer to the act of pouring tea.

by distributing tea thus demonstrates a young bourgeois woman's readiness to act as the woman of the house, announcing her eligibility for marriage.[17] In this way, daily rituals surrounding the proper preparation and presentation of tea speak to labor expectations for women on any number of class-bound levels: just as women of the working classes were expected to deny themselves food and women of the middle class and above were expected to dispense nurture and hospitality while quietly managing household staff, young bourgeois women were expected to ready themselves for marriage and, indeed, to advertise subtly their interest in the marriage mart via the teapot.

If tea encapsulates the idealized image of the home running smoothly and thus both fulfilling and replicating the cultural demand for a nurturing, middle-class domestic order, it simultaneously offers a romantic vision of the female labor of all kinds deemed necessary to create and maintain that home. The attention given to the lady of the house as she effortlessly pours tea erases her managerial responsibilities as well as the work of the female servants that makes the household function. Tea also erases and thus sanitizes the labor of the marriage market, as young women of respectable means are positioned as naturally ready to become wives and mothers, even as their role in preparing and distributing tea, preferably while flirtatiously promising later domestic bliss, shows their thorough training in feminine comportment and domestic administration. Such training in turn ensures the continuation of the respectable, middle-class home that stands as a bastion of British culture. Women can't be seen as angling for marriage or its attendant relative financial security, for open exposure of the economics that make single women like Matty Jenkyns vulnerable would make a young ingénue un- or less marriageable. The work that goes into preparing young women for their place in the domestic order must remain similarly unremarked upon, as a focus upon either their training or efforts to position themselves as bridal commodities would undermine the romanticized vision of courtship that lent allure to the cold hard facts of most women's economic dependency upon men and marriage.

Such dependency is emphasized further by men's participation in daily tea rituals, which Julie E. Fromer highlights through reference to George Gabriel Sigmond's *Tea: Its Effects, Medicinal and Moral*:

> Tea is more particularly adapted for the ordinary beverage of young women; and the individual who, until the day of her marriage, has never tasted wine, or any fermented liquor, is the one who is most likely to preserve her own health, and to fulfill the great end of her existence, the handing down to posterity a strong and well organized offspring, capable of adding to the improvement and to the welfare of the community. To preserve the form and beauty of the [female] sex

---

[17]   Referring to Pansy Osmond's initial plea to prepare and serve tea in *The Portrait of a Lady*, Victoria Coulson argues the similar point that "The tea ceremony has to do with feminine service: a daughter advertises herself as available for domestic appropriation" (84).

is a duty that man owes to himself, not for his sake alone, but for that of future generations. (117; qtd in Fromer 103)

Fromer sees Sigmond's text as indicative of men's need to control the consumption practices of women within their household. In privileging men's participation in tea rituals, however, Fromer's argument neglects the concomitant erasure of women's work and agency necessary to the specific passage quoted above as well as to the larger cultural ramifications of how tea functioned in the British imaginary during the period. Refocusing Fromer's argument, I posit instead that in addition to keeping women away from the dangers of alcohol, Sigmond's association of tea with both healthy offspring and the "welfare of the community" underscores "the great end of [women's] existence": *cultural* as well as familial reproduction. According to Sigmond's logic, young women should drink tea to protect their health and contributions—reproductive and otherwise—to British culture. At the same time, however, respect for young women's decision-making is removed, so that men assume responsibility for protecting the female sex from her own potential bad choices in drink or other matters. In this way, the imperial product of tea is once again reaffirmed as an everyday yet essential part of the bourgeois household, even as the ritual of tea drinking becomes a code for civilization and for women's conformity to conventional domesticity.

The romanticized image of the young woman of the house carefully pouring perfectly brewed tea into delicate china cups suggests a somatic as well as gustatory purity. Tea prepares these women to be good mothers, or as Sigmond puts it, "the efforts of Nature are almost invariably successful and the greater number of females are prepared to fulfill the destiny for which they are ordained" (118). What matters here is how a shared rhetoric of "the destiny for which they are ordained" underpins quite varied inequities *within* Britain's status quo. Preordained, supposedly "natural" distinctions of class and gender coalesce around the tea table to such an extent that they become part of the mystery, witchery and "magic harmony" Mary Elizabeth Braddon associates with Lady Audley's tea preparations. This magic overshadows both the labor and lack of agency demanded of women at every level of the household, instead perpetuating an image of ease, comfort and feminine beauty at the heart of the home. Concocting Britain's national drink thus requires tea leaves, boiling water, and participation in an idealized vision of bourgeois domesticity as the foundation of individual women's fulfillment, proper class divisions, and claims to national belonging.

Even as tea helped to prepare young women for the romance and magic of their place in the British home, the image of women's labor in the tea fields of Ceylon and northern India was harnessed to bolster tea's commercial appeal. Sir Thomas Lipton—a forerunner in the branding of tea—featured his plantations extensively in the packaging and advertising of his goods, thus marking each tin with the exotic locale associated with genuine, high quality teas. The plantation images, however, also assert colonial control in the form of both long, orderly rows of tea shrubs and the stooped figures, often female and dressed in white, pictured picking the leaves.

With the landscape and population governed by British industry, a romanticized, benevolent vision of tea production literally brands Lipton's teas, elevating the leaves to a symbol of imperial success for the colonial administrators, indigenous workers, mercantile investors, and consumers in the metropole alike.

Lipton's celebration of Ceylon as a site for tea emphasizes its plantation holdings (Lipton was a juggernaut in terms of cocoa, coffee and tea production), but occludes the fact that many of the workers were Tamils (an indigenous minority) and members of other exploited groups forced to relocate and work as wage slaves in tea cultivation.[18] Both men and women worked in the fields, but women were valued for their smaller hands, more "delicate" touch, and lower labor costs.[19] Indeed, because child care remained the province of women, children as young as five or six worked beside their mothers picking leaves, since it was established practice on Lipton's estates as well as others to absorb the entire family into the imperial labor force—and at a cut rate, moreover, for women and children did not receive the same kind of remuneration as male laborers, even when they performed exactly the same agricultural tasks.[20] The marketing of tea

---

[18] Workers were recruited by "sardars," independent agents who contracted their workers in aggregate to the plantations. Individual workers were bound to their contracts, usually for five years of service, but often they were not guaranteed promised wages, appropriate nutrition, or safe housing. According to Anandi Ramamurthy, between 1841 and 1849 colonial administrators estimated that a "quarter of Tamil immigrants to Ceylon, indentured to work in tea plantations, died" (109). Nor did the Coolie Acts of 1882 resolve the high mortality rates on tea plantations. During a September 21, 1893 House of Commons debate on Britain's role in legislating labor concerns on tea plantations, Charles Schwann, MP for Manchester North, declared that "coolie labour in Assam was practically a state of slavery" (*Hansard's*, "East India Revenue Accounts" 1828). As support, Schwann quoted a report by the Deputy Commissioner of Sylhet in Assam, Mr Stevenson, which held: "In this matter the law appears entirely one-sided. Everything is in favour of the employer. A labour contract purporting to have been signed by the coolie, but either not executed by him, or executed under a misapprehension, is sent in for registration under Section 111, and registered. It may not be verified for a year afterwards, and suppose it is then canceled, what compensation does the unfortunate coolie receive? He has been, one may say, in wrongful confinement for a year, forced to labour for a màster who had no claim to his services, and liable, if he tried to escape from his *quasi*-slavery, to be pursued, arrested, and sent up for trial like a common criminal, or worse, as these even cannot, in all cases, be held without a warrant" (1828).

[19] According to Rhoda Reddock and Shobhita Jain, on Sri Lankan tea estates well into the twentieth century "plucking, the most labour-intensive task on the tea estate and one which is of highest importance," is done by women because the "estate management prefers to employ women for this job. Both plucking and tipping, done by women, are closely supervised by male foremen (*kangani*)" (12). Women, however, are paid much less than men for their work and are subject to close scrutiny by the *kangani* in and out of the fields. See Crole 204–5; Ramamurthy 119–126; and Reddock and Jain.

[20] Crole reports that children at five or six years help their mothers pick leaves and earn a monthly wage of three shillings for their efforts (203).

leaves through portraits of civilized cultivation—not limited to Lipton—erases the labor and working conditions of these women even as it perpetuates the rhetoric of empire as a humanizing mission, one that women at home should support through their purchases.

Implicit in any Lipton ad is the argument that due to its stringent control of the means of production, consumers trusting Lipton's would avoid adulteration even while contributing to the well-being of workers in the fields. Not all of the women figured in Lipton's ads, however, were shown picking the leaves or waiting for their bundles to be weighed. The following advertisement from *The Illustrated London News* (23 May, 1893) is significant for how the young native girl is figured as drinking tea versus working the fields (Figure 6.1).[21]

Lipton's teas "rich, pure, and fragrant" are available "direct from the tea garden"—the vast Lipton plantation holdings in Ceylon—"to the teapot." Their good taste and purity are represented by the heavily jeweled young woman in South Asian dress, appreciating the cup of Lipton's tea held in her hand. Proclaiming the authenticity of Lipton's products, her appearance, however, belies the experiences of those who actually picked the tea. Part of the wages paid to workers came in the form of tea dust and rice distributed in advance, so that workers remained in perpetual debt to their employers. They could not leave the plantation without permission by owners or overseers, as doing so would be the equivalent of theft for the sustenance that they had not yet labored to repay. The woman figured here, though, replicates a highly romanticized vision of leisure and discerning choice of tea, even as her eerily diminutive hand aligns her with middle-class rather than working-class British femininity. For both the fictive woman pictured in Lipton's advertisement and the bourgeois women in Britain to whom the ad is directed, the mystique of femininity acts as a smoke screen for how their common exploitation is intertwined. Despite their limited agency as tea buyers, British women remain tied to acquiescence and the tea table even as Tamil women workers experience a late-century wage slavery that keeps them tied to the fields without legal redress. The most labor-intensive element of the imperial tea trade—the actual plucking and carrying of the leaves—is women's work, but exactly because it is native women's work, it is erased, only to be replaced with a sanitized image of domestic pleasure. All of these factors coalesce to keep women in Britain aligned with conservative behaviors and gender expectations, while simultaneously rewarding them for their participation in imperialism.

I close my analysis with reference to Ella Hepworth Dixon's *The Story of a Modern Woman* (1894), when Mary, a "new woman" who must support herself after the death of her father, realizes that her guest to tea, the man for whom she has been waiting, has little intention of marrying her:

---

[21]   In her analysis of a different version of this Lipton advertisement (from *The Graphic*, 10 September, 1892) that uses the same image, Ramamurthy emphasizes the figure's sexualized exoticism rather than her cross-class appeal.

Figure 6.1   Direct from the Tea Garden to the Tea Pot. Rich, Pure & Fragrant
Source: The Illustrated London News, 23 May, 1893.

There was a silence which Mary, as hostess, did her best to break. She did not look at him in the eyes any more during his visit. It was almost as if he had struck her. There was a sort of ball in her throat. Her cheeks had got hot; there was colour enough in them now, and her hands shook as she poured out the tea which the maid-of-all-work had brought in. But she must not look as if she cared. A woman—especially in her own house—should always smile. It was on that acquiescent feminine smile that the whole fabric of civilisation rested. And for the next half-hour, as Vincent Hemming discoursed of the unusual opportunities he had enjoyed in Calcutta, in Sydney, and in Ottawa of studying the different systems of government which obtained in various parts of the British Empire, Mary was a model hostess. (166)

Mary knows her duty, and while Vincent might drone on about empire, her job is to smile as she serves tea, for on that "acquiescent female smile ... the whole fabric of civilisation rested." In parallel with Lipton's advertising logic, any violence or coercion inherent in imperial trade is erased, replaced by the image of the smiling English woman offering tea, Britishness, and middle-class allegiance in equal measure.

Works Cited

Anon. "Leaves from the Mahogany Tree: A Cup of Tea." *All the Year Round* 25 July, 1868: 153–6. Web.

Anon. "The Lives and Deaths of the People." *All the Year Round* 8 October, 1864: 198–205. Web.

Arnold, Thomas. "Arnold's Lectures on History." *Blackwood's Edinburgh Magazine* 328.53 (February, 1843): 141–64. Print.

Beeton, Isabella. *The Book of Household Management.* London: S.O. Beeton, 1863. Print.

Braddon, Mary Elizabeth. *Lady Audley's Secret.* NY: Oxford University Press, 1987. Print.

Brontë, Anne. *The Tenant of Wildfell Hall.* NY: Oxford University Press, 2008. Print.

Brontë, Charlotte. *Jane Eyre.* NY: Oxford University Press, 2001. Print.

Broomfield, Andrea. *Food and Cooking in Victorian England: A History.* Westport, CT: Praeger Publishing, 2007. Print.

Browne, Charles. "The Ethnography of Ballycroy, County Mayo." *Proceedings of the Royal Irish Academy* 4 (1896–98): 74–111. Web.

Burnett, John. *Liquid Pleasures: A Social History of Drinks in Modern Britain.* NY: Routledge, 1999. Print.

Carlyle, Thomas. "Occasional Discourse on the Nigger Question." *Critical and Miscellaneous Essays* Vol. 16. NY: Peter Fenelon Collier, Publishing, 1897: 461–94. Print.

Chatterjee, Piya. *A Time for Tea: Women, Labor, and Post/Colonial Politics on an Indian Plantation.* Durham NC: Duke University Press, 2001. Print.

Coulson, Victoria. "Teacups and Love: Constance Fenimore and Henry James." *The Henry James Review* 26.1 (Winter 2005): 82–98. Web.

Crole, David. *Tea: A Text Book of Tea Planting and Manufacture.* London: Crosby Lockwood and Son, 1897. Print.

Day, Samuel. *Tea: Its Mystery and History.* London: Simpkin, Marshall and Co., 1878. Print.

De Quincey, Thomas. "The English in China." *The Uncollected Writings of Thomas De Quincey.* Vol. 2. (ed.) James Hogg. NY: Scribner and Wellford, 1890. 7–36. Print.

Dixon, Ella Hepworth. *The Story of a Modern Woman.* NY: Cassell Publishing, 1894. Print.

"Food and Its Adulterations (Rev.)." *London Quarterly Review* 97 (January to April, 1855): 237–55. Web.

Fromer, Julie E. *A Necessary Luxury: Tea in Victorian England.* Athens, OH: Ohio University Press, 2008. Print.

Gaskell, Elizabeth. *Cranford.* NY: Oxford University Press, 1992. Print.

Gaskell, Elizabeth. *Mary Barton.* NY: Oxford University Press, 2009. Print.

Gaskell, Elizabeth. *North and South.* NY: Oxford University Press, 2008. Print.

Griffiths, John. *Tea: The Drink That Changed the World.* London: André Deutsch, 2007. Print.

Hansard's Parliamentary Debates. London: TC Hansard, 1803–2005. Web.

Hansard's Parliamentary Debates. "East India Revenue Accounts." HC Deb. 21 September, 1893. Vol 17. cc 1794–894. Web.

Haweis, Mary Eliza. *The Art of Housekeeping: A Bridal Garland.* London: Sampson and Low, 1889. Print.

Inglis, Brian. *The Opium War.* London: Hodder and Stoughton, 1976. Print.

Jain, Shobhita, and Rhoda Reddock (eds) *Women Plantation Workers: International Experiences.* NY: Berg, 1998. Print.

James, Mrs A.G.F. Eliot. *Our Servants: Their Duties to Us and Ours to Them.* London: Ward, Lock and Co., 1882. Print.

James, Henry. *The Portrait of a Lady.* NY: Penguin, 2003. Print.

Kowaleski-Wallace, Elizabeth. *Consuming Subjects: Women, Shopping and Business in the Eighteenth Century.* NY: Columbia University Press, 1997. 19–36. Print.

Marx, Karl. *Capital: A Critique of Political Economy.* Vol 1. Trans. Samuel Morse and Edward Aveling. Chicago: Charles H. Kerr and Co., 1921. Print.

Mayhew, Henry. *London Labour and the London Poor.* London: Charles Griffin and Co., 1864. Print.

Miller, Ian. "'A Dangerous Revolutionary Force Amongst Us': Conceptualizing Working-Class Tea Drinking in the British Isles, *c.* 1860–1900." *Cultural and Social History* 10.3 (2013): 419–38. Web.

Mintz, Sidney W. *Sweetness and Power: The Place of Sugar in Modern History.* NY: Penguin, 1985. Print.

Moxham, Roy. *Tea: Addiction, Exploitation and Empire.* NY: Carroll & Graf Publishers, 2003. Print.

Porter, David. *The Chinese Taste in Eighteenth-Century England.* Cambridge: Cambridge University Press, 2010. Print.

Ramamurthy, Anandi. *Imperial Persuaders: Images of Africa and Asia in British Advertising.* Manchester and NY: Manchester University Press, 2003. Print.

Rappaport, Erika. "Packaging China: Foreign Articles and Dangerous Tastes in the Mid-Victorian Tea Party." *The Making of the Consumer: Knowledge, Power and Identity in the Modern World* (ed.) Frank Trentmann. Oxford: Berg, 2006: 125–46. Print.

Reddock, Rhoda and Shobhita Jain. "Plantation Women: An Introduction." *Women Plantation Workers: International Experiences* (eds) S. Jain and R. Reddock. NY: Berg, 1998. 1–16. Print.

Schmitt, Cannon. "Narrating National Addictions: De Quincey, Opium and Tea." *High Anxieties: Cultural Studies in Addiction* (eds) Janet Farrell Brodie and Marc Redfield. Los Angeles: University of California Press, 2002. 63–84. Print.

"Tea and Coffee, 1900." *Parliamentary Papers.* 1902 HC (351) LXX. 363. Web.

"The Scotch Tally-Trade." *Chamber's Journal of Popular Literature, Science and Arts,* 15 (April 6, 1861): 214–16. Web.

Sharma, Jayeeta. *Empire's Garden: Assam and the Making of India*. Durham NC: Duke University Press, 2011. Web.

Sigmond, George Gabriel. *Tea: Its Effects, Medicinal and Moral*. London: Longman, Orme, Browne, Green and Longmans, 1839. Web.

South Briton. "Observations on the Effects of Tea." *The Gentleman's Magazine*, 7 (April, 1737): 213–14. Web.

Wakefield, Edward Gibbon. "England and America." 1833 *The Collected Works of Edward Gibbon Wakefield* (ed.) M.F.L. Pritchard. Glasgow and London: Collins, 1968. 317–430. Print.

Warren, Eliza. *Cookery for Maids of All Work*. London: Groombridge and Sons, 1856. Print.

Warren, Eliza. *Comfort for Small Incomes*. London: Office of The Ladies' Treasury, 1866. Print.

Warrington, Robert. "The Coloration and Glazing of the Teas of Commerce." *The Edinburgh Medical and Surgical Journal* 79 (1853): 373–81. Web.

Waugh, Alec. *The Lipton Story*. NY: Doubleday, 1950. Print.

Yeo, Isaac Burney. *A Manual of Medical Treatment or Clinical Therapeutics*. Vol. 1. London: Cassell and Co., 1893. Web.

PART III:
Imperial Possessions, Commodity Culture, and Colonial Return

Chapter 7

"A cross, a lion and a scroll or two": The Victoria Cross and the Substance of British Imperial Identity

Jason Howard Mezey

The Times reported that the morning of June 26, 1857—the day Queen Victoria awarded the first batch of Victoria Crosses to a parade of recipients in London's Hyde Park—was hot. The warm and humid week averaged 82°, reaching its high point of 92.5° on the 28th (R. Thomson 191–2). *The Times* coverage emphasized the discomfort of those attending the ceremony, especially the vast majority without access to the inner circle of galleries. The class lines in Hyde Park were unmistakably drawn:

> [N]earest to Grosvenor-gate galleries were erected for the accommodation of 7,000 persons, who by a pleasing fiction were denominated the public, though, of course, the distribution of the tickets which admitted to the enclosure was as exclusive as a presentation at Court ... On either side of Her Majesty's position were smaller galleries for the members of the Legislature and Corps Diplomatique, who in virtue of their office were accommodated with seats, while the other portion of the galleries gave only standing room. All the rest of the ground round the enclosed space was left open to the public, who had the usual general license to see as they best could, which, as it happened, was very little indeed. ("Distribution" 5)

The emphasis on the uncomfortable crowd conditions—"in some parts 30 and 40 deep ... under a broiling sun"—established that the crowd was not there to witness the ceremony but to ratify it: "The public, in fact, seemed only invited to contribute a great crowd to the proceedings of the day. They formed a most important portion of the show, and must rest content with having fulfilled that duty, for, as far as the majority of them were concerned, the whole ceremonial might as well have taken place at Stonehenge" ("Distribution" 5). For the attending public, the theme of the morning was the denial of spectacle, a knife twisted all the more cruelly by the Cross itself, "with which all found more or less fault at the very first" ("Distribution" 5). The description that follows spares no sarcasm in depicting these faults:

Than the Cross of Valour nothing can be more plain and homely, not to say coarse-looking. It is a very small Maltese cross, formed from the gun metal of ordnance captured at Sebastopol. In the centre is a small crown and lion, with which latter's natural proportion of mane and tail the cutting of the cross much interferes. Below these is a small scroll (which shortens three of the arms of the cross and is utterly out of keeping with the upper portions) bearing the words, 'For Valour.' Mr Hancock was at first ordered to strike a hundred crosses with steel dies, but the intense hardness of the metal destroyed the dies, and it was at last found necessary to cast them and chase them afterwards. But even with all the care and skill which distinguishes Mr Hancock, the whole cross is, after all, poor looking and mean in the extreme. The merit of the design, we believe, is due to the same illustrious individual who once invented a hat. ("Distribution" 5)

The article found its target not in the symbolism of the Cross itself—which is commended as potentially having "done more towards maintaining the high efficiency of our army than any military distinction founded since the days of Marlborough" ("Distribution" 5)—but rather in both the ceremony surrounding it and the object itself. In other words, *The Times* applauds the recognition of British combat bravery, but suggests that the processionals and emblems of that recognition fell laughably short.

As the Queen awarded these decorations, almost 6,000 miles away a crucial event in Anglo-Indian history was unfolding—the surrender and subsequent massacre of the British contingent in Cawnpore. Cawnpore was a key garrison for the East India Company; it held over 1,000 when it came under attack by rebel forces in early June 1857 (M. Thomson 23). Three weeks of constant bombardment by Nana Sahib's troops had weakened the defenses, which were not prepared for a lengthy siege. Conditions within the garrison were becoming increasingly desperate for the British troops and civilians, hundreds of whom were women and children. On June 26, prompted by the urging of Captain John Moore, General Hugh Wheeler accepted Nana Sahib's proffered terms for surrender, which at first—according to survivor Lt. Mowbray Thomson—consisted of a brief letter: "All those who are in no way connected with the acts of Lord Dalhousie, and are willing to lay down their arms, shall receive a safe passage to Allahabad" (150). The British requested the "honorable surrender of our shattered barracks and free exit under arms, with sixty rounds of ammunition per man; carriages to be provided for the conveyance of the wounded, the women and the children; boats furnished with flour to be ready at the [ghat]" (153). By the time the medal ceremony was reported in *The Times* the following day, many of those who filed down to the Satichaura Ghat (dock) to board boats for their safe passage to Allahabad had been killed in an ambush. The remnants (save a handful of survivors who were able to swim or paddle to safety) would be imprisoned and then murdered two and a half weeks later in the second Cawnpore Massacre, in the infamous Bibighar, where their bodies were disposed of in a dry well.

The simultaneity of the celebratory distribution of the first Victoria Crosses for Valour and the horrifying traumas of the Satichaura Ghat Massacre represents two extremes in Britain's midcentury imperial experience: the ceremony of British imperial success as a staged, royal spectacle versus the deadly violence brought about by the Empire's inability to protect its soldiers and citizens abroad, particularly its women and children. Examining both the material history and the symbolic stature of the Victoria Cross brings these extremes into sharper focus. Born from the logistical failures of military command in the Crimea, the Victoria Cross since its inception has been the embodiment of a democratizing gesture. Any British soldier may win a VC, regardless of rank. At the same time, however, the establishment of the VC attempts to preserve the royal prerogative to remain at the center of British imperialism even while the military was changing into a professional fighting force under civilian command. The physical and ideological substance of this most prestigious decoration tells a history of the British Empire that is built on the strategic evocation of valor as a means of both glorifying the common British soldier while ultimately distracting from the privations of military life and more broadly from the costs of imperial interventions in foreign lands.

The order and decorum of the Hyde Park ceremony achieved its gravitas from the presence of both the queen and the milling crowds, suggesting the support of all England that the new British military honor may be earned by common soldiers. Those who received the first VCs in Hyde Park had fought in the Crimea, a war notorious for command mismanagement and cavalier leadership by senior officers. The VC's acknowledgement that personal gallantry and heroism occurs at every level of military service suggests that valor is a British trait rather than one of class or pedigree. In its invocation of British bravery, the VC reinforced Britain's right to rule, especially important as another imperial challenge, the Sepoy Rebellion, threatened the economic superiority of the East India Company and exposed fissures in the thin ice upon which Honourable John already stood.

First proposed in December 1854 by Captain G.T. Scobell in the House of Commons as an Order of Merit "to be bestowed upon persons serving in the Army or Navy for distinguished and prominent personal gallantry ... to which every grade and individual may be admissible," the VC has never been an everyday object (*Hansard's*, "Medal"). The royal warrant for the VC states that as "there exists no means of adequately rewarding the individual gallant services" of those in the military, the Victoria Cross was instituted to recognize and reward "individual instances of merit and valour" (Smith 207). The wording of these foundational documents concerning the purpose of the VC is significant. Implicit in the calls for the VC are claims to "gallantry" as a kind of broader British cultural inheritance, connecting every man in Britain to a gentlemanly tradition of imperial fortitude and chivalry. Gallantry endows imperial warfare with a potent gendered script: that any soldier or sailor—regardless of rank, class, or station—when needed, may act decisively and with self-sacrifice to protect Crown, country, and the gentler sex.

The meaning of the VC, however, remains rhetorical. Examining the VC as a thing—a thing, moreover, that resists its symbolic intent—reveals the insufficiency of its democratic potential. By definition, the VC is exceptional even while purporting to represent the martial valor that animates every element of British society. Because it is exceptional, the VC occludes the experiences of common soldiers and sailors, many of whom faced poverty during and after their years of service. This chapter attends to the circumstances under which British valor was demonstrated during the Sepoy Rebellion of 1857, particularly the military and cultural imperatives that made a single battle on a single day—the storming of the Sikander Bagh on November 16, 1857—such a defining moment for the Victoria Cross. However, the production of the Cross itself reflects its tenuous place as an object made exalted by its imperial history. Queen Victoria and Prince Albert were astute in their insistence that the VC not be made out of any precious metal, as doing so would suggest that its value might emanate from the physical substance of the medal itself, making it precious as a commodity. Instead, they relied on the alchemy of service to queen and country to turn a very humble, poorly refined bronze into the rarest and most valuable military decoration in the realm. In this way, the VC represents a larger transformative process in which an object's value becomes precious and commodified at least in part because of its initial resistance to commodification. Its meaning as an object becomes further destabilized when accounting for the experiences of the British soldiers who returned home from combat to find their pay withheld, their medical care inconsistent and expensive, and their pensions inadequate. Ultimately, a close analysis of the VC reveals that despite its symbolic import, there was insufficient structural support by military or government officials to provide for the common soldiers upon which the empire depended.

The Origins of the Victoria Cross

In *Awarded for Valour*, Melvin Charles Smith situates the birth of the Victoria Cross at a historical crossroads: "A combination of political uncertainty, royal anxiety, and public outrage came together to create the Victoria Cross. At the heart of these was the controversy concerning the Army's performance in the Crimean War" (29). The Victoria Cross, according to Smith, assuaged all of this uncertainty, anxiety, and outrage, primarily by serving as a public relations bandage for a military apparatus that had been pilloried for its appalling failures in the Crimea.

The incompetence of the British venture in the Crimea has been widely discussed, most significantly by William Howard Russell, the embedded *Times* war correspondent, who in writing about the winter of 1855 describes inadequate clothing and shelter, and a food supply lost to looting by marauding Zouaves (156). Russell spares few details:

> Think of a tent pitched, as it were, at the bottom of a marsh, into which some
> twelve or fourteen miserable creatures, drenched to the skin, had to creep for
> shelter after twelve hours of vigil in a trench like a canal, and then reflect what

state these poor fellows must have been in at the end of a night and day spent in such *shelter*, huddled together without any change of clothing, and lying packed up as close as they could be stowed in saturated blankets. (157)

Many more British died in the Crimea of disease, exposure, and malnutrition than of battle wounds. For Russell, the chief evil resided in the military bureaucracy: "We were cursed by a system of 'requisitions, orders, and memos,' which was enough to depress an army of scriveners, and our captains, theoretically, had almost as much work to do with pen and paper as if they had been special correspondents or bankers' clerks" (155).

The Victoria Cross cannot be divorced from this history of mismanagement, a fact that testifies to the challenge Queen Victoria and Prince Albert faced: to preserve royal influence over the military, even while calls to reform that same military structure under civilian leadership grew louder. Perhaps recognizing that the Crown's symbolism would surmount any barriers between royal and civilian oversight, Victoria and Albert focused on the more emotionally charged awarding of medals as opposed to the more practical military reform undertaken by Parliament. The Victoria Cross was thus the material consequence of a declining royal prerogative to govern the military.

In *The Destruction of Lord Raglan*, Christopher Hibbert chronicles Queen Victoria's obsession with details of the Crimea campaign, which found a particular focus on military decorations:

> Her correspondence with Lord Panmure is full of this. From 28 February until 18 May, when she awarded them herself, she mentions them in almost every letter. 'The Queen said to her wounded Guards when she saw them, she hoped that they would soon have their medals' (28/2/1855); 'When will the medals be ready?' (5/3/1855); 'The Queen has since thought that the value of the medals would be greatly enhanced if *she* were *personally* to deliver them' (22/3/1855); 'How are the medals getting on?' (1/4/1855); 'The Queen wishes to know whether it would be possible for her to distribute the medals *any day* next week?' (14/5/1855). (256n)

Victoria rightly assessed not only the importance of decorations for the maintenance of morale, but also that their status would be elevated if she bestowed them personally. Placing her royal imprimatur on the medals had other implications as well. At stake, Smith argues, was the Queen's role as Commander-in-Chief and the extent to which the position would be under Crown or Parliamentary control. Victoria's position was delicate, as Smith points out, since defending the military status quo in light of the Crimean disaster would never redound to the Crown's benefit (34). The solution, then, was to trade direct authority for symbolic capital, making the institution of the Victoria Cross a face-saving measure that allowed the Crown to have the prestigious role of celebrating the troops while not challenging the civilian reorganization of the military.

This ambivalence was mirrored in the staging of the first conferring ceremony, as noted by *The Times* coverage: the public was invited to play a part in a spectacle to which they were physically if not officially denied access. The symbolic conscription of the British population as ratifiers of the Victoria Cross was engineered to solicit the public's continued support of the imperial enterprise (while also—it was hoped—leading to an increase in enlistments). As news from the Sepoy Rebellion inundated the British press and people, however, England's self-conceptions of British military, racial, and most vitally domestic superiority became threatened. The specter of Indian troops in open revolt against the East India Company was a trial by fire for the British imperial enterprise, troubling the assumptions of heroism and imperial success contained in the VC.

"I think now I shall never stop, if I get a chance again": Race, Gender and Vengeance after Cawnpore

If the ceremony of June 26th in Hyde Park comprised an initial investment in the Victoria Cross as a means to broaden public support for the Victorian military, it yielded its desired return almost five months later. On November 16th, 1857 Sir Colin Campbell effected the second relief of Lucknow, successfully evacuating the remaining British soldiers and civilians by routing enemy forces in intense fighting at two separate (and heavily fortified) locations en route to the embattled Residency.[1] November 16th stands as the day of combat for which the largest number of VCs has been conferred since the Crimean Battle of Inkerman. British soldiers and sailors showed significant bravery that day while operating under conditions of heavy fire. However, the battle outlines and military significance of the Lucknow siege and relief were not exceptional.[2] Campbell admitted that he was unable to accomplish more on the battlefield than reaching and evacuating the besieged Residency; however, such goals were in fact superseded by the imperatives of the rescue mission: "Until the wounded and women are in my camp, the real business of the contest cannot go on, and all the efforts of Government are paralysed" (Shadwell 455–6; qtd in Watson 74–5).

The cultural weight of the Victoria Cross in its infancy is tied to the outsized role the Second Relief of Lucknow, and specifically the Sikander Bagh battle, played in the Mutiny. Any historical analysis of the British heroics in Lucknow that the VC commemorated must attend to the precipitating events at Cawnpore.

---

[1]   In a further coincidence, Campbell had attended the Victoria Cross ceremony in a highly visible official capacity—"The whole of the troops assembled to be under the command of Lieutenant-General Sir Colin Campbell, G.C.B." ("Distribution of Medals in Hyde Park" 9).

[2]   Lucknow's military importance emerged when it became a rallying place for mutineers and a target for British forces to recapture in 1858, but not when Campbell abandoned the city in November 1857, having accomplished his more limited mission.

In his memoir, Mowbray Thomson—one of the two survivors of the Satichaura Ghat massacre who lived to return to Britain—describes Cawnpore as a thriving garrison town located on the bank of the Ganges that was particularly important for its position in defending Oudh (Awadh) against possible invasions from the south:

> Merchants, travellers, faquirs, camels, bullocks, horses, go and come incessantly ... The great Trunk Road which passes close by the city, brings up daily relay of travellers and detachments of troops to the northwards, all of whom halt at Cawnpore, and the railroad, which is now complete from Allahabad, will yet further enhance the busy traffic at this station. The cantonments have not unfrequently contained as many as 6,000 troops, and these increased by the crowd of camp followers have made the population of the military bazaars 50,000 in number. (20–21)

British soldiers lived comfortably in a station separate from Indians in the nearby town, which Thomson describes as "densely packed and closely built as all the human hives of the East are" (21). On the European side, the residents included officers in command of the sepoy troops stationed there, plus foot soldiers and artillerymen, totaling about 300 (M. Thomson 23). There was also a civilian population composed of "the wives, children, and native servants of the officers; 300 half caste children belonging to the Cawnpore school; merchants (some European and others Eurasians); shopkeepers, railway officials, and their families" (ibid.). This mixed population, particularly with women and children integrated into the military population, rendered Cawnpore a particularly troubling target. As S.N. Sen claims, the presence of families limited Major General Hugh Wheeler's ability to evacuate: "Unlike other stations in the North-Western Provinces, Kanpur had a large European and Christian population. Many officers of Her Majesty's 32nd Regiment, then posted at Lucknow, had left their families there, and Wheeler could not expect to remove them to a place of safety in the face of his sepoys, should they prove hostile" (130). Shoring up fortifications, preparing for a siege, and desperately hoping for reinforcements were Wheeler's only options.

Because British reinforcements arrived only after the Satichaura Ghat and the Bibighar massacres, the garrison endured regular bombardments, raids, and counter-raids, causing widespread death due to wounds, illness, and privation. With the garrison in such a parlous state, the surrender terms offered (giving up weapons in return for safe conduct to Allahabad) occasioned a debate that was settled in consideration of the women of the cantonment:

> Sir Hugh Wheeler, still hopeful of relief from Calcutta, and suspicious of treachery on the part of the Nana, for a long time most strenuously opposed the idea of making terms; but upon the representation that there were only three days' rations in store, and after the often-reiterated claims of the women and children, and the most deplorable destitution in which we were placed, he at last

succumbed to Captain Moore's expostulations, and consented to the preparation of a treaty of capitulation. (Thomson 150)

The argument about women and children won the day, although Thomson adds that he and his fellow junior officers sided with Wheeler about rejecting surrender: "Had there been only men there, I am sure we should have made a dash for Allahabad rather than have thought of surrender" (150).

Thomson was particularly sensitive about post-mutiny charges of unmanliness for not resisting to the last European standing, scolding that critics should

> take into consideration in their wine-and-walnut arguments, the famished sucklings, the woe-worn women, who awaited the issue of those deliberations, and perhaps even they will admit, as all true soldiers and sensible citizens have done, that there remained nothing better for our leaders to do than to hope the best from an honourable capitulation. (151)

Thomson's invocation of armchair aversion to surrender firmly plants such ideals in the "olden times" (151). A newer form of heroism, and indeed by extension a newer form of imperial masculinity, tilts in favor of surrender for the sake of "famished sucklings" and "woe-worn women." Thomson recounts in gory detail the manner in which women were worn down by more than woe: they were subject to the same hunger, thirst, disease, and wounds as their men, and often stepped in as ammunition handlers for the soldiers in the trenches and nurses for the wounded behind the fortifications (99–104). On the morning of June 27, however, many women and children—symbols of England's domestic footprint in colonized lands—died when Nana Sahib's forces opened fire on their boats.

Colonel James Neill, who was in Benares, was responsible for leading the relief force that was expected to save the Cawnpore garrison. S.N. Sen attributes the crucial delay in reaching Cawnpore to Neill's bloodlust in putting down the rebellion in Allahabad. By punishing both the civilian and military populations alike, Neill rendered potential supporters hostile and drove away Indians upon whom the British might have ordinarily relied for material support. Andrew Ward shares this assessment, specifying Neill's ill-conceived targeting of a loyal regiment in Benares for disarming and his subsequent executions of suspected rebels as responsible for his failure to provide reinforcements to Cawnpore in the west (256). By the time Neill prepared to mobilize towards Cawnpore, he had been replaced by Henry Havelock, who received a report on July 15th that the survivors of the Satichaura Ghat massacre had been taken prisoner. Encouraging his men the following morning to "[t]hink of our women and the tender infants in the power of those devils incarnate," Havelock fought another battle on the 16th, this time against a force commanded by Naha Sahib himself (Ward 399).

On the following day, Havelock heard rumors of the infamous Bibighar massacre, which were later proven correct. There are gory details aplenty to be read in narratives of the discovery of the massacre site and the well in which many victims were found.[3] A morbidly fascinated British public was anxious to revisit these details and even invent new and more lurid ones, but as John Walter Sherer points out (to his credit) as a witness, "[t]he whole story was so unspeakably horrible that it would be quite wrong in any sort of way to increase the distressing circumstances which really existed. And I may say once and for all that the accounts were exaggerated" (154).[4] During his visit to the battle sites of the Sepoy Rebellion, William Howard Russell both captured the emotional weight of the events at Cawnpore and remained dispassionate in analyzing the basis of this emotion:

> In fact, the peculiar aggravation of the Cawnpore massacres was this, that the deed was done by a subject race—by black men who dared to shed the blood of their masters, and that of poor helpless ladies and children. Here we had not only a servile war and a sort of Jacquerie combined, but we had a war of religion, a war of race, and a war of revenge, of hope, of some national promptings to shake off the yoke of a stranger, and to re-establish the full power of native chiefs, and the full sway of native religions ... Whatever the causes of the mutiny and the revolt, it is clear enough that one of the modes by which the leaders, as if by common instinct, determined to effect their end was, the destruction of every white man, woman, or child who fell into their hands—a design which the kindliness of the people, or motives of policy, frustrated on many remarkable occasions ... But philosophize and theorize as we may, Cawnpore will be a name ever heard by English ears with horror long after the present generation has passed away. (*India Diary* 164–5)

The horror of Cawnpore, then, was not solely confined to the scale and severity of the violence itself, but also to its visibility as an instance of racial conflict in which British men, women, and children were massacred by treachery at the hands of those perceived as an inferior race.[5] Russell's diagnosis asserts that this outcry accentuates the uneasy British consciousness of its presence and role in India.

---

[3] See Ward 427–9.

[4] See Priti Joshi on the impact of the Mutiny on Dickens in his writing of *A Tale of Two Cities*. See also Brantlinger, 202–8 and Sharpe, 63–9.

[5] For greater consideration of the Massacre from a rebel perspective, see Rudrangshu Mukherjee's "'Satan Let Loose upon Earth': The Kanpur Massacres in India in the Revolt of 1857." Mukherjee discusses the racial politics of the Satichaura Ghat Massacre as follows: "Everybody present was implicated in the violence, either directly or as a part of a crowd that watched and exulted. The massacre was a collective affair: an expression of an entire society's hatred and rejection of an alien order. It was a spectacle of rebel power" (110).

The fall of Cawnpore was not solely an inglorious military defeat that called into question Britain's assumptions of racial superiority, but also one freighted with the additional burdens of twice failing to protect British women and children.

> The paramount mission of men like Willie Halliday [Captain, 56th Native Infantry] and Charles Hillersdon [Collector and Magistrate, Cawnpore District] had not been to promote commerce or administer justice or reform Indian society but to make India—especially its cantonments and thoroughfares—safe for their womenfolk. And at no place more than at Cawnpore had Anglo-Indian manhood so utterly failed to accomplish this fundamental mission. The soldiers' grief and outrage thus mingled with an intolerable sense of humiliation and guilt. (Ward 438)

Army Engineer Arthur Moffatt Lang, who was recommended three times for the VC, amplifies Ward's point in his memoirs:

> In the compound stands a tree, marked with bullet holes and sword gashes; in the latter is still long hair; amongst the grass and bushes of the compound, between the house and well, are still strips of clothing and locks of long hair; into that well upwards of 200 bodies of women and children were thrown, many still alive. No one who has seen that spot can ever feel anything but deep hatred to the Nana and his fellow fiends and all his fellow race ... Neill made his high-caste Brahmin and Mussalman sepoy prisoners lick the stains on the floor and wall before he hung them. The gallows on which he hung them is the only pleasant thing in the compound on which to rest the eye.

> ... Every man across the river whom I meet shall suffer for my visit to Cawnpore. I will never again, as I used to at Delhi, let off men, whom I catch in houses or elsewhere. I thought when I had killed twelve men outright and wounded or knocked over as many more at the battle of Agra, that I had done enough: I think now I shall never stop, if I get a chance again. (121)

Lang's regret over showing mercy to Indian men and his determination to make the Indians he will encounter in the future pay for the crimes of Cawnpore are typical responses, as documented in accounts by other English soldiers. This vengefulness provoked the significant consternation of Viceroy Canning and Queen Victoria herself, as documented in Edward J. Thompson's *The Other Side of the Medal*. As Canning wrote to Victoria, "There is a rabid and indiscriminate vindictiveness abroad, even among many who ought to set a better example, which it is impossible to contemplate without a feeling of shame for one's countrymen ... Not one man in ten seems to think that the hanging and shooting of 40,000 or 50,000 men can be otherwise than practicable and right" (Thompson 55). Victoria replied, "Lord Canning will easily believe how entirely the Queen shares his feelings of sorrow and indignation at the unchristian spirit shown also to a great extent here by the public toward India in general" (Thompson 55).

The strategic significance of Lucknow as the only British-held possession in Oudh (which was now entirely in revolt) faded in relation to the public in Britain's reeling emotions and calls for both rescue and vengeance. The fighting to relieve Lucknow, as undertaken first under Henry Havelock's command and then under Colin Campbell's, served several purposes: a popular rescue mission to save women and children; a chance to redeem the failures of Cawnpore; an opportunity to punish as well as defeat rebelling sepoys; and the first step of the larger plan to retake Oudh, and thus India.

The fighting on November 16, 1857—the day before Campbell reached the Residency and began its evacuation—featured the engagement in the Sikander Bagh, a structure that emerges powerfully as a focal point in the overlapping histories of the Mutiny and the VC. Laurence Shadwell, then aide-de-camp to Colin Campbell, describes the building as follows: "The Secunder Bagh [sic] is a large brick building 150 yards square, with walls 20 feet high, and a circular bastion at each corner. It was loopholed, and the roofs of the rooms constructed between the bastions formed an admirable rampart for defence" (10). Put simply, it was a heavily defended obstacle to the troops fighting their way through Lucknow to rescue not just the Registry's original defenders and civilians, but also the forces commanded by Havelock and Outram, who had reinforced them in late September but were unable to break out again.[6] Clearly, there were opportunities for heroism in this situation—Tennyson's poem "The Defense of Lucknow" describes them all—but none of the defenders' action were deemed worthy of the VC. In contrast, the taking of the Sikander Bagh itself produced many VC winners, which points to how specific definitions of heroism, national honor, and masculinity emerged from the experiences of the Mutiny.

Lang, who took part in the battle, explains how Campbell's troops meted out revenge in the walled compound of the Sikander Bagh:

> The effect was electrical; down we dropped the ropes and rushed along too; up sprung 93rd and 53rd and, cheering and shouting 'Remember Cawnpore,' on we went, some at a breach in one of the corner towers and some (with whom I was) over a loopholed mud wall straight at the gate; axes and muskets soon smashed in the gate, and then didn't we get revenge—the first good revenge I have seen! (139)

---

[6] Campbell chose this particular route on the advice of Thomas Kavanagh, a VC winner himself for his improbable journey across enemy lines in native garb and blackface to deliver a message to Colin Campbell that he should approach the city not "by the canal bridge as Outram and Havelock had done, but to strike across country southeast of Lucknow to the Dilkusha, cross the canal north of the Dilkusha by the Martinière, and then advance through the palace area south of the Gumti to the Residency" (Hibbert 338).

Others who witnessed the attack and its aftermath also mentioned similar battle cries and expressed regret for the violence of the British assault. The reaction by Lieutenant Fairweather is particularly noteworthy:

> Among the corpses were those of several women ... I saw the body of a woman lying with a cross-belt upon her and by her a dead baby also shot with two bullet wounds in it. The poor mother had tied the wounds round with a rag ... McQueen [Ensign J.W. McQueen of the 27th Native Infantry] told me he had seen a Highlander bayonet another woman and on his upbraiding him for such a brutal act, he said the man turned upon him like a madman and for a minute he almost expected to be run through with his bayonet himself. (Hibbert 341)

While British masculinity could not tolerate the insult to British womanhood and racial superiority that occurred in the Bibighar, it could—albeit with some degree of shock at seeing a female corpse in the midst of a combat zone—accommodate the killing of Indian women as a corrective to the horrors of Cawnpore.

The intense violence at the Sikander Bagh normalized vengeance as not simply an emotional release but also a legitimate military strategy. In *Martial Races*, Heather Streets asserts that the main participants in the storming of the Sikander Bagh, Highlanders and Sikhs, were conscripted as an adjunct for Englishness, specifically the advancement of England's geopolitical interests in the colonies. In other words, Highlanders and Sikhs were linked by the racist assumption that they took a savage joy on the battlefield in giving their all for the British Empire (12–13). Add to this the objective of rescuing one group of women and children (in the Residency) while avenging another (in Cawnpore), and the individual British valor tested under conditions of heavy fire in Lucknow expressed itself as the slaughter of native troops and noncombatants several times the number of the Bibighar victims.[7] In promoting violent determinants of British heroism, the fighting in the Sikander Bagh becomes a turning point in the history of both the Sepoy Rebellion and the VC.

"Very insignificant, valueless metal"

Thus far, the history of the Victoria Cross as it came of age in the blood-soaked Sikander Bagh demonstrates the celebration of British imperial masculinity as a fist of vengeance. Upon reading Lang's description of the summary execution of 60 sepoy prisoners taken during the fighting—"[T]hey got kicked and spit at and pricked with swords, and always with 'Cawnpore, you scoundrels,' and then they were all shot" (139)—it would seem unthinkable that just nine months earlier Queen Victoria recommended that a particular soldier's name be stricken from the

---

[7]   The assumption that to be awarded the VC, a soldier must kill the enemy would be confirmed in patterns of conferrals during World War One (cf. Smith, note 10).

list of those awarded the VC because of the "very doubtful morality" of his act, which "if pointed out by the Sovereign as praiseworthy, may lead to the cruel and inhumane practice of never making prisoners, but always putting to death those who may be overpowered, for fear of their rising upon their captors" (*Panmure Papers* 355). Despite the qualities of gallantry, merit, and valor emphasized in the royal warrant that established the Victoria Cross (Smith 207), it was, despite frequent recognitions of lifesaving bravery, a reward for violence. In its conception, then, the VC's emphasis on the abstract currency of masculine honor masks the very dirty work of imperial war.

The conjuncture of economics, race, gender, and empire embedded and obscured in bronze has broad implications for the symbolic and material analyses of an object as venerated as the VC. The caution John Plotz gives is particularly relevant:

> There is a familiar rationale for appraising evocative objects, the eloquent signifiers by which a culture makes itself known to itself ... The logical objection to such [anthropological] work is that it generally hears the objects saying nothing that the ambient culture has not carefully instilled. (110)

More valuable, Plotz suggests, are "the slippages that occur between the intended meaning and the actually embodied substance" (110).[8]

For some, the Victoria Cross began its existence as a malfunctioning object, falling woefully short in its symbolic potential due to its pure ugliness. In an editorial that is harshly critical of the arrangements for the June 26th medal ceremony, *The Times* concludes:

> We have forgotten the Medal itself, or the Cross rather, for such it is. Would we could forget it! Never did we see such a dull, heavy, tasteless affair. Much do we suspect that if it was on sale in any town in England at a penny a-piece, hardly a dozen would be sold in a twelvemonth ... Valour must, and doubtless will, be still its own reward in this country, for the Victoria Cross is the shabbiest of all prizes. ("The saying" 9)

For *The Times*, at least, the VC's aesthetic flaws reduced its signifying power as a reward for bravery. The Victoria Cross was made, for better or for worse, to emblematize valorous service to Queen and country, but the pairing of substance and meaning was, like the initial forging attempts, a cumbersome process. The image of hard metal destroying the dies first used to forge them is as apt as any to treat the VC as a cultural artifact using the hermeneutic strategies of Thing Theory.

---

[8] Bill Brown memorably states a similar point when he writes: "We begin to confront the thingness of objects when they stop working for us: when the drill breaks, when the car stalls, when the windows get filthy, when their flow within the circuits of production and distribution, consumption and exhibition, has been arrested, however momentarily" (4).

Bronze was associated with public commemoration due to the tradition of honoring in sculpture those who contributed to the nation and empire (Sullivan 38).[9] However, as bemoaned by *The Times*, the most commemorative and evocative metal was neither the most attractive nor the most malleable, and its forging bred additional inefficiencies. Historian John Glanfield, for example, calculates "that to make 12 crosses with a combined weight of 10oz or 11oz required 47oz of gunmetal because of the wastage in the process" (29). The wastage was due in part to the rejection of as many as two out of three medals for imperfections (Glanfield 29). In light of the need for public commemoration, such inefficiencies of medal production accrued value for the VC. In "'For Valour': Some Metallurgical Aspects of the Manufacture of the Victoria Cross," the anonymous author speculates on production techniques that would be more efficient and less labor-intensive, concluding:

> [N]o doubt today a process could be evolved under special care and attention which would produce the desired quality with less labour and scrap. But tradition is of more importance than efficiency of production in this instance, and even though the metal used is worth only a few coppers, the medals are of considerable value to collectors, and substantial sums of money have been paid for them. (221)

The medal's value as a material object does not derive, then, from the technology that produces it or the aesthetics and worth of the finished product. David Callaghan, former director of Hancocks, the jewelry firm entrusted with the creation of every VC, expresses the divide in value between the medal and its metal more bluntly: "It's made of very insignificant, valueless metal. The metal itself is, I suppose the right word is unstable. It's not nice metal. The more often you use it, the less stable it becomes" (qtd in Clarkson).[10]

In "How the Victoria Cross is Made," published in *The Strand* in February 1901, the anonymous author highlights that each Cross derives its uniqueness from the process of its creation, which in turn has a concrete physical dimension. Because the VC cannot be stamped with a die, it must be first carved as a wax model, which is then used to make a mold of sand, which then receives the melted bronze, which after cooling is shaped, smoothed, and chased using hand tools (163–4). As the extent of the labor is not forgotten, neither is the laborer himself, whose actions are rendered with reference to superhuman skill alongside domestic delicacy:

---

[9]   According to M.G. Sullivan, from the end of the seventeenth century bronze increasingly became a widely used and highly evocative metal for armament production and sculpture (38).

[10]   The bronze used to fashion the VC, unworkable as it was, became part of the Cross mythology, as it was rumored to have come from cannon captured from the Russians after the fall of Sebastopol (and was reported as such in *The Times*). John Glanfield has debunked that story as a myth, but its persistence suggests its continued appeal.

The temperature of this [furnace] is somewhere about 2,000deg. Fahr., a heat almost intolerable for the ordinary individual even to come near. In spite of this, however, the operator watches carefully for the melting of the bronze. When it becomes liquid he withdraws the white-hot pot by means of a pair of long tongs, and pours the molten liquid into the moulds with as much dexterity and with, as a rule, as little loss as a lady pours out a cup of tea in the afternoon. (164)

The skill and artistry that goes into the creation of each VC becomes part of its authenticating stamp, transforming valueless metal into an object of veneration. However, as Callaghan insists, the creative process remains incomplete until the medal is inscribed:

But what makes them unique of course is the information on the back. Until they are issued they are literally valueless. It does actually become priceless once it's been issued because it can be identified with a particular man on a particular day in a particular action, and it's the history which is carried forward. (qtd in Clarkson)

The rituals used to fashion the medal point to the thingness of the VC. The breakage here between the intent of the Cross and the substance of it arises, on one hand, from the idea that there must be a unity between the aesthetics of the object and the bravery it celebrates and, on the other hand, from the confounding disunity between the two. This disunity itself has been incorporated into the mystique of the VC, as Jeremy Clarkson points out: "As Queen Victoria understood all along, the medal itself isn't important. It's the story that goes with it that matters."

If the argument at the heart of Marx's theory of commodity fetishism is that a thing's exchange value overshadows not only its use but also the labor that produced it (164–5), then the Victoria Cross is a non-commodity, in which the aura of the object itself attaches almost exclusively to the labor that produced it. The story of each VC is inscribed on its back, listing the soldier's name and regiment, as well as the military action and date on which the VC was earned. This inscription suggests that the military heroism concretized by the medal remains the originating labor that brought the thing into objecthood, transforming a small, blank, dark medal into a Victoria Cross. Yet Marx's description of creating commodities is the same as creating VCs:

[T]he products of labour become commodities, sensuous things which are at the same time suprasensible or social. In the same way, the impression made by a thing on the optic nerve is perceived not as a subjective excitation of that nerve but as the objective form of a thing outside the eye. In the act of seeing, of course, light is really transmitted from one thing, the external object, to another thing, the eye. It is a physical relation between physical things. As against this, the commodity-form, and the value-relation of the products of labour within

which it appears, have absolutely no connection with the physical nature of the
commodity and the material [dinglich] relations arising out of this. (164–5)

The Victoria Cross represents a fetishized object, to be sure, but the fact that its
labor and material production are lovingly described warns us to consider a more
systemic sort of fetishism: covering up the true meaning of the soldier's labor and
recasting the inherent violence at the heart of the imperial mission. Like the fetish,
the Victoria Cross is summoned by the British Empire as a central prop in the story
Empire tells to itself about the human cost of its imperial aspirations.[11]

Returning to Britain

For the soldiers in the British army who fought in the Crimean War and the Sepoy
Rebellion, however, the most relevant information about cannons was not the
provenance and workability of their bronze but rather where they were aimed
and whether they were loaded with grapeshot or cannonballs. Just as the VC's
role as a sanctified relic of war contrasted sharply with its modest appearance
and unworkable metal, so too stood this portable celebration of individual valor
in sharp distinction to the lack of resources afforded to the soldiers and sailors
whose bravery was celebrated. As *The Times* rightly identified on June 27, 1857,
the broadly democratic appeal inherent in the VC as an award attainable by the
common soldier was subsumed by the royalty-focused, class-divided spectacle of
its presentation. The split identity of the Cross as an object that constantly pushed
back against its prescribed meanings emerges more powerfully and systemically
when considering the material conditions in which a soldier lived while fighting
for, and returning home to, Great Britain.

While the full extent of the privations suffered by British soldiers in the
Crimean War was the subject of considerable public outrage, the standard of
living of rank-and-file British soldiers was not very high to begin with, nor was it

---

[11]   Fashioning the VC from one of the spoils of war gives it a new interpretive
possibility, ushered in by Nicholas J. Saunders, who refers to it as "[p]erhaps the most
unexpected example of metal trench art," a description that evokes the trauma of war more
clearly than any of the medal's other characterizations (*Trench Art* 30). Defined as "'Any
item made by soldiers, prisoners of war, and civilians, from war *matériel* directly, or any
other material, *as long as it and they are associated temporally and/or spatially with armed
conflict or its consequences*'" (Saunders, "Bodies of Metal ..." 45), Trench Art carries
with it the same democratizing connotations as the Victoria Cross, an art object regardless
of the humble and often deadly origins of its materials and medal winners regardless of
rank. However, the term "trench art" does not ultimately hold up, as the VC lacks the
collective grieving associated with the medium. The Victoria Cross does not commemorate
those who fell in battle during the Crimean War, nor is it meant to evoke the trenches
surrounding Sebastopol; instead, the potential for mourning has been subsumed by the state
and transformed into a celebration of military glory.

going to improve more speedily than what Peter Burroughs describes as military reform's "former unhurried pace along the grooves of gradual amelioration and piecemeal replacement" (183).[12] Alan Skelley points out that although one shilling per day was widely known to be the standard army salary, the Queen's Shilling was seldom if ever that (182). Through pay stoppages that were meant to cover "messing expenses, clothing and equipment replacement, washing, hair-cutting and barrack damages" (183), as well as hospitalizations or disciplinary fines (183), the typical soldier's net salary was greatly reduced, much of it ending up back in military coffers. The upshot was that "throughout the whole of the period 1856 to 1899 the army was consistently able to compete in financial terms with only the very lowest paid of civilian occupations" (181–2). Failures to make one's pay were often considered the fault of the profligate or undisciplined individual soldier rather than the institutionally sanctioned function of the company store. The stoppage system was so extreme that after 1856 a minimum net salary of one penny per day had to be established for soldiers to earn anything (184).

The military's low wages, coupled with a lengthy enlistment period, undermined recruitment, a crucial problem given the constant need to defend or expand vast colonial holdings.[13] The Victoria Cross was viewed in its initial stages, a good two decades before the circumstances requiring reform would be addressed, as one way of alleviating that concern. As Henry Pelham, Duke of Newcastle, wrote in his capacity as Secretary of State for War: "Such a reward would have more effect in the Army than the grant of Commissions, and the sight of one of these crosses on the breast of a soldier returned home invalided would bring more recruits than any of the measures we can now adopt" (248–9). Pelham's rhetorical excess is unfortunate, suggesting that the remote possibility of earning a rarely-bestowed military honor would counterbalance better pay, more humane treatment, a shorter enlistment, and more secure prospects upon discharge.[14] As things stood, however, even though the pay soldiers earned without stoppages doubled from 1856–76, recruiting continued to be sluggish (Skelley 189).

Military recruitment was not helped by the persistent concern of soldiers not receiving the pay that remained after stoppages. On June 22, 1855, August Stafford, MP from Northamptonshire Northern, rose in the House of Commons to claim that he

---

[12] According to Burroughs, "[o]ne reason for this relapse was that the outcry had reflected emotional outrage, not a secure basis for prolonged, constructive pressure; unfocused denunciations of the way the army was run produced no coherent, detailed programme of change" (183).

[13] By 1847, enlistment was usually for 12 years; prior to this, enlistment had been for 21 years (Spiers 119).

[14] In total, 182 VCs were awarded for actions during the Sepoy Rebellion; out of 41,000 troops, this would have produced a rate of .44 percent, or roughly one VC for every 225 troops. See Glanfield 41–2.

had a long list of names placed before him of men who had suffered the greatest hardships in consequence of the retention of the pay due to them. The sums they claimed varied in amount, a great majority of the claims amounting to 5*l.* and 6*l.*, and yet many of these men had been compelled to pawn their clothes to enable them to meet their relatives, or, after having received a small pittance with their furlough, to proceed to their several places of destination. (*Hansard's*, "Arrears of Pay to Soldiers")[15]

Bury MP Frederick Peel, who was Undersecretary of State for War, replied that the only way to make payouts quickly would be to take the soldiers at their word for how much they were owed; thus, the only way to resolve the situation with greater accuracy would be to wait for more documentation (*Hansard's*, "Arrears of Pay to Soldiers"). The response that the documentation for how much was owed was lost was an insufficient explanation, as it amounted to penalizing the soldiers for bureaucratic incompetence. The issue was raised again on July 13, 1855, this time by Lt. Col. Brownlow W. Knox, MP of Great Marlow, who quoted accordingly from *The Times* about an 11-month pay gap among a group of soldiers invalided from the Crimea: "They complain most earnestly, as they want the money. Some of the non-commissioned officers have wives and families to support, and have as much as 10*l.* due to them" (*Hansard's*, "Arrears of Pay to Wounded Soldiers").

In response, Peel seems to have resorted to the time honored tactic of seeing which of multiple explanations might stick: the number affected was "inconsiderable," the claims of those "to whom some difficulties occurred" "were gradually being disposed of," and though there was a gap in pay, it was only a 7-month gap rather than an 11-month gap, as "those men had been receiving their full pay ever since their arrival in England" around the previous April (*Hansard's*, "Arrears of Pay to Wounded Soldiers"). While an August-to-April pay gap is clearly preferable to an August-to-July pay gap, the refrain of military arrears suggests the extent to which soldiers' pay—like their boots, food, or overcoats—was delivered on a schedule more suited to the rules and loopholes of military bureaucracy than to the needs of the soldiers.

Because it was awarded with a pension of £10 per year, the VC directly engages with the crucial issue of the soldiers' material circumstances during and after enlistment. Most soldiers did not enjoy such monetary benefits after leaving military service. Skelley lays out the matter bluntly: "The insufficiency of army pensions, both in terms of the number and the size of the allowances awarded each year is nowhere better demonstrated than by the number of ex-soldiers reduced to destitution and to dependence on civilian institutions yearly" (210). Such dependence raised the issue of the state's responsibility, if any, for how its soldiers were treated after serving many years, suffering privations, and sustaining wounds for the British military, an obligation the British state failed to meet, and continued

---

[15] Stafford had raised this issue before, during the session on the previous day, as well as—according to his opening statement—six times prior since February 1855.

to fail even through the process of military reform. According to Skelley, after reaching a level of 47.7 percent total pensions per total discharges from 1861–5, and peaking at 50.5 percent from 1876–80, the total number of pensions per discharges dropped to 21.6 percent in 1896 (209). In fact, Lord Palmerston, recently made Prime Minister, echoed Peel's sentiments when he stated:

> Pensions for wounds, for widows, and provisions for orphans, were liberally made. But on the return of peace, Committees were appointed to inquire into the amount of the Army Estimates, and Reports were made as to the great and heavy amount of the charge. Government was then urged to pare down and diminish the provisions made in the moment of liberality, and the allowances made were taken away on the plea of an economical prudence. (*Hansard's*, "Army Estimates—Supply")

Calculations that favor a reduced number of pensions with reduced funds find their counterpart in the practice of private charities caring for former soldiers, despite the strenuous objections made by those like Colonel Frederick North, MP of Hastings, who said he was "unable to see the justice of providing for the widows and orphans of one class in the army and not for those of another. It was both mean and impolitic in a great nation like this, to send round a begging box, calling on the public to do that which he maintained the State was bound to do" (*Hansard's*, "Amy Estimates—Supply").

Unfortunately, the begging box was figuratively and sometimes literally the best option. Such was particularly the case for the widows and children of deceased soldiers. As Myna Trustram points out in her trenchant examination, *Women of the Regiment: Marriage and the Victorian Army*, "[t]he first move towards making any provision for women and children in the event of the death of a soldier occurred in 1881. Widows of NCOs and men who were killed in action, or who died as a result of wounds received in action, became eligible to receive a gratuity of one year's pay" (93).[16] Furthermore, Trustram states that although soldiers' families were placed in a different classification from other people receiving poor relief and thus entitled to assistance without entering the workhouse, "there was much local variation and confusion over the procedure to be adopted" (143). Any assistance provided was left to the discretion of administrators in individual localities, producing a situation in which the means of sustenance for soldiers' wives and children was a matter of political and financial wrangling between local authorities, the Poor Commissioners, and the War Office.

------

[16]   For more details on the regulations that required a commanding officer's approval of a soldier's marriage, see Trustram. Such approval—restricted to a small minority of soldiers—determined whether wives were "on" or "off the strength of the regiment," and thus whether wives and children were eligible for Army housing, food, medical services, and transportation.

For soldiers who returned to England either discharged or invalided out of service, there were limited options for post-military employment. In its coverage of the ceremonial awarding of the first VCs in Hyde Park, *The Times* reports on the disparities among some VC holders between the military glory they achieved and their current economic statuses, identifying former sergeant George Walters, who found employment as a police officer—"Surely for such a man a better post may be found than that of a constable at 18s. a-week"—and another who was dressed as a park keeper ("Distribution" 5). However, as Skelley writes, "The pensions paid to police constables and to private soldiers were frequently compared between 1856 and 1899. As with wages, comparisons leave no doubt that the constable was much better off" (210). In short, the implication was that Walters was one of the fortunate ones, especially when considering his additional annual pension of £10, as provided for in the VC warrant, added to his yearly wages of nearly £47. It is true that there were some options available, as well as some measure of concern in Parliament about the plight of the unemployed soldier. On May 2, 1876, Sir Henry Havelock, MP of Sunderland and himself a VC holder, moved

> [T]hat a Select Committee be appointed to inquire –1st. How far it is practicable that Soldiers, Sailors, and Marines who have meritoriously served their Country should be employed in such Civil Departments of the public service as they may be found fitted for; 2nd. How far it is practicable, in order to form and retain an efficient Reserve Force, for the State to become the medium of communication between private employers of labour and Soldiers of the Army Reserve and Militia Reserve who desire to obtain employment ... (*Hansard's*, "Motion for a Select Committee")[17]

However, the government either could not or would not contribute sufficiently to account for the total number of soldiers who needed employment upon their return, causing organizations like the Army and Navy Pensioner's and Time-Expired Men's Society and the National Association for the Employment of Reserve and Discharged Soldiers to take up the slack. One such organization, the Corps of Commissionaires, is noteworthy in part because it still exists today as a security

---

[17] Havelock was the son of Henry Havelock, the general who commanded the march towards Cawnpore to recapture it from Nana Sahib, and then broke through the siege in the First Relief of Lucknow but was unable to break out again. For an account of the younger Havelock's VC, which was granted "provisionally [thus skirting the typical review process] in the field by his own father, Brigadier General Henry Havelock," see Smith 66. He concludes: "[T]he Havelock VC was widely accepted in India as pure favoritism. The blatant nepotism of the provisional bestowal was only reinforced by Havelock senior's recommendation of a bar for the VC for a later act of heroism by Havelock junior before the original award had been confirmed by the home government" (66–7).

services firm.[18] Founded by Captain Edward Walter in 1859 for the employment of wounded soldiers, the Corps of Commissionaires was the subject of a news item and fundraising appeal in *All the Year Round*. The unsigned article contains a restatement of what was widely known, that a military pension was too little to support a soldier, and thus to be a commissionaire meant that "the life that was committed to forced idleness and poverty becomes honorably useful, and is saved from the pinch of want" (62). However, as one might imagine, there were some strict guidelines for joining the Corps of Commissionaires:

> No man can be a Commissionaire unless he has served in the Army, Navy, Militia, or Police, and earned a pension. His character must bear the strictest examination. Preference is given to men who have been severely wounded when on duty. Soldiers of good character but broken health, whose temporary pensions have expired, may be Commissionaires if they deposit twenty-five pounds in the savings-bank of the corps, which money will be liable to forfeiture in case of dishonesty proved against them in a court of justice. (63)

While Corps members had to pay into a Sick and Burial Fund, a Clothing Fund, and a General Fund to cover sick days, uniforms, and expenses, it is the cost of admission in particular that set up a barrier against those who were beset with the difficulties the Corps was supposed to alleviate. A soldier with a pension who could afford such fees would certainly benefit from his association with the Corps, but his ability to do so would suggest that he stood on firmer ground financially than many of his unfortunate comrades. For a soldier with an expired temporary pension to furnish £25 would be an impressive and difficult feat. In four examples given by Skelley, the largest daily pension granted was 1s 2d per day for three years (206)—amounting to £63 17s 6d for a £21 5s 10d annual income—with lesser examples totaling £12 3s 4d per year, £13 13s 9d per year, and £9 2s 6d per year.[19] An invalided soldier whose pension had expired could not have joined the Corps of Commissionaires without some connections who could have put up the money for him, thereby restricting one of the best post-military opportunities available to those of the middle class or above.

More to the point, a soldier's eligibility for the Corps hinged in large part on a determination of character, which was doubtless important for an organization with highly visible members that as of 1864 was seeking an £8,000 endowment through subscriptions (*All the Year Round* 65). However, the emphasis on character returns to the assumption that a soldier's life was more dissolute than an average

---

[18] For more information, see Skelley and what is now called Corps Security, http://www.the-corps.co.uk/.

[19] Calculations for annual incomes derived from Skelley's base figures of 1s 2d per day for three years, 8d per day for two and a half years, 9d per day, and 6d per day (206). In addition, Skelley points out that permanent pensions could only be awarded to soldiers who had served at least a full 14 years and were invalided as a result of their service.

citizen's. As stressed by the Corps's founder Edward Walter in the February 12, 1876 issue of *The Times*: "I do not think that the soldier is so much ill-used as misused; it is generally his own fault if he is not a better man in most respects on leaving the service than when joining it ..." (8). This statement reflects long-held beliefs and stereotypes about the morality of the British soldier, or as the Duke of Wellington phrased it early in the century, that "the army was composed of 'the scum of the earth, ... fellows who have all enlisted for drink'" (Dinwiddy 320). Such assumptions were strongly class-based, as the low military pay "necessitated that the army rely on only the poorest classes of society to fill its ranks—men who were either in trouble with the law or who could find few alternatives to real hunger" (Streets 21). In fact, as Streets claims, "Britons of nearly every class believed that soldiers of the line were uneducated, immoral, and prone to drink and violence" (21). With a reigning attitude about enlisted men and a War Office frustrated with low rates of recruitment but remaining complacently incremental about improvements in pay, pensions, and enlistment terms, the returning soldier was set up to be a particularly vulnerable member of society, and those who succeeded, it seemed, did so in spite rather than because of the structures set up around them.

The instability of daily life for former soldiers was most poignantly evident in the records of those invalided out of service due to mental instability. According to Kathleen Jones, England at midcentury had made significant strides in caring for the mentally ill: "The prospects for the treatment of the insane seemed bright. There was a new spirit of humanity in treatment, and a tentative approach to what we would now call social therapy ... There was a new concept of mental nursing which stressed the treatment of the patient as a sick individual, not a dangerous 'case'" (2). However, Parliamentary discussion of the care of soldiers who had been deemed lunatics focused on cost, the status of particular facilities, and interactions between military asylums and local communities, often without recognition of the mental illnesses and psychological traumas that might accompany life as a British soldier. For instance, in Parliamentary sessions on June 18, 1860 and April 5, 1864 members expressing their concern over the case of a soldier who, in the words of Colonel North, "had become a lunatic in consequence of wounds he had received in the service of his country. The case, which had occurred at Rochester, had come on for hearing before the mayor. This man was set adrift in the streets of Chatham with a non-commissioned officer in plain clothes to watch him" (*Hansard's*, "Supply—Army Estimates").[20] The author of an unsigned

---

[20]   Chatham is also mentioned by J.W. Henley, MP from Oxfordshire, who concluded that "[t]he manner in which a poor lunatic soldier had been turned out in the neighbourhood of Chatham, in order to raise a legal question as regarded the parochial authorities, was not a good sample of Government treatment of these poor creatures" (June 18, 1860); and Philip Wykeham-Martin, who stated: "Within his recollection it was the practice that ... the moment [a soldier] became hopelessly insane he was removed from Chatham parish to the unfortunate parish of St. Margaret, Rochester, and at ten o'clock at night turned loose into

note in the *British Medical Journal* described this practice as an example of "[t]he superb contempt entertained by the military authorities for the civil power" (945). In a letter published two weeks later in the same journal, G.R. Dartnell, Deputy Inspector-General of Hospitals, placed the case in the context of the larger bureaucratic machine that transferred mentally ill soldiers from hospital to hospital, with the eventual goal of the soldiers "being forwarded on to their respective parishes" (989).

Dartnell paints a bleak picture of the medical establishment subject to the demands of the War Department without regard for the patients' health. He would do the same in his House of Commons testimony about facilities for soldiers who were classified as lunatics. Dartnell explained that the lunatic hospital at Yarmouth, which he directed for two years, closed when the Navy reclaimed the buildings, as they were owned by the Admiralty (Robertson 273–4). Indeed, it appeared that facilities marked for use as asylums for lunatic soldiers were often deemed inadequate or simply repurposed for other military needs, which deepened dependence on local charities and taxes to attend to soldiers who would not be cared for by the Government. As a result the Netley military hospital to accommodate the insane was planned. In June 18, 1860, Sir Joseph Paxton, MP from Coventry, rose to state that the Netley hospital:

> had been one of the most mismanaged of all our public buildings … Land had first been purchased on the Southampton Water. Then money was asked for the foundations. Step by step the outlay had risen to £350,000, and no doubt it would amount to £400,000 before it was finished. It was a hospital for accommodating 1,000 men, and it would cost £400 per man, while in a sanitary point of view it was a most improper site for a hospital … The sun hardly penetrated the long corridors, and it was internally ill-arranged. It appeared to be got up for a show in Southampton Water, and not as a hospital for invalided soldiers. (*Hansard's,* "Supply—Army Estimates")

Lord Palmerston was even more negative in his own assessment of Netley:

> My strong impression is that, if completed on the present plan, it will be a charnel-house instead of a sanatorium … [T]he wards will have no sunlight, there will be no means for thorough draft, and shaft ventilation is a poor substitute for it … For my part, I would rather pay for throwing into Southampton Water every brick and stone that has now been laid than be a party to completing a building which would be likely to send thousands upon thousands to a premature grave. (*Panmure Papers* 347–8)

---

the street, with a notice sent to the proper authorities to catch him and keep him until his settlement was ascertained" (April 5, 1864).

The asylum was established at Netley, and it remained operative until 1978.[21] However, the path to get there was paved with long neglected cases of British soldiers, invalided for psychiatric reasons, bounced from military asylum to military asylum, from government facility to private facility to public charity. As was the case with soldiers' pensions, the care of the mentally ill soldier after his return home was marked by some good intentions and high ideals that were shot through with bureaucratic dysfunction. In this way, though in a format that was not as public as a story in *The Times* or a despatch from William Howard Russell, the mismanagement of the Crimean War continued for decades.

The VC, in this sense, was a whitewash, the conferring of an exalted status upon a group of people who were celebrated publicly but systemically told to be happy with what they got when they got it, if they ever did. Soldiers continued to exhibit gallantry, bravery, and self-sacrifice, continued to win the VC, and continued to be feted and gazetted for having done so. Ultimately, though, holders of the VC were a small sample of a much larger group of people, many of whom were in the military because their options were limited, and who—when they left—found themselves with a similar lack of options.

Conclusion

When Lord Michael Ashcroft talks about the Victoria Cross, he presents himself as a collector of intangibles. Acquiring Victoria Crosses since 1986, Ashcroft describes his drive to own the world's largest collection as "almost obsessive," stemming from the stories he heard from his father, a veteran of World War II. As he explains in a profile published by the *Telegraph*, his fascination with his father's combat experiences took the rather safer form of collecting:

> Lord Ashcroft's fixation with bravery led to his resolve one day to own a Victoria Cross. He bought his first in 1986, when he was 40. As he held it in his hand, reading the citation that told the story of its holder, he felt a surge of pride. 'I wanted more. I set my heart upon building a formidable collection,' he says. And an obsession was born. Today, he owns 164 VCs, the largest private collection in the world. 'The collection is, simply, my pride and joy,' he says. Its value for Lord Ashcroft can only be measured in terms of respect and sentiment, but it is estimated to be worth more than £30 million. (Craig)

---

[21]   However, had Panmure followed through on his plan to hurl every brick and stone into Southampton Water, he would eventually have had to contend with the foundation stone, which was laid by Victoria herself in 1856 to commemorate the end of the Crimean War. Under the stone, according to Julie Piggott, was a casket that contained several coins, several medals, and one Victoria Cross (16).

The paragraph presents a story of origins, in this case, the origins of a desire to collect that sprang into being with the direct physical contact between the collector and the collected item. According to Ronald Bishop, the story laid out in the *Telegraph* conforms to a typical biographical narrative: "It starts with infatuation with an item, usually at a young age. The item either catches the collector's eye or is linked somehow to the collector's family. It evokes pleasant memories. Once the connection with the item is forged, the collector embarks on a single-minded pursuit of the items" (Bishop 122).

In this case, the collecting story of origins serves the purpose of providing a mellow and moving side of a wealthy, hard-edged, Tory critic of Tories. In less sympathetic publications, Ashcroft's obsession with the VC furnishes a revealing look into the character and aspirations of a peer who purchased his peerage after pledging to no longer live in tax exile (Siddique). In a harsh commentary, "Lord Ashcroft Passes the Buck," Michael White writes:

> Credit: I am amazed to hear that it really is the case that Ashcroft's collection of up to 160 Victoria Crosses–the largest in the world, allegedly worth £30m–is going on show at the Imperial War Museum. Splendid, splendid, you may feel.
>
> Yes, but it's going to be called the Lord Ashcroft Gallery which strikes me as a judgment in questionable taste. Courage is something you can't buy, but buying a collection of VCs and naming their new home after oneself is close to trying.

White's line about the buying of courage is an easy shot to take, but of greater interest is the notion itself of the Cross as concrete, portable, collectible bravery. It is easy to imagine the incredibly wealthy Ashcroft, whose net worth as of this writing is valued by Forbes at £1.4 billion ("Michael Ashcroft"), collecting VCs out of respect for their rare quality of courage in the face of life-threatening circumstances, rather than for the accumulation of more wealth (although it is equally easy to imagine that well-heeled collectors like Ashcroft may drive up the price any collectible object might earn for its collector). More importantly, however, we are witnessing another form of alchemy at work. If the original VC could turn worthless bronze into a priceless symbol of courage, then Michael Ashcroft could transform the VC into an investment with returns of sharply increased cultural capital, as can be seen in his donation of his Victoria Cross collection to the Imperial War Museum.

> As Susan Pearce writes, 'to give material freely to museums is a meritorious act which conveys famous immortality.' And so although donors rid themselves of the problems of storage and upkeep, they retained symbolic ownership—a manifestation of what Annette Weiner calls 'the paradox of keeping-while-giving.' Collecting was civilizing; subsequently to donate to a worthy museum ensured that such an act remained visible in perpetuity and secured a lasting connection between person and object. (Alberti 564)

Ashcroft as both accumulator and celebrator of acts of bravery represents a larger split in the life of the Victoria Cross, in which the symbolic freight of the award frequently became detached from any act of courage shown by its recipient. We cannot see the medals representing valor without first entering into the gallery that bears Ashcroft's name. He becomes an aspirant to the role of privileged conduit between the Victoria Cross and the public who can admire them as mediated through him: his collection on display at the Imperial War Museum, his coverage in the newspapers, the sales of his book *Victoria Cross Heroes*. If the public life of the Victoria Cross is more about the recognition given to the House of Lords peer who collects them instead of the soldiers who earned them, then does the VC remain an object of veneration for the brave act of a soldier, or has it turned into a different kind of thing?

To understand the transformative process in which not just bravery but also national honor can be commodified, it is useful in closing to turn to the theories of Arjun Appadurai:

> Let us approach commodities as things in a certain situation, a situation that can characterize many different kinds of thing, at different points in their social lives. This means looking at the commodity potential of all things rather than searching fruitlessly for the magic distinction between commodities and other sorts of things. It also means breaking significantly with the production-dominated Marxian view of the commodity and focusing on its total trajectory from production, through exchange/distribution, to consumption.

> But how are we to define the commodity situation? I propose that *the commodity situation in the social life of any 'thing' be defined as the situation in which its exchangeability (past, present, or future) for some other thing is its socially relevant feature.* Further, the commodity situation, defined this way, can be disaggregated into: (1) the commodity phase of the social life of any things; (2) the commodity candidacy of any thing; and (3) the commodity context in which any thing may be placed. (13)

Appadurai's words provide cause for reflection: the social relevance of the VC is certainly its exchangeability, from the State to the soldier, from the auction house to the collector, from the collector to the museum.

According to the venerable Spink and Son Auction House, the first two Victoria Crosses that were successfully auctioned sold for a combined £37 in 1884. (A VC was auctioned in 1879 but failed to sell.) Thus began a new phase in the life of the VC, when the public could more fully embrace its value as a commodity, one that would make it possible to assign different monetary values to different VCs based on rarity, condition, and of course the uniqueness of the feats of courage that won them. In 1894, a VC sold for £155, "a record price that would last for the next twenty-five years" ("Victoria Cross at Auction"). On July 2, 2014, Ashcroft purchased the VC and accompanying medals of Colonel John Duncan

Grant for £340,000 ("Victoria Cross for Cheltenham"). Awarding the VC is now only the first step of a long process that leads to the circulation of that which was never meant to be circulated, and the commodification of that which could not be commodified. This process is nothing new, but in the hands of Michael Ashcroft, it is much more publicly visible and much more costly. What remains hidden, however, is the VC's inability to carry out its democratic potential. Though the inscription on the back of the VC of rank, name, and date of combat gives the medal its value in today's market, the inverse was not true. In Victorian Britain, the creation of the Cross acknowledged that common soldiers and sailors were necessary to maintain empire, but for many, there was little space or support once their service concluded.

Works Cited

Alberti, Samuel J.M.M. "Objects and the Museum." *Isis* 96 (2005): 559–71. Print.

Appadurai, Arjun. "Introduction: commodities and the politics of value." *The Social Life of Things: Commodities in Cultural Perspective* (ed.) Arjun Appadurai. Cambridge: Cambridge University Press, 1986. Print.

Ashcroft, Michael. *Victoria Cross Heroes*. London: Headline Review, 2007. Print.

Bishop, Ronald. "It's Not Always About the Money: Using Narrative Analysis to Explore Newspaper Coverage of the Act of Collecting." *The Communication Review* 6 (2003): 117–35. Print.

Blomfield, David (ed.) *Lahore to Lucknow: The Indian Mutiny Journal of Arthur Moffatt Lang*. London: Leo Cooper, 1992. Print.

Brantlinger, Patrick. *Rule of Darkness: British Literature and Imperialism, 1830–1914*. Ithaca: Cornell University Press, 1988. Print.

Brown, Bill. "Thing Theory." *Critical Inquiry* 28.1 (2001): 1–22. Print.

Burroughs, Peter. "An Unreformed Army? 1815–1868." *The Oxford History of the British Army* (gen. ed.) David G. Chandler (assoc. ed.) Ian Beckett. 1994. Oxford: Oxford University Press, 2003. 161–86. Print.

Clarkson, Jeremy. *The Victoria Cross: For Valour*. Dir. Richard Pearson. Chrysalis Television. 2003. Web.

Craig, Olga. "Lord Ashcroft Interview: Our Bravest of the Brave." *Telegraph*, 16 October, 2010. Web.

Dartnell, G.R. "Military Lunatics." *British Medical Journal*, 3 December, 1859: 989–90. Web.

David, Saul. *The Indian Mutiny, 1857*. London: Penguin, 2003. Print.

Dinwiddy, J.R. *The English Historical Review* 97.383 (1982): 308–31. Print.

"Distribution Of The Victoria Cross For Valour." *The Times*, 27 June, 1857: 5. *The Times Digital Archive*. Web.

Douglas, George and George Dalhousie Ramsay (eds) *The Panmure Papers, Being a Selection from the Correspondence of Fox Maule, Second Baron Panmure,*

Afterwards Eleventh Earl of Dalhousie, K.T., G.C.B. Vol. 2. London: Hodder and Stoughton, 1908. Web.

"'For Valour': Some Metallurgical Aspects of the Manufacture of the Victoria Cross." *Metal Treatment and Drop Forging* 23 (1956): 222, 221. Print.

Glanfield, John. *The Bravest of the Brave: The Story of the Victoria Cross.* Stroud: Sutton, 2006. Print.

Hansard's Parliamentary Debates. London: TC Hansard, 1803–2005. Web.

Hansard's Parliamentary Debates. "Army Estimates—Supply" HC Deb. 2 March, 1855, Vol. 137, Col. 63–76. Web.

Hansard's Parliamentary Debates. "Arrears Of Pay To Soldiers" HC Deb. 22 June, 1855, Vol. 139, Col. 21–4. Web.

Hansard's Parliamentary Debates. "Arrears Of Pay To Wounded Soldiers—Question." HC Deb. 13 July, 1855, Vol. 139, Col. 852–3. Web.

Hansard's Parliamentary Debates. "Medal For The Army In The Crimea." HC Deb. 19 December, 1854, Vol. 136, Col. 505–7. Web.

Hansard's Parliamentary Debates. "Motion For A Select Committee." HC Deb. 2 May, 1876, Vol. 228, Col. 1987–98. Web.

Hansard's Parliamentary Debates. "Public Lands And Buildings (Local Rates)—Resolution." HC Deb. 5 April, 1864, Vol. 174, Col. 479–500. Web.

Hansard's Parliamentary Debates. "Supply—Army Estimates." HC Deb. 18 June, 1860, Vol. 159, Col. 589–616. Web.

Hansard's Parliamentary Debates. "Treatment Of Insane Persons In England And Wales." HC Deb. 6 June, 1845, Vol. 81, Col. 180–202. Web.

Hibbert, Christopher. *The Destruction of Lord Raglan: A Tragedy of the Crimean War, 1854–55.* Boston, MA: Little, Brown, 1961. Web.

Hibbert, Christopher. *The Great Mutiny: India 1857.* NY: Viking, 1978. Print.

"How the Victoria Cross is Made." *The Strand* March 1901: 170–73. Web.

Jones, Kathleen. *Mental Health and Social Policy, 1845–1959.* 1960. Abingdon: Routledge, 1998. Print.

Joshi, Priti. "India, Britons, and Charles Dickens's *A Tale of Two Cities.*" *Nineteenth-Century Literature* 62.1 (2007): 48–87. Print.

Martineau, John. *The Life of Henry Pelham, Fifth Duke of Newcastle, 1811–1864.* London: John Murray, 1908. Web.

Marx, Karl. *Capital: A Critique of Political Economy.* Trans. Ben Fowkes. NY: Vintage, 1977. Print.

"Michael Ashcroft." *Forbes*, n.d. http://www.forbes.com/profile/michael-ashcroft/. Web.

Mukherjee, Rudrangshu. "'Satan Let Loose upon Earth': The Kanpur Massacres in India in the Revolt of 1857." *Past & Present* 128 (1990): 92–116. Print.

Paton, Alex. Review of *Spike Island: The Memory of a Military Hospital*, Philip Hoare. *British Medical Journal*, 6 July, 2002. Web.

Piggott, Julie. *Queen Alexandra's Royal Army Nursing Corps.* London: Leo Cooper, 1975. Print.

Plotz, John. "Can the Sofa Speak? A Look at Thing Theory." *Criticism* 47.1 (2005): 109–18. Print.

Robertson, C. Lockhart. "*The Military Lunatic Hospital*; a Summary of the Minutes of Evidence taken before the Select Committee on the Medical Department (Army) so far as they relate to the re-establishment of that Hospital. By C. Lockhart Robertson, M.B. Cantable, &c., &c., &c." *The Asylum Journal of Mental Science* 3 (1857): 271–6. Web.

Russell, William Howard. *My Diary in India, in the Year 1858–9*. Vol. 1. London: Routledge, Warne, and Routledge, 1860. Web.

Russell, William Howard. *Russell's Despatches from the Crimea, 1854–1856* (ed.) Nicolas Bentley. NY: Hill and Wang, 1966. Print.

Saunders, Nicholas. "Bodies of Metal, Shells of Memory: 'Trench Art' and the Great War Re-Cycled." *Journal of Material Culture* 5.1 (2000): 43–67. Print.

Saunders, Nicholas. *Trench Art*. Princes Risborough: Shire, 2002. Web.

Sen, Surendra Nath. *Eighteen Fifty-Seven*. Delhi: Publications Division, Ministry of Information and Broadcasting, 1957. Print.

Shadwell, Lawrence. *The Life of Colin Campbell, Lord Clyde*. Vol. 1. Edinburgh and London: William Blackwood and Sons, 1881. Web.

Sharpe, Jenny. *Allegories of Empire: The Figure of Woman in the Colonial Text*. Minneapolis: University of Minnesota Press, 1993. Print.

Sherer, John Walter. *Daily Life During the Mutiny: Personal Experiences of 1857*. London: Swann Sonnenschien, 1898. Web.

Siddique, Haroon. "Profile: Lord Ashcroft." *The Guardian*, 1 March, 2010. Web.

Skelley, Alan. *The Victorian Army at Home: The Recruitment and Terms and Conditions of the British Regular, 1859–1899*. London: Croom Helm, 1977. Print.

Smith, Melvin Charles. *Awarded for Valour: A History of the Victoria Cross and the Evolution of British Heroism*. NY: Palgrave Macmillan, 2008. Print.

Spiers, Edward M. *The Late Victorian Army, 1868–1902*. Manchester: Manchester University Press, 1992. Print.

Streets, Heather. *Martial Races: The Military, Race and Masculinity in British Imperial Culture, 1857–1914*. Manchester: Manchester University Press, 2004. Print.

Sullivan, M.G. "Brass Sculpture and the Ideology of Bronze in Britain 1660–1851." *Sculpture Journal* 14 (2005): 30–40. Print.

Tennyson, "The Defense of Lucknow." *Archives of Empire, Volume I: From the East India Company to the Suez Canal* (eds) Barbara Harlow and Mia Carter. Durham: Duke University Press, 2003. 542–5. Print.

"The Corps of Commissionaires." *All the Year Round*, 27 August, 1864: 62–6. Web.

"The Distribution Of Medals In Hyde Park." *The Times*, 25 June, 1857: 9. *The Times Digital Archive*. Web.

"The Saying That The English Are Not A Military People." *The Times*, 27 June, 1857: 9. *The Times Digital Archive*. Web.

"The Siege Of Lucknow." *The Times*, 6 May, 1858: 11. *The Times Digital Archive.* Web.

"The Victoria Cross." *The Times*, 29 June, 1858: 10. *The Times Digital Archive.* Web.

"The Victoria Cross at Auction Part 1: 1856–1983." *Spink*, 13 January 2011. Web.

"The Week." *British Medical Journal*, 19 November, 1859: 945. Web.

Thompson, Edward. *The Other Side of the Medal.* 1926. Westport: Greenwood, 1974. Print.

Thomson, Mowbray. *The Story of Cawnpore.* London: Richard Bentley, 1859. Web.

Thomson, Robert Dundas. "Second Quarterly Meteorological Report at St. Thomas's Hospital for 1857." *The Lancet*, August 22, 1857. 190–92. Web.

Trustram, Myna. *Women of the Regiment: Marriage and the Victorian Army.* Cambridge: Cambridge University Press, 1984. Print.

"Victoria Cross for Cheltenham College's Lieutenant John Duncan Grant sold at auction for £340,000." *Gloucestershire Echo*, 9 July, 2014. Web.

Walter, Edward. "Army Reform." *The Times*, 12 February, 1876: 8. *The Times Digital Archive.* Web.

Ward, Andrew. *Our Bodies Are Scattered: The Cawnpore Massacres and the Indian Mutiny of 1857.* NY: Holt, 1996. Print.

Watson, Bruce. *The Great Indian Mutiny: Colin Campbell and the Campaign at Lucknow.* NY: Praeger, 1991. Print.

White, Michael. "Lord Ashcroft Passes the Buck." *Guardian*, 20 September, 2010. Web.

Chapter 8

Monkeys in the House: Commodities and Competing Fetishisms in Late Victorian Popular Culture

Bradley Deane

The most wondrous sea change in the Victorians' relationship to their material world was the intensifying disposition Marx called commodity fetishism. Drawing on a long history of European derision of West African religious practices, Marx appropriated fetishism as a metaphor for the misapprehension of commodities under capitalism, thereby turning Europe's own scorn for the belief in magical objects back upon itself. In the decades that followed the first volume of *Capital* (1867), Marx's metaphor proved particularly prescient. Advertisers began to encourage—far more vigorously than the economists ridiculed by Marx—fantasies of desirable objects wholly abstracted from any understanding of the social processes that produced them, objects acting with a miraculous agency all their own as they promised impossible benefits. But Marx's fetish metaphor was equally prophetic because the ostensibly primitive regions that had inspired it had become vital sources of British industry's materials, goods, and labor. As the empire expanded, partly to guarantee those new commercial interests, advertisers mystified products in flamboyantly imperialist terms, thereby enacting a paradox that would have delighted Marx: the shadowy terrains of backward superstition were to be subdued and enlightened by a nation of consumers who were themselves eager to buy supernaturally potent commodities stamped with the frontier's exotic glamour.

Cultural historians have compellingly argued that the commodities of late Victorian advertising not only reflected Britain's increasingly imperial self-image, but indeed contributed to the consolidation and escalation of imperialist ideology. "In the hands of 1890s advertisers," Thomas Richards has contended, "the commodity was represented as the bulwark of Empire—as both a stabilizing influence and a major weapon in England's struggle against a bewildering variety of enemies" (142). The triumphant outward march of an ever-widening British influence implied by ads for Bovril or Pears' Soap was coupled with a centripetal movement of the frontier into the Victorian household as commodities festooned with signs of colonial exoticism or imperial might were produced for domestic consumption. Such jingo kitsch, as Richards calls it, "removed Empire from the domain of political struggle by moving it into the home, where ... it became an unthreatening decorative fixture" (134). True to Marx's account of fetishism, Richards's reading of the imperial iconography of late Victorian merchandise suggests that the reassuring sense of commodities' mystical ability to conquer the world or tame the unfamiliar came at the cost of understanding the exploitative and often bloody conditions of production and circulation, both at home and abroad, that made such commodities possible. Anne McClintock's influential analysis of imperial commodity fetishism offers a more complicated view than Richards's, especially because she fuses Marxist and psychoanalytic models of fetishism, reading the fetishized commodity as an ambivalent site at which desire struggles with disavowal. Still, for McClintock, imperialist ideology and commodity fetishism were, in the end, reciprocally legitimating dimensions of late Victorian culture: "commodities were mass-marketed through their appeal to imperial jingoism, [and] commodity jingoism itself helped reinvent and maintain British national unity in the face of deepening imperial competition and colonial resistance" (209).

In the pages of Victorian popular literature, however, we can trace another view of material culture and its fetishes, one in which the seemingly magical commodities circulating through the empire do not so quiescently rest on the mantelpieces of British homes, one in which they guarantee neither the superiority of Victorian values nor the stability of the social structures that bolstered dreams of imperialist consumerism. The key to this alternative view lies in the discourse of fetishism with which the late Victorians were themselves most familiar, a discourse they knew not from Marx or Freud but from contemporary anthropologists such as E.B. Tylor. In the anthropological context, the fetish object was equally resonant with imperial concerns, since the discourse of fetishism was born out of the intercultural contact of European powers and their Others, in what William Pietz has called the "abrupt encounters of radically heterogeneous worlds" (6). Yet by the second half of the nineteenth century, the fetish object began to figure as a fulcrum on which two opposed interpretations precariously balanced: on one hand, the religious worship of objects appeared to the Victorians a barbarous practice beyond which their civilization had evolved; but on the other, they recognized in primitive fetishism an uncomfortably familiar image of their own relationship to their things. The subversive potential of the anthropological fetish object rested in the reversibility of its associations, its competing implications of cultural differences and uncanny similarities. It was a material point of contact which might confirm the Victorians' chauvinistically flattering self-image or might, just as easily, serve as a mirror that reflected back their own superstitions, idolatries, and cruelties.

I will argue that the anthropological notion of the fetish reveals Victorian attitudes toward consumerism and imperialism that remain largely invisible in Marxist and psychoanalytic accounts of commodity fetishism. Where critics such as Richards and McClintock show how material goods could be pressed into the ideological service of hegemonic British capitalism, this chapter will supplement that narrative by emphasizing ways in which relations with the objects of empire could provide a critique of economic practices and colonial chauvinism. I call this subversive image of the imperial object the anthropological fetish, largely because the kind of cross-cultural comparisons elaborated by E.B. Tylor as he defined his fledgling discipline typify the modes of thought through which this critique operated. I do not mean to suggest, however, that all anthropologists and ethnographers agreed on this subject, or that the critique was restricted entirely to their studies.

In fact, the subversive possibilities intimated by the anthropological fetish are most vividly dramatized in popular fiction, particularly within the genre of stories that Patrick Brantlinger has called the "imperial gothic." During the romance revival of the late nineteenth century, many such stories fantasized about colonial objects with actual magical properties, escalating imperial commodity fetishism to its irrational extreme and thereby staging a challenge to a society in which domestic comfort was predicated on the consumption of goods from across the globe. Drawing upon the anthropological understanding of the fetish, these stories articulate a counter-tradition to the commodity fetishism so frequently depicted in Victorian advertising. The commodity may be fetishized, but in these stories the fetish refuses to be commodified. By resisting and even reversing the dynamic of commodity fetishism, these colonial objects reveal the dehumanizing and violent conditions of production that commodity fetishism masks. My chief example will be one of the most memorable tales of horror from the turn of the century, W.W. Jacobs's "The Monkey's Paw." Before exploring Jacobs's story, though, we must consider a few advertisements that illustrate the logic of commodity fetishism as Victorianists have generally come to understand it; these advertisements will demonstrate the forms of fantasy and wish-fulfillment that would be turned on their heads in Jacobs's tale.

From Washing to Wishing: Soap as Imperial Commodity Fetish

The case of the British soap industry exemplifies the ways in which material changes in late nineteenth-century production fueled the escalation of imperial commodity fetishism, both because the industry had come ever more to depend on raw materials imported from the colonial world and because it spent so lavishly on the kinds of ads and branding strategies that typified Britain's increasingly consumerist economy. As a commodity, soap was one of the nineteenth century's great success stories. Before routine washing was popularized by the Duke of Wellington,[1] soap was regarded as an occasional luxury rather than an everyday need, yet by the end of the century, the standards of cleanliness afforded by regular washing of bodies, clothes, and domestic interiors had become one of the principal signs of Victorian virtue and a mark of civilization itself. Figures for the

---

[1] On Wellington's influence, see David Linday and Geoffrey Bamber's *Soapmaking Past and Present*, which offers the year 1815 as the turning point in British washing habits (12).

consumption of soap across Victoria's reign bear out the increasing centrality of soap in daily life: the number of tons of soap consumed in Britain doubled in the 30 years between 1831 and 1861, and multiplied another two and a half times in the following 30 years; consumption per capita also rose precipitously between 1861 and 1891, from 8 to 15.4 pounds per year.[2]

Ironically, the increasingly ubiquitous bars and boxes of soap became signs of the national character only as soap production itself became a global enterprise. The great improvements in soap manufacturing processes largely replaced tallow (rendered fat, chiefly from domestic and Australian livestock) with cheaper and more appealing vegetable oils from regions opened to the British by late nineteenth-century imperial expansion: coconut oil imported from Fiji and New Guinea, cottonseed oil from Egypt, and palm kernel oil from West Africa. In 1889, W.H. Lever, master of the powerful manufacturing company Lever Brothers, built his great factory-town, Port Sunlight, where he had easy access to seaborne imports and could eventually maintain the firm's own ships. By the early twentieth century, the company began to claim its own territories overseas, acquiring 30,000 acres in the British Solomon Islands to grow coconuts as well as a concession to develop 2 million acres of palm forests in the Belgian Congo.[3] The enormous productive capacities of the soapmakers' international network, however, would have amounted to little had they not also produced a corresponding consumer desire. Using what Lever himself called the "hypnotic effect" of advertising, soap manufacturers attempted to convince the public that their products fulfilled needs that consumers never knew they had, and the manufacturers turned to ads to imbue their products with a supernatural aura of desirability. "The whole object of advertising," wrote Lever, "is to build a halo around the article" (qtd in Wilson 21).

Soap manufacturers thus became leaders in new styles of advertising and branding, and from the late 1880s, the pages of illustrated weeklies were dominated by their prominent ads, most notably from three major brands: Lever's Sunlight (a laundering soap), Pears' Soap (which cornered the toilet and complexion market), and Brooke's Monkey Brand (for pots, pans, and nearly every other object or surface in the household). Together these ads created a range of potential meanings for their commodities that had less to do with the efficacy of their cleansing properties than with ideals of Britain's moral innocence, racial purity, and imperial strength. Soap manufacturers well understood the commercial value of investing their products with a fetishizing halo of significations. In 1895, the Philadelphia-based company that made Monkey Brand, Benjamin Brooke and Co., was valued at £250,000, the great bulk of which—more than £189,000—was reckoned as the worth of the brand established by its London advertising office ("Brooke v. Commissioners" 671). When Lever bought Brooke and Co. in 1899, he retained

---

[2] I derive these figures from Charles Wilson's *The History of Unilever*, 9; and Linday and Bamber, 12.

[3] Lever Brothers also eventually purchased what had once been the Royal Niger Company. See *The Story of Port Sunlight*, 12.

the man responsible for the company's renowned advertising campaigns, Sydney Gross, and gave him a seat on the Lever Brothers board.

As cultural historians have since recognized, much of the power of these ads stemmed from their use of the symbolic palette of the late Victorian imperial imagination, which enabled them to depict soap as a medium through which British values flowed outward to a benighted and dirty world even as the wealth and exotic glamour of the colonies flowed back to ease and glorify life in the British home. In the famous jingoistic ads for Pears', the commodity could act as the civilizing mission's magical agent, capable of autonomously transforming the globe even without the aid of soldiers or missionaries.[4] An ad called "The Birth of Civilization," for example, depicted a crate of soap washed up on some savage shore and discovered by a dark-skinned native.[5] This fetishized representation of soap depended not only on erasing the human struggle of imperialism, but also—by reimagining Britain as the source of soap rather than as the primary market for a product manufactured from imported materials—on reversing the actual trajectory of the process of production. Omitting the dependence of British production on foreign material and labor, the ads could thus present a flattering portrait of the stark differences—of race, progress, and civilization—that elevated the imperial center decisively above the periphery of the frontier.

Other soap ads, however, admitted that the wider world might transform life in Britain. For instance, Brooke's Monkey Brand, as a household cleaner rather than a toilet soap, found its ideological destination in the already civilized home rather than in the dirty hands of dusky foreigners. The monkey mascot of the brand, as in the 1894 ad "Adopted by John Bull" (Figure 8.1), appears as an ambassador from some nonspecific colonial space (of the sort, like sub-Saharan Africa or the Indian subcontinent, that Victorians associated with monkeys), who brings to the domestic interiors of Britain the miraculous powers of his soap. Pledging his love for England and promising to "make those homes look cheerful and bright," the monkey holds up a brightly polished frying pan to his patron so that John Bull may see his own satisfaction mirrored back to him in his possession. By 1894, Monkey Brand and its mascot were already well established by years of advertisements, so the implication that the monkey had just been adopted by Britain suggests the need to maintain the monkey's fresh exoticism, to imagine him as always having just arrived. In an ad from 1890 (Figure 8.2), this exoticism is underscored by the monkey's position in front of the ferns in the background, which make him appear as though he has not entirely stepped out of the jungle. The monkey's primitive and alien mystique enhances the fetishistic qualities of the commodity, particularly in reinforcing the soap's promise of an alchemical transformation of household possessions that "Makes Tin like Silver, Copper like Gold, Paint

---

[4]   For an extended analysis of soap as an agent of civilization and imperial progress, see Anandi Ramamurthy's *Imperial Persuaders*, 24–62.

[5]   The "Birth of Civilization" ad is reproduced in McClintock (224), Richards (121), and Ramamurthy (47).

Figure 8.1   Adopted by John Bull
Source: The Graphic, 5 May, 1894.

Figure 8.2   Will Do a Day's Work in an Hour
Source: The Graphic, 31 May, 1890.

like New." Here again, the brightly polished frying pan has been taken out of the kitchen and into a room where it is of no use except as an object of appreciation in its own right, an object whose purpose has become to reflect the character of the British consumers, thus teaching them to admire themselves admiring their things. Divorced from the actual work of cooking, the frying pan has been subsumed into the representational logic of the fetishized commodity, the same logic that transforms the reality of colonial labor relations into the figure of a lovingly subservient monkey who brings to Britain his magical soap.

In its analysis of the imperial commodity fetish as a mystified object that integrates consumerist desires with the fantasy of benign empire by concealing the social relations that enable its own production and circulation, my reading of these Monkey Brand ads follows a conventional line of interpretation. McClintock, whose work on the fetish also includes an analysis of a Monkey Brand ad, has drawn similar conclusions, though with more attention to gender: "Soap is masculinized, figured as a male product, while the (mostly female) labor of the workers in the huge, unhealthy soap factories is disavowed. At the same time, the labor of social transformation in the daily scrubbing and scouring of the sinks, pans, and dishes, labyrinthine floors and corridors of Victorian domestic space vanishes" (217). Here McClintock's reading focuses more on the erasure of women's work rather than that of the colonial labor emphasized in my reading, but both conclusions are compatible, and both are consistent with Marx's model of commodity fetishism. Yet the same Marxist premises that allow us to read these images in this way also render the ads themselves relatively insignificant as cultural agents; in the end, it is not advertising that makes commodities fetishes (although ads may compound the subjective effect), but the very production of objects as commodities to be exchanged. Fetishism for Marx is a structural characteristic of capitalism, and no awareness of hidden social relations can alter it.

It is in fact through a turn from Marx's fetish to Freud's that McClintock develops a deeper and richer account of the cultural work performed by these ads. The psychoanalytic fetish allows us to disavow threatening realities (domestic labor, colonial unrest, atavistic degeneration) by displacing them onto an object or image (monkeys or Monkey Brand soap) which can then be symbolically controlled. We might thus manage our anxieties, but because fetishes are produced by the disavowal of a reality to which we have already been exposed, traces of the anxiety remain legible in the inevitable contradictions of the fetish itself. It is in this sense that McClintock contends that "Like all fetishes, the monkey is a contradictory image, embodying the hope of imperial progress through commerce while at the same time rendering visible deepening Victorian fears of urban militancy and colonial misrule" (217). In this model of fetishism, the ads become more consequential in their own right: not only does the fetish become complex, contradictory, and richly interpretable (as opposed to Marx's account, wherein the contradictions are structural and fetishes are merely mystifications), but it takes on the important cultural work of enabling society to tame its anxieties. McClintock suggests that, ultimately, even the contradictions expressed in the fetish, whether semi-conscious anxieties or "subterranean flows of desire and taboo" (213), are manipulated by advertising's consumerist spectacles, so that "commodity jingoism itself helped reinvent and maintain British national unity in the face of deepening imperial competition and colonial resistance" (209).[6]

My point is not that one or the other of these two models of the fetish better describes the Victorian experience of their material world as it knit together ideas of home and empire, although it is worth acknowledging that the two approaches yield conclusions more disparate than we tend to allow.[7] Instead, I want to draw attention to a blind spot in both approaches, which, in their implication that the Victorians were puppets of capitalist production or jingoist spectacle, obscure the degree to which the Victorians were themselves consciously concerned by, and openly critical of, their relationship to the objects of imperialist consumerism. Indeed their own anthropological discourse on fetishism in the latter half of the century provided a vocabulary with which they could challenge consumerist acquisitiveness or the chauvinist hierarchies of civilization and race. The anthropological fetish became available as a privileged site of contact between the British self and the foreign Other, a physical object that acted as a point of articulation between the social practices of two seemingly incompatible material cultures. Breaking down binary differences between the empire's rulers and its colonial subjects, the fetish could reflect the imperialist critique of barbarity or superstition back upon the Victorians themselves: imagine John Bull peering into the polished frying pan to see not his own face, but the monkey's.

The Anthropological Fetish as Critique

Tylor's method of comparative anthropology is rightly remembered for its patronizing attempts to cast contemporary non-Western social practices as the primitive precursors of Europe's more evolved culture. Yet Tylor's method also compelled attention to the connections between East and West, and to the survival of putatively barbarous practices in his own society. In *Primitive Culture* (1871), fetishism serves as one of his chief examples of the way that apparent differences

---

[6] More recently, Elaine Freedgood's *The Ideas in Things* has also argued for the value of a psychoanalytic interpretation of imperial commodity fetishes, as in her analysis of the references to Negro Head Tobacco in Dickens's *Great Expectations*: "This global commodity fetish is paradoxically closer to Freud's idea of the fetish than to Marx's in that it proffers a *partial* knowledge of social relations, rather than a complete repression or reification of them. It provides for a less veiled form of exchange; indeed, the social relations of production—in the form of slaves used to advertise tobacco—become commodified twice over: as slaves and as 'brand' material. And once commodified, negro heads can still both serve and potentially disrupt the system that has rendered them symbolic" (96).

[7] On logical discrepancies between Marxist and Freudian understandings of the fetish, see Francis Mulhern's "Critical Considerations on the Fetishism of Commodities," 482–3.

are blurred by deep continuities and persistent survivals: "Far on into civilization," he writes, "men still act as if in some half-meant way they believed in souls or ghosts of objects" (500–501). While Tylor openly disdains primitive superstition (and only tacitly implicates Christianity as a vestige of the same irrational impulse), he nevertheless turns repeatedly to fetishism to illustrate cross-cultural continuities, treating it as an expression of "a system of religious philosophy which unites, in one unbroken line of mental connexion, the savage fetish-worshipper and the civilized Christian" (501–2). The popular press often reinforced the possibility that fetishism as a practice did more to unite than distinguish savagery and civilization. An 1883 article called "Fetishism" in *All the Year Round*, for instance, elaborated Tylor's views by comparing West African beliefs with those that exist "to this day, in our own society": the article's examples include "horse-shoes nailed on to stable-doors, and the sixpences with holes, which many people carry about for luck" (227). Such fetishes reveal, as they had for Tylor, "how the whole human race is united by one invisible thread" (229). The fetish emerges as the preeminent symbol of human unity, a reminder even more forceful, the article concludes, than the rhetorical catholicity of Christian doctrine: "We like to talk in missionary meetings of our 'poor black brethren,' but until we consider this question of fetishism perhaps we do not realize how much they really are our brethren" (229).

The cultural continuity of fetishism that fascinated late Victorian anthropologists even turns up in soap advertising, as we find in a Monkey Brand ad from 1899 (Figure 8.3). Like its predecessors, the ad emphasizes the soap's supernatural efficacy, in this case the ability to bring both brightness and good luck. Yet this ad's symbolic logic departs from the others: the thaumaturgical promise of the soap is enhanced not only by the mysterious exoticism of the mascot, but also by the familiar horseshoe charm that frames him. The convergence here of the imperial commodity fetish with what anthropologists saw as a classic British fetish demonstrates the ability of fetishistic iconography to breach the Manichean boundaries of jingoism. Appealing simultaneously to the exotic powers of the commodity and to homegrown British superstition, the ad also humanizes the well-coiffed monkey and represents him—through his watch chain and fob and his cigarette—as a consumer in his own right. Having discarded his pan, the monkey has himself become the funhouse reflection of the spectator.

Yet the ambiguities presented by the fetish's cultural promiscuity were not always treated so optimistically. Even before Tylor, the charge of fetishism had been widely used as a critique of British culture, and of its material culture more specifically. Marx was not the first to invoke fetishism as a metaphor for the absurdities of the modern world of objects, and his own use of the term may owe something to the indirect influence of the trope's frequent repetition. For instance, James Byrne's comparative study of religion in 1859, while in no way sympathetic to Marx's general argument, nevertheless offers an analogy that presages *Capital*: "Just as the miser first loved money for what it could purchase, and then loved it for itself, so the fetish-worshipper first supposed the holy thing to be the medium

Figure 8.3   Brightness Brings Good Luck, Monkey Brand Brings Brightness
Source: The Illustrated London News, 29 April, 1899.

of divine influence, and then attributes divinity to itself' (282). Not only does the derisive parallel Byrne draws between a capitalist practice and fetish-worship remind us of the spirit of Marx's metaphor, but his equation of the love of money for itself and a fully developed fetishism recalls Marx's portrayal of money as the purest form of the commodity fetish. Other writers similarly drew on fetishism to deprecate Victorian willingness to put relationships with objects before the claims of other people. John Hollingshead's 1861 essay on "Fetishes at Home" attacks the fiercely possessive materialism of "the fetish worshippers of civilization, who exist in fruitful abundance around me" (109). In Hollingshead's account, Victorian fetishes take the form of objects purchased for the household and then guarded with a savage and potentially violent jealousy: "Sometimes the fetish is a china punch-bowl, a Wedgwood vase, a Sèvres dessert-plate, or a tea-service. If any man by accident should injure any of these fetishes, let him beware, for civilization has its modes of revenge, not less effective, because deliberate and refined, than the rude, impulsive vengeance of the despised African" (113). Anticipating Tylor's argument, Hollingshead concludes that fetishistic beliefs permeate Victorian material culture, revealing a fundamental unity between an ostensibly civilized race and its foreign antitheses:

> and so we go on, from year to year, with our little likes, our great antipathies, our little weaknesses and our little strength, our shallow doubts and our deep convictions, our virtues and our crimes; and possibly it may turn out, when the great account is at length cast up, that the petty history of one degree of latitude and longitude does not differ very materially from the petty history of another, and that there is not a wonderful difference, after all, between white and whitey-brown, and black, red, pink, olive, blue, and yellow men. (114–15)

In arguments such as Hollingshead's, the binary distinctions of imperialist ideology crumble. The very commodities used as material proof of Britain's advanced civilization or racial superiority become tokens of a lurking barbarism, and the domestic spaces thought to enshrine the best of Victorian virtues instead shelter the crude idolatry of the tea service.

The Monkey's Paw

By the end of the nineteenth century, many popular novels and stories had taken up the theme of the fetish in this anthropological mode; perhaps the most pointed example is Grant Allen's *The British Barbarians* (1895), in which a man from the twenty-fifth century travels back in time to study the taboos and fetishes that the Victorians elaborated in their worship of Mammon.[8] Yet a range of other

---

[8]   Allen's time-traveler, Bertram Ingledew, regards his Victorian hosts in the same anthropological terms in which they speak of primitive foreigners, causing much

fanciful romances represented foreign objects as actually magical, a trope which further subverted imperialist confidence in the superior powers of British reason. Such stories—sometimes comical, sometimes chilling—amount to a popular counter-tradition to imperial commodity fetishism. The supernatural objects of the colonies are no longer so harmlessly domesticated, but exercise a power of their own, particularly the power to dismantle difference between the British and their Others. Like fetishized commodities, they are granted a mysterious agency; unlike those commodities, however, their effect is not to erase imperial labor but to unveil it. The troubles of the frontier are reproduced in the Victorian home, thus exposing the colonial violence suppressed by commodity fetishism, and even suggesting that the British themselves have been objectified by their own consumer culture.

W.W. Jacobs's great contribution to this group of stories was his taut triumph of the macabre, "The Monkey's Paw." First published in 1902, the story was quickly celebrated as a masterpiece of supernatural fiction. A dramatic version was staged at the Haymarket Theatre the following year, and the story has since been firmly established in British and American popular culture, routinely anthologized and frequently adapted for cinema, radio, and television. While it continues to enjoy a long cultural afterlife, the story is best understood in its original context as a document of the horrors that haunted the intersection of empire and material culture at the *fin de siècle*. The story describes an idealized English family, suggestively called the Whites, comprised of two genial, grey-haired parents and their son, a clever, jovial young factory hand named Herbert. The Whites lead a comfortable, lower middle-class life, occupying a villa in a new suburb of the sort that had begun to spring up at the end of the nineteenth century to house the swelling ranks of clerks. In the story's first scene, the Whites are visited by an old friend, Sergeant-Major Morris, who has returned after 21 years of service in India, and who regales them over drinks with tales of "strange scenes and doughty deeds; of wars and plagues and strange peoples" (31). When Mr White muses that he would like to visit India, too, "to see those old temples and fakirs and jugglers," Morris shakes his head and tells him, "Better where you are" (31–2). The exchange signals the exotic allure of Eastern magic on which imperial commodity fetishism draws, but also introduces the story's first warning against such enticements.

Morris reluctantly produces an actual fetish in the anthropological sense: a mummified monkey's paw, which he explains was enchanted by a fakir to grant three wishes. Morris regards the paw as dangerous and tosses it in the fireplace, but Mr White snatches it from the flames and presses Morris to take some money for it, thus drawing the fetish into the comforting field of exchangeable commodities. The Whites can then playfully fantasize about their new possession, which Mrs

---

consternation among the British chauvinists. "I forget every minute," Ingledew apologizes, "that *you* do not recognize the essential identity of your own taboos and poojahs and fetishes with the similar and often indistinguishable taboos and poojahs and fetishes of savages generally" (196).

White observes, "Sounds like the *Arabian Nights*" (35). Busily preparing their dinner, she proposes that her husband "might wish for four pairs of hands for me" (35), a wish that at once recalls the miraculous labor-saving powers of Monkey Brand soap and suggests the transformation of Mrs White into a domestic parody of a multi-armed Hindu goddess. Young Herbert links these Orientalist associations with a more explicitly imperial suggestion: "Wish to be an emperor, father" (36). But Mr White cannot imagine anything he needs: "'I don't know what to wish for, and that's a fact,' he said slowly. 'It seems to me I've got all I want'" (37). Herbert convinces him to make a modest wish for £200, just enough to clear the debt on the villa. As he wishes, the paw twists repulsively in his hand, but nothing else happens. The family retires for the night, leaving Mr White alone staring into his hearth, seeing in the fire a series of ominous faces that culminates in one "so horrible and so simian" that he hurries off to bed (39). Imagining human faces giving way to a simian one in the fire might not amount to seeing a monkey's face reflected in the frying pan, but it is enough to remind Mr White disquietingly that his new possession had a living origin overseas.

Through the remainder of the story, the life of the Whites catastrophically deteriorates. Mr and Mrs White get their £200 the next day, but they receive it from a representative of the factory where Herbert works, Maw and Meggins, who brings it with the news that Herbert has been caught in the machinery and so fearfully mangled that his corpse is barely recognizable. Ten days later, Mrs White suddenly realizes they could use the paw again, and Jacobs represents her as frighteningly hysterical as she wildly demands that her reluctant husband wish Herbert back. Shortly thereafter comes a foreboding pounding at the villa's door, and as Mrs White scrambles to unlock it, her husband "frantically breathe[s] his third and last wish" (53). Jacobs leaves the content of that final wish for the reader to surmise, but whatever it was, the pounding at the door ceases. Mr White hears his wife's "long loud wail of disappointment and misery" as the door opens on the deserted and lonely suburban street (53), an external sign of the utter alienation which has now penetrated the Whites' home.

Jacobs's story rewrites old themes of folklore into a vision of horror tailored for the new age of consumerism. The venerable tale of three imprudently used wishes is common enough to enjoy a category of its own in the Aarne-Thompson folktale classification system: type 750, the "foolish wishes." Typically these are comic stories involving outlandishly poor decisions: in a common European variant, a woman squanders a wish by asking for a sausage, whereupon her angry husband wishes the sausage magically affixed to her nose, so that the couple must spend their last wish detaching it.[9] Jacobs's innovation was not only to darken the

---

[9]   There is even, as Mrs White suggests, a variant of the three wishes story in the *Arabian Nights*, though it seems unlikely she would have read it unless she had managed to find one of the privately printed copies of Richard Burton's unexpurgated translation. In this lewd version the protagonist wastes his wishes in disastrous attempts to alter the size of his penis.

tone of such narratives but to recast the trouble with wishes. While the folklore versions invite us to mock the idiocy of their characters, "The Monkey's Paw" sympathetically presents a family whose wishes begin modestly and remain entirely understandable. The problem is not foolishness or avarice but desire itself; it is not the content of the wishes that brings catastrophe but the very act of wishing. Jacobs emphasizes the Whites' original contentment not only to amplify the horror of their later desolation, but to indicate that they already had all they needed; as Mr White acknowledges, "It seems to me I've got all I want" (37). But the introduction of the fetish in the household generates dissatisfaction, unmooring desire from necessity and utility. It is in this way that "The Monkey's Paw" most powerfully responds to the insinuations of the Monkey Brand ads, which, by taking the frying pan off the fires of the stovetop and repositioning it nearer the hearth, reveal the characteristic ambition of contemporary advertising as the production of previously undiscovered desires. The story speaks to emerging consumerist anxieties by intimating that the deepest horror is the haunting suspicion that even relatively sensible desires, once unchecked by immediate demands of need or use, cannot be ultimately satisfied, but lead instead to the ruinous proliferation of desires, the wish for more wishes.[10]

Like the advertisements we have examined, Jacobs's story entwines consumerism with imperialism, but in his darker vision, the horror of desire is coupled with the dreadful consequences of colonial entanglements. We have seen already that the Indian origin of the paw inspires the Whites to interpret it in imperial terms: hence Herbert's suggestion that his father wish to be an emperor and Mrs White's allusion to the *Arabian Nights*. Yet the anthropological fetish does not simply put the Whites in mind of the exotic, but claws away at the imagined boundary between the domestic scene and the colonies. The description of India as a place "of wars and plagues and strange peoples" turns out by the story's end to be a fair characterization of the Whites' own home. Herbert's death leaves his parents profoundly heartsick, and they become alienated strangers to one another and to the monster we imagine outside the door. The household also becomes a scene of literal and metaphorical violence: Mr White tries forcibly to restrain his wife when they hear the pounding on the door, which Jacobs describes as a "perfect fusillade of knocks" (52). Mr White is similarly compared to a soldier when he learns of his son's death: "On the husband's face was a look such as his friend the sergeant might have carried into his first action" (44).

---

[10] Jacobs's story offers an explicit moral that differs from the point I make here about consumerist desire. Morris tells the Whites that the paw has been enchanted by the fakir with the aim of teaching a lesson to those who would tamper with fate. But this metaphysical point is unsatisfactory even in the story's own terms: if the fakir wanted to dissuade people from challenging fate, he would have done better to refrain from creating the paw, which is the only apparent means by which fate might have been challenged to begin with. At best, this seems a rather nasty case of mystical entrapment.

But if the Whites become linked to the violence of colonialism, they are also joined by the fetish to the natives on whom British aggression was turned, particularly through the story's subtle but insistent implication of the continuity between the monkey itself and the Whites. Though the object at the tale's center is a paw, the narrator obsessively draws attention to the Whites' own hands; the words "hand" and "hands" appear nearly two dozen times in this short tale, making this the most commonly used noun in the text. If, as Aviva Briefel has argued, the disembodied hands that appear so frequently in *fin-de-siècle* stories about the East stand synecdochically for the colonial production of commodities,[11] we can perceive the paw as mediating the connection between the Whites as English workers and their foreign counterparts; Herbert, as what the Victorians would call a factory hand, renders the association stronger still. At every turn the story reproduces the colonial scene in the English home, bringing not only its wonder but its violence, associating the Whites' own hands with an objectified reminder of colonial labor.

Yet the story's most explicit indictment of the objectifying effects of mass production follows from Herbert's grisly fate, which reveals that he had become less than human to his masters even before his parents' desperate wish brings him trudging back from the graveyard. The second of the Whites' visitors, the unnamed representative from Maw and Meggins, can barely meet the eyes of the elderly couple to whom he brings his news, and Jacobs uses him to underscore the callous inhumanity of the system that had used Herbert. Note the man's behavior in the wake of his announcement:

> [Mr White] sat staring blankly out at the window, and taking his wife's hand between his own, pressed it as he had been wont to do in their old courting days nearly forty years before.
>
> 'He was the only one left to us,' he said, turning gently to the visitor. 'It is hard.'
>
> The other coughed, and rising, walked slowly to the window. 'The firm wished me to convey their sincere sympathy with you in your great loss,' he said, without looking round. 'I beg that you will understand I am only their servant and merely obeying orders.' (44)

---

11   In her "Hands of Beauty, Hands of Horror," Briefel argues that the anxiety generated by the repeated motif of the disembodied Eastern hand "emanates from its ambiguous position as an artifact that is itself a source of production" (258). In the mummy stories she examines, the objectified hand refuses to be tamed, but instead makes the English into "inferior replicas," thus putting "the English subjects in their place as the sterile products, not producers, of a technological age" (262). The colonial fetish in "The Monkey's Paw" has much the same effect.

The representative uncomfortably shrugs off Mr White's gentle appeal, giving the lie in his actions to the "sincere sympathy" he has been dispatched to mouth, and taking refuge from the claims of humanity by clinging to his place as an obedient functionary. "I was to say that Maw and Meggins disclaim all responsibility," he proceeds to tell the thunderstruck parents. "They admit no liability at all, but in consideration of your son's services, they wish to present you with a certain sum as compensation" (44–5). Herbert is thus assigned a price and abstracted into a commodity in his own right; he has been brought, as the paw had been earlier in the story, into a vast and inhuman network of exchange values. On both the domestic and colonial fronts, then, the magical fetish here lays bare precisely what commodity fetishism obscures.

By contrasting the different representations of imperial objects in Monkey Brand ads and "The Monkey's Paw," I do not mean to suggest that the latter responds directly to the former, that the ads somehow inspired the story. Any number of ad campaigns might be used to illustrate imperial commodity fetishism, and these coexist with dozens of popular stories about dangerously magical objects from the colonies. For instance, the many late Victorian stories about mummies, as Nicholas Daly has argued, thematize what he calls a "cultural recoil" to imperialism, one in which "domestic space is ... experienced as foreign" (100), and in which commodities "take on a life of their own, and collectors face their own objectification" (102). To the list of mummy stories by such popular writers as Bram Stoker and Rider Haggard, we might also add other tales that are in this respect partly related to "The Monkey's Paw," such as Arthur Conan Doyle's "The Brown Hand" (1899), Rudyard Kipling's "The Mark of the Beast" (1890), and H.G. Wells's "The Lord of the Dynamos" (1895) or "The Magic Shop" (1903).[12] Some of these stories are at least implicitly anti-imperialist, as is arguably the case with Jacobs's. Others are thoroughly imperialist but in a mode that decries consumerism and sees the frontier as a pre-capitalist arena in which the degenerating strength of Britain might be restored. But whatever their politics individually, these stories collectively complicate the assumptions about fetishism we have derived from the spectacular pageant of advertising. They remind us that the Victorians themselves could be critical of the interlocking vices of consumerist materialism and imperial prejudice, and they enrich our understanding of the complex fantasies Victorians entertained about the objects that circulated through their empire and into their homes.

---

[12]   For more comical versions of the disruption of British life by a colonial fetish, see F. Anstey's *Vice Versa* (1882) and *The Brass Bottle* (1900). D.H. Lawrence's "The Rocking-Horse Winner" (1926) would later closely parallel "The Monkey's Paw" by using supernatural elements to dramatize the ruinous proliferation of material desires in the British household, though its only explicit link to empire is the name of the final winning horse, Malabar.

Works Cited

Aarne, Antti. *The Types of the Folktale: A Classification and Bibliography*. Trans. Stith Thompson. 2nd edn, 1961. Helsinki: Academia Scientarium, 1987. Print.

Allen, Grant. *The British Barbarians: A Hill-Top Novel*. NY and London: G.P. Putnam's Sons, 1895. Print.

Anstey, F. *Vice Versa: Or a Lesson to Fathers*. 2nd edn, NY: D. Appleton & Co., 1882. Web.

Anstey, F. *The Brass Bottle*. 2nd edn, NY: D. Appleton & Co., 1900. Web.

Brantlinger, Patrick. *Rule of Darkness: British Literature and Imperialism, 1830–1914*. Ithaca: Cornell University Press, 1988. Print.

Briefel, Aviva. "Hands of Beauty, Hands of Horror: Fear and Egyptian Art at the Fin de Siècle." *Victorian Studies* 50.2 (2008): 263–71. Print.

"Brooke & Co. (Limited) v. Commissioners of Inland Revenue." *The Weekly Reporter* 44 (1895–1896): 670–72. Print.

Byrne, James. "The General Principles of the Religions of Mankind." *Dublin University Magazine* 54 (September 1859): 279–99. Print.

Conan Doyle, Arthur. "The Brown Hand." *Round the Fire Stories*. NY: McClure Co., 1908. 287–307. Web.

Daly, Nicholas. *Modernism, Romance, and the Fin de Siècle*. Cambridge: Cambridge University Press, 1999. Print.

"Fetishism." *All the Year Round*, 18 August, 1883: 226–9. Print.

Freedgood, Elaine. *The Ideas in Things: Fugitive Meaning in the Victorian Novel*. Chicago: University of Chicago Press, 2006. Print.

Hollingshead, John. "Fetishes at Home." *Ways of Life*. London: Groombridge and Sons, 1861. 108–15. Print.

Jacobs, W.W. "The Monkey's Paw." *The Lady of the Barge*. 1902. NY: Dodd, Mead and Co., 1911. 27–53. Print.

Kipling, Rudyard. "The Mark of the Beast." *The Phantom 'Rickshaw and Other Stories*. NY: Charles Scribner's Sons, 1899. 170–91. Web.

Lawrence, D.H. "The Rocking-Horse Winner." *Selected Stories*. NY: Penguin, 2007. 269–85. Print.

Linday, David T.A., and Geoffrey C. Bamber. *Soapmaking Past and Present: Special Edition to Commemorate 100 Years of Soapmaking, 1876–1976*. Nottingham: Gerard Brothers Ltd, 1976. Print.

Marx, Karl. *Capital: A Critique of Political Economy*. Vol. 1. Trans. Ben Fowkes. 1976. London: Penguin, 1990. Print.

McClintock, Anne. *Imperial Leather: Race, Gender, and Sexuality in the Colonial Contest*. NY: Routledge, 1995. Print.

Mulhern, Francis. "Critical Considerations on the Fetishism of Commodities." *ELH* 74 (2007): 479–92. Print.

Pietz, William. "The Problem of the Fetish, I." *Res* 9 (Spring 1985): 5–17. Print.

Ramamurthy, Anandi. *Imperial Persuaders: Images of Africa and Asia in British Advertising*. Manchester: Manchester University Press, 2003. Print.

Richards, Thomas. *The Commodity Culture of Victorian England: Advertising and Spectacle, 1851–1914*. Stanford: Stanford University Press, 1990. Print.

The Story of Port Sunlight. Port Sunlight: Lever Brothers, 1953. Print.

"The Three Wishes, or the Man Who Longed to See the Night of Power." *The Book of a Thousand Nights and a Night*. Vol. 6. Trans. Richard Francis Burton. n.p. 1885. 180–81. Print.

Tylor, Edward Burnett. *Primitive Culture*. 1871. NY: Henry Holt and Co., 1883. Print.

Wells, H.G. "The Lord of the Dynamos." *Selected Stories* (ed.) Ursula K. Le Guin. NY: Random House, 2004. 203–11. Print.

Wells, H.G. "The Magic Shop." *Selected Stories* (ed.) Ursula K. Le Guin. NY: Random House, 2004. 260–270. Print.

Wilson, Charles. *The History of Unilever: A Study in Economic Growth and Social Change*. Vol. 1. London: Cassel and Co., 1954. Print.

Chapter 9

Lady Montagu's Smokers' Pastils and *The Graphic*: Advertising the Harem in the Home

Kellie Holzer

The first issue of *The Graphic*, December 4, 1869, features an advertisement for Smokers' Pastils remarkable for its endorsement by a deceased celebrity:

> *Through all my travels few things astonished me more than seeing the beauties of the Harem smoking the Stamboul. After smoking, a sweet aromatic Lozenge or Pastil is used by them, which is said to impart an odour of flowers to the breath. I have never seen these breath lozenges but once in Europe, and that was at Piesse and Lubin's shop in Bond Street.* —Lady Montagu

Lady Mary Wortley Montagu, wife of the British Ambassador appointed to the Ottoman Empire, lived in Istanbul between 1716 and 1718. Her status as an imperial celebrity derived in part from being the first known western woman to enter an Oriental harem and describe the "mysteries" of this veiled lifestyle in her letters home.[1] Lady Montagu died in 1762—nearly a century prior to the establishment of the Bond Street perfumers Piesse & Lubin. Thus the endorsement, a rhetorical form that ostensibly relies on the authenticity of its speaking subject for its persuasive power, is entirely invented.

The Smokers' Pastils advertisement capitalizes on the midcentury British public's fascination with the Oriental harem via a metonymic chain of commodities that links the Occident to the Orient, ultimately prompting the middle-class figure that critic Lori Anne Loeb names the "consuming angel" to identify with her racial other. The British reader of the Smokers' Pastils advertisement identifies with Lady Montagu's class and racial privileges of mobility and observation and thus

---

[1] A popular account of Lady Montagu's short residence in Istanbul was posthumously published in 1763 as *Turkish Embassy Letters*. Montagu's descriptions of Turkish women in the baths have been richly analyzed as cross-cultural feminine descriptions that subvert patriarchal voyeurism (Billie Melman), a uniquely feminine scopophilia (Indira Ghose), or European woman's appropriation of the masculine gaze and her consequent complicity with Orientalism or with the masculine prerogatives of Aestheticism (Meyda Yegenoglu, Janaki Nair and Elizabeth Bohls).

is, initially, positioned to see with Lady Montagu, "the beauties of the Harem smoking." But further, the advertisement brings the floral-scented lozenge from the harem into English homes, promising the female reader that her breath can be sweetened just like that of the Turkish ladies. Piesse & Lubin link the "Stamboul" or hookah with the tobacco-consuming practices of the English home, inviting the female reader to adopt the leisured behaviors of elite Oriental women. The advertisement signals how the period's nascent commodity culture could re-cast common assumptions about middle-class Victorian femininity, sexuality, and race in surprisingly flexible ways, offering a construction of gendered English identities that exceeds what Simon Gikandi has called the "now familiar dialectic of identity and difference."[2]

Probably because pastilles were a fairly mundane household item (common both as candy and as a medication for treating throat ailments), Piesse & Lubin resorted to using the fantasy of the harem to sell the product. The *faux* Lady Montagu endorsement was cleverly timed, as the harem figured prominently in Victorian public discourses in several ways. It was an object of fascination described in fiction and in ethnographic and travel writing. It was a symbol for all that threatened the sanctity of the private sphere and the institution of marriage. It was a tourist destination, particularly after 1869 when the opening of the Suez Canal made travel to the Middle East more accessible to middle-class travelers. And it was deployed to promote both Victorian feminist and anti-feminist agendas. My analysis of the Smokers' Pastils advertisement begins with the questions, *how else* does the harem figure into English domestic culture and economy? And how can the representation of a lozenge materialize a set of relations between the consuming angel and her Oriental counterpart, the odalisque? I argue that the advertisement's invitation to female cross-racial identification provides further evidence that ideological constructions of racial difference were contingent particularly in the context of imperial capitalism—that lines drawn between the metropolitan ruling culture and the cultures of the ruled were tenuous, permeable.[3] The advertisement's location in *The Graphic*, a middle-class weekly illustrated newspaper, suggests that under certain conditions the institutions of capitalism would not hesitate to draw equivalences between women in different cultures, appealing to British aspirations of social mobility and overriding racial difference to reinforce patriarchal structures of authority and imperial commerce.

---

[2]   In historiography, Englishness has been conceptualized as a national identity shaped through racial differentiation and fashioned in response to conflict with a threatening, typically exotic other: see Linda Colley and Kathleen Wilson. Gikandi puts pressure on this dialectic, detailing British identity as a more ambivalent cultural phenomenon, staged as both "radically different and yet inherently similar" (2). He writes that while the dialectic between identity and difference is an "enabling condition for the project of postcolonial studies, it has never been clear where the identity between colonizer and colonized ends and the difference between them begins" (2).

[3]   On the contingency of colonial categories of difference, see Ann Laura Stoler.

The following analysis considers the ways that the Smokers' Pastils advertisement differentiates consumers by gender and sexuality by using the language of imperial fantasy to translate the "thing"—the hard candy—into a commodity. At the same time, the advertisement's narrative obscures the material histories of the production of pastils and related commodities of Victorian smoking culture. I begin by locating the advertisement in its historical context and tracing the Victorian trope of the harem in order to arrive at another way of understanding how British middle-class domesticity was structured by everyday practices and material objects derived from Oriental cultures.

Puffing Trends I: The Harem as Commodity–Spectacle

Many scholars have noted that advertisements bear witness to a commodity's historical context.[4] The Smokers' Pastils historical moment was characterized not only by a swiftly evolving middle-class consumer culture and rapid developments in the institution of advertising, but also by a fascination with Middle Eastern modes of domesticity that gained visibility through the tourism industry and the increased accessibility of the women's quarters in Middle Eastern households. This fascination with harems was reinforced by sensational news stories and fictions about bigamy cases in the British Isles.[5] These trends intersect and converge in the Smokers' Pastils advertisement as a commodity-spectacle. The term "commodity-spectacle" usefully indicates the way that advertisements combine economic and cultural forms. At once artistic (or literary) and commercial, such representations transcend the imperative to buy; they are narratives of exchange-value that invent social relations. The contextualization of the Smokers' Pastils advertisement below demonstrates that in industrial modernity, the commodity-spectacle (the basis for modern Victorian commodity culture) mediates between the domestic and the colonial.

Piesse & Lubin's 1869 advertisement occupies a transitional place in the emergence of the late Victorian advertising industry. The nineteenth century witnessed advertising move from the public sphere—literally, the streets—into the middle-class home with the expansion of newspaper circulation and the rise

---

[4] My conception of advertisements as economic representations that organize social life relies on work by Thomas Richards and Lori Anne Loeb. Building on Guy Debord's insights on commodities as spectacle, Richards argues that advertising is the semiotic side of capitalism: the commodity transformed into language and spectacle, a discourse that inscribes subjects. Loeb sees advertisements as carriers of culture, historical documents that reveal cultural ideals. See Asa Briggs, as well.

[5] The 1860s saw a publishing boom in sensation fictions with bigamy plots that were based on real-life news stories such as the 1861 Yelverton case in which Theresa Longworth discovered that the Hon. William Charles Yelverton, whom she had married in secret, had married another woman. See Jeanne Fahnestock and Rebecca Gill.

in income and in leisure time for reading. At midcentury, most advertising still consisted of bills haphazardly posted on hoardings and sides of buildings or distributed in the streets, hawkers calling out formulaic and time-tested slogans, sandwich-boards, and advertising van men (Richards 45). Loeb describes the period between 1850 and 1880 as an "advertising craze" stimulated by the abolition of the advertising duty, increased professionalization (e.g. the rise of the designer and agent), the recognition of the middle classes' expansion and potential as a market, and new techniques in illustration (5). In this context, as a translation of a thing into a narrative, the form of Piesse & Lubin's advertisement is fairly primitive: confined to the narrow, uniform, back-page columns of *The Graphic's* advertisement section, it lacks the lavish illustrations of *fin-de-siècle* ads (Figure 9.1). In spite of the enlarged headline in bold typeface announcing the product, "Smokers' Pastils.—" the text itself does not quite register the significance of the commodity, which is ultimately subordinated to the fascinating narrative of Lady Montagu's endorsement.[6] The advertisement is also rhetorically primitive, as marketing strategies go: there is no argument, appeal, or imperative to shop. It is, rather, an ethnographic description of a scene followed by information about the store and the price: "Sold in boxes, 2*s*.—2, New Bond St., London."

And yet if the Smokers' Pastils advertisement is visually and rhetorically primitive, it is modern in the topicality of its content and in its narrative excess through which it articulates social relations beyond mere economic exchange. It employs an artificial and extravagant means of stylizing the product—floral breath lozenges—creating a lifestyle of luxury and leisure around the pastille by citing a stereotype of Oriental domesticity. The narrative effectively detaches the commodity from the milieu of its production, and relocates the product's consumption to a fantasy harem inside the English home. The advertisement's narrative is a mode of sensationalistic journalism that functions by creating a commodity-spectacle: its narrative excess participates in a larger cultural transition from earlier modes of spectacle such as melodrama to the fetishization of the commodity, a discursive staging of the thing that elevates it sensationally through narrative out of the realm of material exchange altogether.

By transforming a mundane commodity into an exoticizing and eroticizing narrative, the advertisement draws on the logic of masculine imperial fantasy discourse, combining the conventions of sensation journalism, ethnographic description, and travel writing.[7] One implication of this is that, as with all Orientalist discourse, the advertisement bears no relation (or obligation) to "truth." This sketchy relationship to objective truth—here embodied in the imagined category

---

[6] According to Richards, "In the sensation advertising of the 1860's the commodity did not speak at all: it was still a trivial thing, so trivial that it had to be hidden away, veiled with outrageous rhetoric, deprived of its attributes, and offered for public consumption as something other than an article of manufacture" (70).

[7] For a germinal discussion of masculine entitlement in travel writing and ethnography, see Mary Louise Pratt.

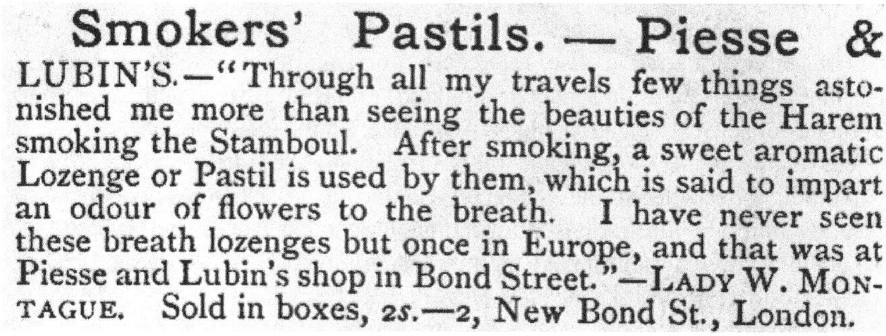

Smokers' Pastils. — Piesse &

LUBIN'S.—"Through all my travels few things astonished me more than seeing the beauties of the Harem smoking the Stamboul. After smoking, a sweet aromatic Lozenge or Pastil is used by them, which is said to impart an odour of flowers to the breath. I have never seen these breath lozenges but once in Europe, and that was at Piesse and Lubin's shop in Bond Street."—LADY W. MONTAGUE. Sold in boxes, *2s.*—2, New Bond St., London.

Figure 9.1   Smokers' Pastils
Source: The Graphic, 4 December, 1869.

of the harem "beauties"—was already a target of critique within the advertising industry. Gimmicks such as fabricated product endorsements were rampant in early nineteenth-century advertising, as Abraham Hayward indicated in an article entitled "The Advertising System" printed in the *Edinburgh Review* in February 1843. In this article, Hayward provides a taxonomy of the "most shameless arts of puffery" by charlatans, quacks, and self-promoters in every occupation (16). Hayward's taxonomy is useful to placing Piesse & Lubin's Smokers' Pastils advertisement into a larger context of puffing trends. Targeting the hyperbolic testimonials of supposedly real customers, Hayward notes that some particularly inventive advertisements cited royal patronage to legitimate the claims within.[8] One advertisement that Hayward mocks is for a dietary supplement called "The *Raccahout des Arabes*." According to the advertisement, the French discovered and imported this "cure for leanness" said to be the "preparation on which the Dey of Algiers fattened his Harem" and to be "held in high esteem throughout the East" (Hayward 12). Like the Smokers' Pastils advertisement, this advertisement cites a travel narrative in which a Captain Harris describes an African country where one of the ruler's 15 wives became her husband's favorite with recourse to the *raccahout*. The *Raccahout* advertisement indicates that a precedent had already been set for Piesse & Lubin's appeal to English ladies to imitate the lifestyles and beauty

---

[8]   Hayward cites a particularly humorous example of one advertisement's attempt to gain legitimacy: "Mr Cockle's Antibilious Pills are recommended by a long list of patrons, containing ten Dukes, five Marquises, seventeen Earls, eight Viscounts, sixteen Lords, one Archbishop (Armagh), fifteen Bishops, the Adjutant-General, the present Attorney-General, the late Attorney-General, the Advocate-General, Sir Francis Burdett, Sir Andrew Agnew, Alderman Wood, and Mr. Sergeant Talfourd … This list might give rise to curious speculations as to the comparative biliousness of the higher classes" (6).

regimens of non-white women across the empire.[9] Significantly, the *Raccahout* advertisement's narrative also references polygamous modes of domesticity, inviting the housewife (in France or England) to further participate imaginatively in modes of self-exoticization and self-eroticization via consumption.

Its inclusion in *The Graphic* of December 4, 1869 serves to amplify the commodity-spectacle of the Smokers' Pastils advertisement, since this issue features multiple illustrations drawing on Orientalist tropes and evoking the sexual and imperial fantasies of the newspaper's readers. In this issue, national and domestic concerns like the Houseless Poor Act and the latest Parisian fashions compete with imperial news items and images based on paintings by celebrated Orientalist artists Gustav Richter and Jean-Léon Gérôme. The cover features an engraving of Richter's bejeweled "Egyptian Girl" looking coyly away from the viewer (Figure 9.2).

The reader's interest in empire indicated (or created) by the cover image is reinforced throughout the journal by illustrated features and news stories about imperial commerce and politics such as the full-page engraving of the "Pasha's Couriers." This illustration of two turbaned messengers flying out the entrance of a crumbling fort accompanies a news item about Algiers, where "[t]he Pasha himself has cast aside the pipe of contemplation and seized the sabre of revenge," his idle leisure disrupted by proclamations of war against the French infidels ("Pasha's Couriers" 15). This story engages Victorian stereotypes about French colonialism and Oriental violence and excess, dramatizing the ways that colonial politics disrupt the luxuries of Oriental idleness.

The reader's interest in empire is next captured by two illustrated articles about the Suez Canal, a buzzing topic in December 1869. The first article, "The Suez Canal," incorporates a large woodcut entitled "Bird's Eye View of the Suez Canal" and a series of six small ethnographically styled woodcuts of "Scenes on the Banks of the Suez Canal." This article addresses the need to widen and deepen the canal to allow larger vessels to pass through, a problem of engineering and planning that the writer surmises may reanimate "the old apprehensions as to the commercial success of the undertaking" ("Suez Canal" 15). The second article, entitled the "Opening of the Suez Canal," displays portraits of the Khedive of Egypt and M. de Lesseps inset into an article praising de Lesseps' honorable motivation "to promote commercial intercourse between the West and the East" and reassuring readers that the recent differences between the Ottoman Sultanate and the Egyptian Khedive would be neutralized by the "Powers of Europe" that share a common interest in the commercial passage ("Opening" 20). This news item gestures at the Levantine

---

[9]   Adjacent to the Smokers' Pastils advertisement readers of *The Graphic* would find two additional advertisements from Piesse & Lubin for equally exotic substances for consumption in the English home: fragrant essences of Frangipani, Patchouly, and Ylang-Ylang, as well as "Pestachio Nut Toilet Powder" promising to impart to browned or reddened skin a "natural whiteness." All three Piesse & Lubin advertisements invite the "consuming angel" to identify with her racial Other.

Figure 9.2   Gustav Richter, "Egyptian Girl"
Source: The Graphic, 4 December, 1869.

antagonisms that threatened the success of Europe's and England's traffic in India, China, Australia and other "regions of the East," invoking the near eastern "Orient" as an obstacle to English national and imperial prosperity. The conflict between Turkey and Egypt alluded to in the article is reinscribed through the juxtaposition of two portraits of Levantine women in the bound volume of the first six months' numbers of *The Graphic*.[10] The frontispiece of the first bound volume of *The Graphic* (June 1870) features an engraving of Richter's "An Odalisque" (Figure 9.3), followed by the title page, introduction, and an index, and then the reader encounters Richter's "Egyptian Girl," the cover image of the first issue, discussed above. The representations share visual cues: both portraits depict a woman with dark eyes, elaborate jewelry and headdress, and low neckline. Together, Richter's portraits of Eastern women suggest the commercial appeal of the harem. Overall, the repeated cross-referencing of Levantine women and imperial commerce in the articles, engravings, and advertisements reinforces that the Victorian home was organized as much around titillating imperial commodity–spectacles as around material goods and news from the empire.

The advertisement's power to bring aspects of Oriental domesticity into the Victorian home discursively performs an apt reversal of the trajectory of British intrusions into actual harems—intrusions facilitated by the opening of the Suez Canal. Not only did this new route "promote commercial intercourse between the West and the East," it also prompted the rapid expansion of mass tourism to the Orient encouraged by guide books and organized trips like those of Thomas Cook's to Palestine and Egypt beginning in 1869 (Melman 35). As travel to the Orient became more accessible to the middle classes, more Muslim households opened up to curious tourists and travel writers. Harem visits became "a staple of the tourist itinerary" (Lewis 14). The increasing safety and ease for women traveling to the Middle East resulted in the development of a genre authored by western women that Billie Melman has called "harem literature," a mode of writing aligned with ethnography in its interest in the customs and manners of the harem and its inhabitants. Reina Lewis describes the popularity of harem writing in *Rethinking Orientalism*: "any book that had anything to do with the harem sold. Publishers knew it, booksellers knew it, readers knew it and authors knew it" (13). Western women writers excelled in this genre because they could access spaces from which male travelers were barred. Marked by the domestication and humanization of the harem, such writing also began to reflect early western feminist desires for greater independence—or at least the right to own property, as Ottoman women could. In short, women's harem literature exhibited conflicting tendencies to cross-cultural

---

[10]   Formal distinctions should be made between individual newspaper numbers and annual or semi-annual bound volumes of the same periodicals. Bound volumes were popular library additions for many middle-class Victorians. The volume of *The Graphic* that I examined, published in June 1870, is part of the collection at the University of Washington, Seattle. Sadly, as of July 2012, the frontispiece is missing from the volume.

AN ODALISQUE
FROM A PICTURE BY RICHTER

Figure 9.3   Gustav Richter, "An Odalisque"
Source: The Graphic, June 1870.

comparison, identification and sympathy especially along lines of gender, as well as the reiteration of racial or cultural difference.

The Smokers' Pastils advertisement capitalizes on the popularity of harem tourism and literature in a way that likewise differentiates its readers by gender and sexuality. Eastern harems were opened up for the spectatorial consumption and exploitation by British tourists and travel writers; the advertisement relies on similar spectatorial devices. Although the advertisement contains no illustrations, its imagery and diction locate it in the realm of the visual, a locus of asymmetrical power relations. The advertisement invites the reader's gaze by invoking representations of odalisques and Turkish baths already in circulation. This invocation, functioning grammatically as an imperative to look at the beauties of the harem, organizes reading subjects into a male/female binary. It does this by participating in two familiar discourses of mid-Victorian writing, Aestheticism and Orientalism, both of which helped to structure and maintain hierarchies of social power in imperial England. In Aesthetics as it was elaborated in the eighteenth century, the viewing subject is understood to be masculine and a gentleman (Bohls 9). The distinctly masculine sense of entitlement operating in the gaze of aesthetic contemplation is akin to that operating in the gaze of the Orientalist subject—the male explorer, traveler, ethnographer, trader, soldier, or diplomat.[11] However, while the Smokers' Pastils advertisement participates in Orientalist discourse, especially insofar as it was manifest in women's harem literature, it does so in a way that, rather than domesticating the exotic, *exoticizes the domestic* by inserting the possibility of the harem into the drawing room of the middle-class home.[12] Importantly, from the perspective of commodity culture, this prospect is not a threat to English domesticity. Rather, the harem "beauties" are invited in as examples of the good life. They are to be envied for their leisure, their self-indulgences, and even their sexuality. In short, the female reader as a consuming angel is invited to imitate the odalisque.

To further contextualize this invitation to identify across constructs of racial difference, we might return to the scene of the early eighteenth century and Lady Montagu's letters from the Turkish Embassy. As scholars such as Ghose, Lewis

---

[11]   Said provides an example of this in his description of the relationship of material, sexual, and discursive domination between Gustave Flaubert and Kuchuk Hanem, the Egyptian courtesan. Flaubert's account of Kuchuk Hanem in his travel writings "produced a widely influential model of the Oriental woman; she never spoke herself, she never represented her emotions, presence, or history. *He* spoke for her and represented her. He was foreign, comparatively wealthy, male, and these were historical facts of domination that allowed him not only to possess Kuchuk Hanem physically but to speak for her" (Said 6).

[12]   This possibility was alternatively a fantasy and a threat. See Fahnestock and Kaori Nagai, both of whom analyze the deceased wife's sister marriage controversy. Fahnestock argues that debates over legalizing such marriages in the 1860s were symptomatic of bourgeois bigamy fantasies. Nagai addresses the ways that the legalization of such marriages in British settler colonies represented the threat of polygamous relations in English homes.

and Bohls have noted, Lady Montagu's position in the Turkish baths and harems was complex. As a woman she was accustomed to being an object of the male gaze; yet in the harem or the baths she was at once spectator (appropriating the masculine gaze and narrative authority) and spectacle (the object of the Turkish women's interested gazes). Lady Montagu was no doubt familiar with the stereotypes circulated by her male contemporaries of Turkish women as oversexed houris. Indeed, excerpts from Alexander Pope's letters to Lady Montagu while she was traveling through Turkey in 1717–1718 exhibit the twinned Enlightenment tropes of the lascivious odalisque and the jealous Ottoman. Pope writes to Lady Montagu regarding her imminent arrival in Turkey: "[you will soon be] in the land of Jealousy, where the unhappy women converse but with Eunuchs, and where the very cucumbers are brought cutt [sic]" (qtd in Melman 72). In contrast to male writers' fantasies, Lady Montagu's description of the women in the baths in Sofia emphasizes her own position as an oddity and the "obliging civility" of the Ottoman ladies (Montagu 58). In this well-known passage, Lady Montagu not only reverses the direction of the typical male writer's powerful curiosity by placing herself under the objectifying gaze of the bathers, she also directly contradicts the male writers' stereotypes: "there was not the least wanton smile or immodest gesture amongst them" (Montagu 59). Scholars agree that in the *Turkish Embassy Letters* Montagu had undertaken to revise male writers' exoticizing and eroticizing stereotypes of Oriental women.[13] However, as Bohls points out, Montagu's aristocratic status still aligns her with the privileged masculine subjectivity of the Aesthetic viewer.[14] That is, her careful representations of the Ottoman ladies still participate in their objectification. In appropriating the male gaze in her representation of the women, Montagu has usurped masculine aesthetic and authorial privilege, but has not relinquished the racial privilege inherent in the power to create and circulate such representations.

Just as Montagu's racially privileged spectator position in the Turkish women's quarters was complicated by her culturally prescribed gender status as both an erotic and aesthetic object, we must read the Smokers' Pastils advertisement as operating with the same complications for its female readers. This tension between women's objecthood and their status as subjects, agents or spectators

---

[13]   Lewis summarizes: "Writing against the already prevalent codification of the polygamous harem as a space of sexual depravity and random cruelty, Montagu's observations took a culturally relativist stance" (13). Montagu's eyewitness account influenced later harem descriptions by western women. Lewis writes, "Her willingness to evaluate the harem, seen in men's (imaginary) accounts as the ultimately 'other' space of the Orient, in relation to Western domestic gender relations, was to become typical of Western women's harem literature" (13).

[14]   Bohls observes that Lady Montagu compares Turkish women to the beautiful goddesses populating great European works of art by Guido and Titian in order to undermine degrading masculine depictions. Montagu's "description of the women's baths boldly turns the language of aesthetics as a rhetorical weapon against Orientalist stereotypes, but cannot leave aesthetics' troubling power dynamics entirely behind" (Bohls 24).

is clearly replicated in the advertisement and the way it hails male and female readers differently. The former are encouraged to "look" with the potential to have or possess the beauties of the harem through the metonymic chain of objects to which the advertisement points: pastil, tobacco, hookah, harem. The latter are encouraged to "look" with the potential to identify with the lazy sensuality of the odalisque, to imitate or imaginatively become another one of the beauties of the harem. While the advertisement might stimulate a male reader's desire to possess both materially and sexually the "commodities" it displays, the female readers are positioned at once as spectator–consumer and commodity–spectacle.

This complex positioning of the female reader reveals an alternative way that the harem figured in Victorian discourse: as a catalyst for a mode of capitalist consumption that would produce the middle-class English woman (the "consuming angel") as a sexual subject. This mode of consumption hinged on the operation of an analogy between English women and Oriental women, an analogy that also appears strategically in Victorian feminist deployments of the trope of the harem. I use the term "analogy" not in the sense of an ontological comparison but rather as an idiomatic equivalence of function. Thinking analogically in this sense means transferring attributes from a familiar source entity (here, the analogue is the stereotype of the odalisque) to another entity (the middle-class wife). This cognitive process identifies relations between the two entities inferentially; analogies create knowledge about the target entity that previously was not available (i.e. the housewife is sensual). The advertisement's deployment of the harem as the stage for its commodity–spectacle produces an effect of cross-cultural equivalence, not a literal likeness but an imagined unity via a shared sexual identity: non-reproductive yet compulsory heterosexuality. As analogies tend to do, the advertisement's inferred comparison of housewife to odalisque occludes the very real power hierarchies among eastern and western women, even if only temporarily. In the next part of my argument, I explore the historical precedents of this analogy by tracing the ways that the harem figured in nineteenth-century feminist discourse.

Analogy and the Uses of the Harem

For British social reformers, the trope of the harem indexed a general concern with practices of female seclusion in the Orient and a disapproval of what they perceived as Oriental domestic despotisms. Social reformers and early feminists often conflated Indian, Turkish, Algerian, and other cultures' practices of female seclusion in the same way that plural wives in Asian cultures were conflated with concubines. In such writing, the terms "purdah" and "zenana" (both of Persian origin, variously denoting "screen," "veil," or "women's quarters"), "harem" (Arabic, suggesting both the veil and the physical confinement of women), and "seraglio" (an Italian word adapted from the Latin for "enclosure") all came to be associated with polygamy and female incarceration. Thus we can speak of an undifferentiated Victorian trope of the harem as a general equivalent of the "gilded cage," a cruel imprisonment and typically a sign of that barbarism against which England needed to distinguish itself. In short, the harem functioned as a signifier of the superiority of western culture—a superiority, feminists argued, that could be reconfirmed by giving more rights and opportunities to English women.

Victorian feminist deployments of the trope of the harem had a noteworthy antecedent in Mary Wollstonecraft's *A Vindication of the Rights of Woman* (1792). For Wollstonecraft the harem stood for a barbarism already lurking *within* England and English homes—suggesting a dangerous likeness between English women and odalisques and between English men and Oriental despots. In *Vindication* she indicts middle-class English women for willingly subjecting themselves to the frivolous training which makes them "fit only for a seraglio!" (10). In other words, in the current state of things middle-class English women are no better than odalisques.[15] Here and elsewhere in *Vindication*, Wollstonecraft is reacting to Rousseau's assertion in Émile that women ought to be granted little liberty. Rousseau had written, "For my part, I would have a young Englishwoman cultivate her agreeable talents, in order to please her future husband, with as much care and assiduity as a young Circassian cultivates her's, to fit her for the Haram of an Eastern bashaw" (qtd in Wollstonecraft 86). In response, Wollstonecraft urges English women to reject the gilded cage. "In a seraglio," Wollstonecraft writes:

> all these arts are necessary; the epicure must have his palate tickled, or he will sink into apathy; but have women so little ambition as to be satisfied with such a condition? Can they supinely dream life away in the lap of pleasure, or the languor of weariness, rather than assert their claim to pursue reasonable pleasures and render themselves conspicuous by practising the virtues which dignify mankind? (29)

Here Wollstonecraft at once pleads against the comparison of English women to Oriental women and deploys the threatening analogy between them to rail against despotism in English homes.

Nineteenth-century feminists adapted such rhetoric about the condition of women and the trope of harem from the writings of Mary Wollstonecraft, as well as those of James Mill[16] and later social evolutionist thought.[17] In Victorian

---

[15]   While she paints a negative portrait of the unambitious, idle, pleasure-loving Oriental woman in order to chastise her English sisters, Wollstonecraft saves her severest criticism for the despotic English men who prevent women from developing their faculties of reason and virtue and who fit their wives and daughters out for the harem: "the husband who lords it in his little haram thinks only of his pleasure or his convenience" (73).

[16]   On female seclusion as evidence of the degraded condition of Oriental women, see Mill 309.

[17]   Thus Henrietta Müller, active in the women's suffrage movement in the 1880s and the daughter of the renowned Orientalist scholar Max Müller, could declare in 1894—nearly

feminist rhetoric the figure of the Oriental woman was the victim of the violent excesses of Oriental domesticity such as "suttee," child marriage, polygamy and seclusion. Like Flaubert's Kuchuk Hanem, a definitive Orientalist representation that Said described as "[l]ess a woman than a display of impressive but verbally inexpressive femininity," the Oriental woman continued to be the mute object of Victorian reform projects which included not only education and religious salvation for the racial other, but education, suffrage, and property rights for English women (Said 187). Inderpal Grewal writes that "women in England fought for their rights with frequent references to the subordination and incarceration of Asian women" (64). Likewise, according to Antoinette Burton, "Feminist writers who constructed arguments about the need for female emancipation built them around the specter of a passive and enslaved Indian womanhood" (63). Burton continues, "[d]isdain for the harem became an essential part of feminist emancipationist argument. Seclusion was thought to be the equivalent of degradation, and harem life 'dull and vacuous to the last degree'" (66).

Late twentieth-century harem scholarship like that by Grewal and Burton cited above tends to engage the discursive tradition of nineteenth-century feminism in a way that emphasizes the instrumentality of constructions of racial difference for Victorian women and overlooks analogies drawn between English and Asian women in Victorian writing. In *Burdens of History* (1994), Burton argues that nineteenth-century feminism, far from organizing in terms of a global sisterhood to combat patriarchal oppression, actually reinforced constructions of the racial difference of colonized women in order to make bids for greater liberties and rights. Similarly in *Home and Harem* (1996), Grewal writes regarding the suffragist movement, "[t]here was little consciousness of any solidarity on the part of Englishwomen with the oppressed in the colonies" (74). Both of these texts do the important work of revealing the complicity of Victorian feminism with imperialism. That is, when Victorian feminists considered the harem, it was often as a symbol of a racially distinct despotic form of rule by domination, wherein women were incarcerated and oppressed. Such a discourse could as easily be mobilized to justify colonization and the civilizing mission as it could be adapted to argue for women's emancipation at home in England, and then by extension to British women across the empire.

But neither Burton nor Grewal explore modes of relations other than the political between English women and colonized women. Billie Melman's book *Women's Orients* offers one alternative. Analyzing 200 years of western women's travel writing, Melman argues:

> Travel and the encounter with systems of behaviour, manners and morals, most notably with the systems of polygamy, concubinage and the sequestration of females, resulted in analogy between the polygamous Orient and the travelling

80 years after Mill's *History*—that "intelligence and status of the women of a country are a measure of its civilization" (qtd in Burton 83).

women's own monogamous society. And analogy led to self-criticism rather than cultural smugness and sometimes resulted in an *identification with the other* that cut across the barriers of religion, culture and ethnicity. (8, emphasis added)

Melman's analysis points to an affinity between western and eastern women, a not-quite gender solidarity that, though structured by the politics of empire, could also extend beyond relations of economic and political power. Melman's rich archive narrates the story of English women's infiltration in Oriental domesticity. Meanwhile, as I suggest above, the Smokers' Pastils advertisement in *The Graphic* indexes the reversal of that narrative. Having infiltrated the English home, Piesse & Lubin's advertisement prompts that female cross-racial identification initiated by Lady Montagu and condemned by Mary Wollstonecraft.

Melman's analysis gestures at cross-racial identification as an alternative social relation between English and Asian women. I offer a second alternative, that of an analogy—an idiomatic equivalence of function—made possible through Victorian commodity culture. The Smokers' Pastils advertisement stages *material* relations between English women and their racial other, bringing everyday household things into the equation. In my reading, the advertisement destabilizes and denaturalizes the Victorian (and all too often, Victorian*ist*) binary of home and harem through the implied circulation of things. In the harem *within* the English home as it is constructed by the advertisement, idleness signifies not racial inferiority but the economic privilege of leisure realized in things like hard candies and the trappings of smoking culture. In terms of consumer capitalism, the advertisement piques bourgeois aspirations of social mobility and it grounds these aspirations in patriarchal fantasies of English women's sexual promise. That is, conspiring with other imperial images in *The Graphic* of Levantine women, the Suez Canal, and Algeria, all of which allude to Orientalist paintings of the harem, the advertisement constructs English women as sexual beings. And it does so, in part, through its cheeky inference that the angel in the house might indulge in smoking. Pipes, cigars, and cigarettes are no less phallic than Pope's infamous cucumbers. With the aid of everyday things that require puffing and sucking, the middle-class woman of the house is eroticized as an odalisque in a scene from Orientalist art.

In Orientalist painting, while the racial difference between the Muslim and non-Muslim male is very much kept intact, distinctions of race grow more ambiguous when it comes to representing the woman in the harem. In a selective survey of nineteenth-century Orientalist painting, Ivan Kalmar notes that the implied viewer of such paintings as those by Ingres, Delacroix, and Gérôme is not the Muslim lord of the harem but the European male: "He has penetrated the Muslim man's harem, encountering no opposition. (Presumably his Muslim opponent has already been defeated.) The odalisque is waiting for *him*" (220). While the prototypical audience for Orientalist paintings of harem inhabitants is the white male, the figure of the odalisque is rendered as racially *white*. Kalmar argues:

> It is European women that are here the willing prisoners in a harem that has been taken into the imagined possession of a male European spectator ... To this extent, the orientalist harem painting is not a projection of the East into the West, but a perverse projection of the Western woman into the subject position of a powerless sex slave. (222)

Kalmar's words suggest that for Victorians, the harem continued to spark male fantasies of domination over women of any color or creed, even though its "secrets" had been penetrated and revealed in harem literature. Like Orientalist painting, to which the advertisement alludes through visual invocations of the reclining odalisque freshening her breath after smoking the "Stamboul," the advertisement sexualizes English women in everyday acts of idle consumption such as smoking in the privacy of their own homes.

As Grewal and others have argued, "home" may have been most recognizable as a discursive contrast to "harem," but ideas about home had already assimilated imaginary aspects of Oriental domesticity, just as homes themselves were populated with things from the Orient. Indeed, homes in England were as transformed by contact with colonial subjects and imperial commodities like tobacco, as homes in the empire were transformed through contact with the subjects and objects of the Occident. To unpack the way that exotic objects of Victorian smoking culture could alter English domesticity, generating material relations between women in England and their racial others, I turn now to the production and consumption of pastils and tobacco products. Historians have shown that smoking was primarily a masculine activity; as I will suggest, the historical archive may be opened up in a way that enables us to see smoking as a feminine activity and an affectation as well. I trace the feminization of the commodity—exemplified in the literary figuring of cigarettes as feminine—and the feminization of the labor force to illustrate how English women's position in the economy and culture of smoking was as complex as that of Lady Montagu in the Turkish baths or of the female readers of the Smokers' Pastils advertisement.

Puffing Trends II: The Lady is a Cigarette is a Lady, or "girls, girls everywhere"

If the implied spectacle in the Smokers' Pastils advertisement is not an Asian woman but an English woman as I have argued above, the commodity implicitly lying at the end of that metonymic chain imagined in the advertisement is neither pastils, nor tobacco products, nor the abstract labor that goes into the production of pastils and tobacco products, nor the pipes or papers that aid the consumption of tobacco products, but women's idle bodies. In a germinal example of the feminization of the commodity, Marx wrote that commodities "are things, and therefore lack the power to resist man. If they are unwilling, he can use force; in other words, he can take possession of them" (178). Using language that echoes the discourses of Aesthetics and Orientalism, Marx indicates that owner and object are gendered roles. Piesse & Lubin's advertisement replicates the gendering of imperial capitalism on the most minute scale, indexing at once the industrialization entailed in the manufacture of pastilles, the gendering of the labor force in the production of the tobacco products the pastilles are supposed to remedy, and the twinned consumption practices of Oriental and Occidental women. Essentially the Smokers' Pastils advertisement places an entire series of commodities in relation to one another: the pastil with the cigarette and the hookah, the consuming angel and the odalisque. All of these commodities are more or less able to be possessed by the male readers of *The Graphic*. The advertisement narrates material relations between English women and their racialized others, setting up the mirror in which one commodity sees its own value in the image of another.

The advertisement begins this work by naming the commodity, the pastille, and its equivalent value in shillings and pence. Despite their French name, pastilles were a rather quotidian domestic object. Pastilles, drops, and lozenges were well known in the parallel realms of chemistry and medicine, perfumery, and domestic economy as vehicles for spreading good odors (or for veiling unpleasant ones) and for medicinal purposes. For example, acidulated drops, also known as lemon lozenges, were used to soothe sore throats and coughs, as evidenced in *Punch*'s amusing review "Malibran's Pastille Papers" from November 16, 1844, a review not of the product itself but of the manufacturer's press release materials comprising endorsements by various singers and dramatists who had lost their voice until taking a pastille made them veritable chanticleers.[18] Advertisement pages in *The Lady's Newspaper* of March 27, 1852 indicate that pastilles or lozenges were popular home remedies for various "Disorders of the Pulmonary Organs" such as "Difficulty of Breathing" and "Redundancy of Phlegm." According to another article in *The Lady's Newspaper* from February 23, 1856 entitled "The Toilette Table," pastilles were also a popular mode for perfuming one's apartments. The article provides a recipe for homemade pastilles (artfully shaped mounds of ingredients which would then be burned as incense), a compound requiring equal parts powdered benzoin, myrrh and tolu; essence of cloves, nutmegs and lavender; and an ounce of nitrate of potass; all blended together into a stiff paste with something mysterious called mucilage of tragacantha and left to dry.

The recipe in *The Lady's Newspaper* calls to our attention the human labor behind the Smokers' Pastils—labor obscured twice over by the commodity form itself and by the representation of that commodity in the advertisement. Pastilles could be made by hand at home by industrious housewives, in a chemist's or

---

[18]   The reviewer writes, "Recently we have been favoured with a box of lozenges, which, we presume, have been sent us for the purposes of review, and also to cure us of any little hysterical attacks, lowness of spirits, loss of voice, or tightness of the throat we may be subject to." The *Punch* reviewer humorously continues, "The Lozenge Correspondence brings into play the literary powers of many distinguished persons, whose effusions we shall proceed to notice ..." (212).

perfumer's shop, or they might be an artisanal specialization of elite chefs like the Royal Confectioner.[19] According to the description in chemist Arnold Cooley's *Cyclopaedia of Six Thousand Practical Receipts, and Collateral Information* (1854), the procedure for making pastilles by hand was complicated:

> Lozenges made by melting one half of the sugar in a brass or iron pan, lipped to the right, with a little flavored water, then adding the other half of the powdered sugar, previously warmed, and dragging small portions of the grouty mass out by a wire, so as to fall on a stone or metal slab or plate, rubbed with a little powdered starch or sweet oil, are called '*drops*' by the confectioners, and '*pastilles*' (pastilli) by the French. (Cooley 406)

The ingredients for pastilles and lozenges ranged from the mundane to the exotic. Rose pastille drops called for ½ oz. water, 3 ½ oz. sugar, a few drops of essence of roses, and a few drops of prepared cochineal. Ginger pastille drops required essence of Jamaican ginger, whereas peppermint pastilles called for essence of peppermint. Essences, or essential oils, were distilled from aromatic plants and herbs found in exotic colonial climes and imported for use in English homes and laboratories.[20] If the pastille business depended, in part, on colonial products, it was also advanced by domestic industrialization in the decade leading up to Piesse & Lubin's 1869 advertisement. A number of patents were registered for improved lozenge-manufacturing machines, including a machine for more efficiently cutting the sugar into drops and one that would facilitate printing multi-colored pictures on the lozenges. Handicraftsmen were not necessarily put out of business by the rationalization of the pastille-production process. The existence of *The Royal English and Foreign Confectioner: A Practical Treatise on the Art of Confectionary in all its Branches, Comprising Ornamental Confectionary Artistically Developed* (1862) suggests that artisanal confectioners might still have served an elite clientele.

Cigarette production followed a similar trajectory as that of pastilles, progressing from being hand-made in the 1850s using fine papers and exotic Turkish shag, to being mass-produced using the new Bonsack machine (which was invented and patented in the US in 1881 and purchased for proprietary use

---

[19]   Charles Elmé Francatelli's 1862 tome, *The Royal English and Foreign Confectioner: A Practical Treatise on the Art of Confectionary in all its Branches* offers instructions for creating Rosolio Pastilles: drops made of boiled sugar and colored pink, blue, green or yellow and cast in small impressions with various designs, which could be made in the shape of haricots, coffee beans, or raspberries.

[20]   For instance, according to the Economic Volume of the 1908 *Imperial Gazetteer of India*, "The exports of seeds containing essential oils have been steadily increasing for some years; in 1876–7 they amounted to Rs. 29,000 and in 1903–4 to 12–3 lakhs" (179).

in the UK in 1883 by the Wills Brothers).[21] Common lore has it that the cigarette was popularized in England following the Crimean War when British troops had copied their Turkish allies' practice of rolling loose tobacco in scraps of newspaper.[22] Cigarettes on the mass market were made by women, whose smaller, more delicate fingers were considered ideal for handling the leaves and rolling the tubes of fine paper. According to historian Matthew Hilton, at the time the Bonsack machine came into use in the early 1880s in Britain, "cigarettes were still hand rolled by large teams of girls and young women, the most skilled of whom could make several a minute. Consequently, they were expensive and only purchased by an elite clientele, a niche market which the manufacturers believed did not hold much potential for expansion" (84).

The labor behind cigar production in the colonies was likewise gendered and eroticized. As trade periodicals such as *Cope's Tobacco Plant* show,[23] tobacco was an object of masculine connoisseurship. Writers for these periodicals traveled to exotic places like Cuba to observe the cultivation of tobacco and the production of cigars. These writers extolled the "'sylph-like,' 'sweet-sixteen'-year-old female cigar rollers touching every part of an object that now lay between their lips" (Hilton 25). One writer for *All the Year Round* became rather obsessed with the young female workers in a Cuban factory:

> There was not a male worker to be seen. They were all girls, the majority of them very young, and every one of them held at that moment a handful of tobacco leaf, which she was rolling into a cigar ... It was a busy scene. Girls, girls everywhere, all neat and tidy and cheerful, many of them exceedingly pretty. The effect of these four thousand white fingers nimbly plying their task was that of a dancing light—like the sunlight glistening through rustling leaves. (qtd in Hilton 25)

In this quotation, the travelogue fantasy of the native woman's productive labor is complicated by the racialization of her body. Her "white fingers" serve as a gendered substitute for the hands of English factory "Hands," appendages to industry and empire alike. The girls are Cuban—that is, native—yet industrious and tidy, their white fingers rolling the cigar that will make its way to the lips

---

[21]   The Bonsack machine could produce 300 cigarettes a minute; this boom in manufacturing made the cigarette a more egalitarian commodity. And, of course, advertising produced a mass market for the new abundance of cigarettes in circulation; see Matthew Hilton.

[22]   This story is still widely disseminated in popular form on the World Wide Web and occasionally in academic histories of tobacco production and consumption, although some historians question the details. See W.E. Alford.

[23]   See Hilton for a discussion of tobacco periodicals as a discourse that legitimated masculine modes of consumption and helped to fashion a bourgeois–liberal masculine identity.

of the consumer. The repetition of the word "girls" as in "they were all girls" and "girls, girls everywhere" raises the specter of the harem. The prospect would be tantalizing to the male reader at home in England: implicitly, he was denied a "drop to drink," like the ancient mariner. But the commodity itself becomes a substitute for the pretty young girls the gentleman cannot possess. Smoking becomes a way to consume the Cuban factory girls. Thus the young female cigar-rollers are sexualized, made available by proxy, their physical labor pledged to pleasuring that species of bourgeois armchair-traveler, the smoking gentleman, a demographic perhaps comprising the very readership of *The Graphic*.

The feminization of the tobacco rolling labor force found a neat corollary in the feminization of the commodity, the cigar or the cigarette, in popular discourse.[24] Women and smoking were figured as alternative modes of consolation, or as rivals. For instance, J.M. Barrie's 1890 book *My Lady Nicotine* anthropomorphizes tobacco in feminine form in the title, while in the first chapter the narrator explains regretfully how he came to choose matrimony over his beloved bachelorhood smoking habit. Lord Byron's 1823 poem, "The Island" Canto II, includes an elaborate apostrophe suggesting that tobacco rivals the ladies in the harem for the attention of their lord: "Sublime tobacco! Which from east to west / Cheers the tar's labour or the Turkman's rest; / Which on the Moslem's ottoman divides / His hours, and rivals opium and his brides" (ll. 448–51). Subsequently, the poet casts "sublime tobacco" in feminine form, writing, "Yet thy true lovers more admire by far / Thy naked beauties—Give me a cigar!" (ll. 458–9). Tobacco is here gendered and sexualized: men prefer it undressed. Perhaps a more overt reminder that women were as consumable as tobacco products—both could "go up in a puff of smoke"—is found in Ouida's popular novel *Under Two Flags* (1867), which features a female character named "Cigarette." Her name signifies her deviance from normative English femininity: the narrative makes clear that Cigarette is not just a coquettish young woman but also sexually experienced. Her name also predicts her fate—to be extinguished while protecting the man she loves by shielding his body from a firing squad.[25] Cigarette's fate reinforces the likeness

---

[24]   The tradition of personifying tobacco as female dates to the Elizabethan era; see Dolores Mitchell. For late nineteenth-century evidence of this tradition Mitchell cites Rudyard Kipling, who "referred to his Havana cigars as 'a harem of dusky beauties fifty tied in a string'" (294).

[25]   In the scenes leading up to her death, her body is figured as a cigarette: "A dusky scarlet fire burned through the pallor of her face" (361), and her hands were "brown, scorched, feverish" (366). At the moment of Cigarette's death, "the heavy smoke rolled out upon the air, the death that was doomed was dealt" and that "the flash of fire was not so fleet as the swiftness of her love" (386). Then (for Ouida stretches Cigarette's death over several pages), the "color was fast passing from her lips, and a mortal pallor settling there in the stead of that rich bright hue, once warm as the scarlet heart of the pomegranate" (389–90). And finally, a "shudder shook her as, for the moment, the full sense that all her glowing, redundant, sunlit, passionate life was crushed out forever … overwhelmed her" (390).

of women and tobacco products as consumable, addictive, never satiating—the perfect commodity.

Cigarette's fate dramatizes the dual positioning of the female readers of the Smokers' Pastils advertisement. Just as they would have been both spectator and spectacle in a harem, they were as likely to be consumers of tobacco products as to be conflated with them. Popular discourse about tobacco in the nineteenth century indicates that smoking was gendered; that is, the historiography of smoking seems to support the notion that the tobacco consumer was by and large male, or at least mannish.[26] Hence it is now a historical commonplace that respectable women did not smoke in the Victorian era. But this commonplace may be the result *not* of a dearth of primary evidence attesting to the existence of lady smokers, but of how the archive is handled by historians in such a way that obscures evidence that ladies did smoke. Historians have focused on how smoking became a means of modeling or constructing masculinities or class identities.[27] Yet smoking was clearly catching on with the ladies, especially after the popularization of cigarettes made with the lighter "Virginian" tobacco in the later 1860s.[28] It appears that the history of the female smoker prior to the 1880s has yet to be written. I broach the topic here to establish background for the insinuation in the Smokers' Pastils advertisement that its female readers might smoke too.

At midcentury, tobacco usage varied among the classes by mode of ingestion and place. Men and women in the lower classes smoked pipes in the home or outdoors—witness Gabriel Betteredge's own pipe-of-contemplation habit in *The Moonstone*—as did undergraduates and artists who sought to offend Mrs. Grundy.[29] Gentlemen smoked cigars, and because smoking in the presence of ladies was considered uncouth, middle- and upper-class men tended to take their cigars in the smoking room at their club.[30] When "respectable" women smoked at all, it was likely in private.[31] Publicly, smoking was associated with loose morality or aspirations to masculinity, and ladies not only eschewed pipes,

---

[26]   The historical archive linking women and smoking seems to open up only after the cigarette-manufacturing boom in the 1880s, and more so in the early twentieth century when the industry began to target women, promising them greater independence. See Rosemary Elliott, Mitchell, and Penny Tinkler.

[27]   Hilton's *Smoking in British Popular Culture 1800–2000* is exemplary of such work.

[28]   G.L. Apperson claims that cigarette smoking by women began to be more common in the 1860s (220). Asa Briggs, too, indicates that although smoking culture seemed a masculine prerogative, women too became smokers especially after the introduction of the cigarette (241).

[29]   On the provincial aspects of pipe-smoking, see Apperson.

[30]   Ouida once described the smoking room of a club in Orientalist terms, as "that chamber of liberty, that sanctuary of the persecuted, that temple of refuge, thrice blessed in all its forms throughout the land, that consecrated Mecca of every true believer in the divinity of the meerschaum, and the paradise of the narghilé" (qtd in Hilton 34).

[31]   Smoking in private was, apparently, an established tradition among ladies. Gilman and Xun cite Horatio Busion, a seventeenth-century traveler to London, who described

cigars, and cigarettes in public, but they also vehemently complained of their menfolk partaking in the smelly habit.[32] Primary sources exhibit a general rhetoric of disapproval in both elite and popular literary and periodical texts. Common images from the nineteenth century include women leaving the table after dinner while the men remained to enjoy their cigars, signs in railway cars prohibiting smoking (until the 1850s), and notices put up in public parks requesting gentlemen to mind the ladies' sensitivities.

Indeed, prior to the "New Woman" debates, literary precedents for the lady smoker were few and far between, and generally reflected the conventional stance described by G.L. Apperson in his anecdotal *The Social History of Smoking* (1914): "Respectable folk in the middle and upper classes would have been horrified at the idea of a pipe or a cigar between feminine lips; and cigarettes had been used by men for a long time before it began to be whispered that there and there a lady—who was usually considered dreadfully 'fast' for her pains—was accustomed to venture upon a cigarette" (217).[33] In Eliza Lynn Linton's 1880 novel *The Rebel of the Family*, the provocatively "mannish" Bell Blount smokes cigarettes and claims to "know the value of nicotine," equating it with liberty (143). Certain midcentury cartoons in *Punch* provide further evidence of the alarming associations of women's smoking habits with "bloomerism."[34] The associations of smoking with bloomerism and other modes of imitative masculinity were not only the subject of pictorial lampoon but were also bemoaned in women's writing. In *A Woman's Thoughts About Women* (1860), Dinah Mulock Craik complains that women are trained to be so helplessly dependent upon others that "'An independent young lady' and 'a woman who can take care of herself'—and such-like phrases, have become tacitly suggestive of hoydenishness, coarseness, strong-mindedness, down to the lowest depth of bloomerism, cigarette-smoking, and talking slang" (17).

In spite of so much historical evidence to the contrary, it is hard not to sense a mild form of admiration, if not approval, of such feminine independence in other popular images and representations. For instance, what prompted the publishers

---

the city's female inhabitants' pipe-smoking habits: "Gentlewomen moreover and virtuous women accustom themselves to take it as medicine, but in secret" (13).

[32]   Hilton writes, "The cigar also helped to divide domestic space as women's complaints against the smell that lingered on the upholstered furniture and heavy drapery of Victorian drawing rooms provoked many men to set aside a special room in their house for the smoking habit" (52).

[33]   The familiar story of Charles Dickens encountering three lady cigar smokers at a hotel in Geneva in 1846 illustrates a common mid-Victorian attitude toward women smoking. Dickens allegedly reported: "I showed no atom of surprise; but I never *was* so surprised, so ridiculously taken aback, in my life; for in all my experience of 'ladies' of one kind and another, I never saw a woman—not a basket woman or a gypsy—smoke, before!" (qtd in Forster 291–3).

[34]   See cartoons entitled "Bloomerism: An American Custom" and "Woman's Emancipation" in *Punch* July-December 1851, or an illustration entitled "Progress of Bloomerism or, a Complete Change" in *Punch's Pocket Book*, 1852.

of the yellowback novel *Revelations of a Lady Detective* (1864) to print what must have been a scandalous cover image of the eponymous "lady detective" with red petticoats showing while smoking a cigarette?[35] Meanwhile, periodical news items attest to the growing popularity of cigarette-smoking for ladies on the Continent. In 1858, David W. Bartlett reported having seen, more than once, "well-dressed women smoking cigarettes" in the famous night cafés of Paris (29). And starting in November 1870, the image on the cover of the yellowback *Lady Detective* was echoed in a new series in *Punch* entitled "Cigarette Papers," featuring a tough-looking bluestocking, wearing spectacles, shorter skirts, with a cigarette hanging off her lip and walking a bull dog.

These popular images and narratives, a girl named "Cigarette" included, all seem to suggest that smoking did not always necessarily "unsex" or masculinize a woman. The Smokers' Pastils advertisement participates in this alternate discourse, hyper-sexualizing the figure of the respectable housewife by positing an idiomatic equivalence between her and her racial others. And it achieves the analogy by obscuring the central contradiction of the commodity: the leisured consuming angel cannot also be the industrious housewife making pastilles in her kitchen, nor can she be the eroticized, nimble-fingered tobacco-rolling female worker. By reverently upholding the "beauties" of the harem as symbols of harmless, idle self-indulgence, the advertisement invites English women to participate in the secluded pleasures of smoking, and to veil their habit by sucking on floral lozenges, rather than to labor at producing either of these products. The cost of such transgression for the consuming angel is her own self-commodification.

The advertisement points to how gender and sexuality are produced through everyday activities—material social practices like reading a newspaper, smoking a cigarette, or taking a pastille to veil the pestiferous pastime. When such material social practices revolved around imperial commodities, they could alter existing socio-political relations. The advertisement renders imperial constructions of female racial difference temporarily insignificant, revealing another way to conceive of middle-class Victorian domesticity as racialized. Here, the domestic sphere is not racialized through the reiteration of sexual difference between English and Oriental women, but through the operation of an analogy between the two, an analogy derived through the circuits of imperial commerce and contributing to the gendering of Victorian commodity culture.

Works Cited

Alford, B.W.E. W.D. & H.O. *Wills and the Development of the U.K. Tobacco Industry 1786–1965*. London: Methuen, 1973. Print.

---

[35] I am grateful to Dagni Bredesen for sharing this image as part of her paper "Substantiating the First Female Detectives in Victorian Popular Print Culture," given at NAVSA Yale, 2008. See also Bredesen 2010.

Apperson, G.L. *The Social History of Smoking*. London: Martin Secker, 1914. Print.

Barrie, J.M. *My Lady Nicotine*. London: Hodder & Stoughton, 1890. Web.

Bartlett, David. *Paris: with Pen and Pencil*. NY: Hurst & Co., 1858. Web.

Bohls, Elizabeth. *Women Travel Writers and the Language of Aesthetics, 1716–1818*. Cambridge: Cambridge University Press, 1995. Print.

Bredesen, Dagni (ed.) *The First Female Detectives: The Female Detective (1864) and Revelations of a Lady Detective (1864)*. Ann Arbor, MI: Scholars' Facsimiles and Reprints, 2010. Print.

Briggs, Asa. *Victorian Things*. London: B.T. Batsford Ltd, 1988. Print.

Burton, Antoinette. *Burdens of History: British Feminists, Indian Women, and Imperial Culture, 1865–1915*. Chapel Hill: University of North Carolina Press, 1994. Print.

Byron, George Gordon. *The Complete Works of Lord Byron*. Vol. 1. Paris: Baudry's European Library, 1847. Print.

Colley, Linda. *Britons: Forging the Nation 1707–1837*. New Haven, CT: Yale University Press, 1992. Print.

Collins, Michael. "English Art Magazines Before 1901." *Connoisseur* 191 (March 1976): 198–205. Print.

Collins, Wilkie. *The Moonstone*. 1868. NY: Oxford University Press, 2000. Print.

Cooley, Arnold. *A Cyclopaedia of Six Thousand Practical Receipts, and Collateral Information*. NY: D. Appleton, 1851. Web.

Craik, Dinah Mulock. *A Woman's Thoughts About Women*. London: Hurst and Blackett, 1858. Web.

Elliot, Rosemary. *Women and Smoking Since 1890*. NY: Routledge, 2007. Print.

Fahnestock, Jeanne. "Bigamy: The Rise and Fall of a Convention." *Nineteenth-Century Fiction* 36.1 (1981): 47–71. Web.

Forster, John. *The Life of Charles Dickens*. Vol. 2. Philadelphia: J.B. Lippincott, 1874. Web.

Francatelli, Charles Elmé. *The Royal English and Foreign Confectioner: A Practical Treatise on the Art of Confectionary in all its Branches*. London: Chapman and Hall, 1862. Web.

Ghose, Indira. *Women Travellers in Colonial India: The Power of the Female Gaze*. Delhi: Oxford University Press, 1998. Print.

Gikandi, Simon. *Maps of Englishness: Writing Identity in the Culture of Colonialism*. NY: Columbia University Press, 1996. Print.

Gill, Rebecca. "The Imperial Anxieties of a Nineteenth-Century Bigamy Case." *History Workshop Journal* 57.1 (2004): 58–78. Web.

Gilman, Sander L. and Zhou Xun. Introduction. *Smoke: A Global History of Smoking* (eds) Sander L. Gilman and Zhou Xun. London: Reaktion Books, 2004. 9–28. Print.

Grewal, Inderpal. *Home and Harem: Nation, Gender, Empire, and the Cultures of Travel*. Durham, NC: Duke University Press, 1996. Print.

Hayward, Abraham. "The Advertising System." *Edinburgh Review* 77 (February 1843): 1–43. Print.

Hilton, Matthew. *Smoking in British Popular Culture 1800–2000.* Manchester: Manchester University Press, 2000. Print.

Hunter, William Wilson, William Stevenson Meyer, Richard Burn, James Sutherland Cotton, and Herbert Hope Risley (eds) *Imperial Gazetteer of India.* Vol. 3. Oxford: Clarendon Press, 1908. Web.

Kalmar, Ivan Davidson. "The *Houkah* in the Harem: On Smoking and Orientalist Art." *Smoke: A Global History of Smoking* (eds) Sander L. Gilman and Zhou Xun. London: Reaktion Books, 2004. 218–29. Print.

Leech, John. "Bloomerism: An American Custom." 1851. *Mr Punch's Victorian Era.* London: Bradbury, Agnew, 1887. 119. Web.

Leech, John. "Progress of Bloomerism, or a Complete Change." 1852. Bodleian Library, Oxford. *VADS Collection. John Johnson Political and Satirical Prints.* Web.

Lewis, Reina. *Rethinking Orientalism: Women, Travel and the Ottoman Harem.* New Brunswick, NJ: Rutgers University Press, 2004. Print.

Linton, Eliza Lynn. *The Rebel of the Family.* Orchard Park, NY: Broadview, 2002. Print.

Loeb, Lori Anne. *Consuming Angels: Advertising and Victorian Women.* NY: Oxford University Press, 1994. Print.

"Malibran's Pastille Papers." *Punch*, 16 November, 1844: 212. Web.

Marx, Karl. *Capital: A Critique of Political Economy.* Vol. 1. Trans. Ben Fowkes. NY: Vintage Books, 1977. Print.

Melman, Billie. *Women's Orients: English Women and the Middle East, 1718–1918.* Ann Arbor, MI: University of Michigan Press, 1992. Print.

Mill, James. *The History of British India.* Vol. 1. 5th edn, London: James Madden & Co., 1848. Print.

Mitchell, Dolores. "Women and Nineteenth-Century Images of Smoking." *Smoke: A Global History of Smoking* (eds) Sander L. Gilman and Zhou Xun. London: Reaktion Books, 2004. 294–303. Print.

Montagu, Lady Mary Wortley. *Turkish Embassy Letters.* 1718. London: William Pickering, 1993. Print.

Nagai, Kaori. "A Harem in the Home: The Deceased Wife's Sister Bill and the Colonisation of the English Hearth." *The Erotic Empire: Sexuality, Gender and Power in Britain and Beyond.* Special issue of *Australasian Victorian Studies Journal* 8 (2002): 45–59. Print.

Nair, Janaki. "Uncovering the Zenana: Visions of Indian Womanhood in Englishwomen's Writings, 1813–1940." *Journal of Women's History* 2.1 (1990): 8–34. Print.

"Opening the Suez Canal." *The Graphic*, 4 December, 1869: 20. Print.

Ouida. *Under Two Flags.* Philadelphia: J.B. Lippincott Co., 1900. Web.

"Pasha's Couriers." *The Graphic*, 4 December, 1869: 13–15. Print.

Pratt, Mary Louise. *Imperial Eyes: Travel Writing and Transculturation.* NY: Routledge, 1992. Print.

Richards, Thomas. *The Commodity Culture of Victorian England: Advertising and Spectacle, 1851–1914*. Stanford: Stanford University Press, 1990. Print.

Said, Edward. *Orientalism*. NY: Vintage Books, 1979. Print.

Stoler, Ann Laura. *Carnal Knowledge and Imperial Power: Race and the Intimate in Colonial Rule*. Berkeley: University of California Press, 2002. Print.

"Suez Canal." *The Graphic*, 4 December, 1869: 15–16. Print.

Tinkler, Penny. *Smoke Signals: Women, Smoking and Visual Culture*. Oxford: Berg, 2006. Print.

"Toilette Table." *The Lady's Newspaper*, 23 February, 1856: 115. Web.

Wilson, Kathleen. *The Island Race: Englishness, Empire and Gender in the Eighteenth Century*. NY: Routledge, 2003. Print.

Wollstonecraft, Mary. *A Vindication of the Rights of Woman*. 1792. NY: W.W. Norton, 1988. Print.

"Woman's Emancipation." *Punch* 21 (1851): 3. Web.

Yegenoglu, Meyda. "Supplementing the Orientalist Lack: European Ladies in the Harem." *Inscriptions* 6 (1992): 45–80. Print.

Index